NATALIA KOBYLKINA

NAVIGATING
SUCCESS

HOW CAN YOU BUILD A MILLION-DOLLAR BUSINESS?
YOUR GUIDE TO BUSINESS DEVELOPMENT

2022

AUTHORITIZE™ LTD

Published by Authoritize Ltd
14, Croydon Road, Beddington,
Croydon, Surrey CR0 4PA UK
+44 (0)20 8688 2598
www.authoritize.co.uk

ISBN 978-1-915465-01-6

Natalia Kobylkina: author

Loft D'art: cover design

Olga Juravleva: cover photo photographer

Maya Stoilova: translator

Cristina Slattery: editor

Boriana Damianova: printed book design and layout

For Authoritize - Alexandra Truta Creative Director

Success always leaves a mark.

I dedicate this book to my lovely parents and my family.

To my husband—thank you for the love, patience, and support!

I also dedicate this book to all my followers, who are as brave as me. You change your life for the better every single day! Thank you for inspiring me and thank you for the strength you have given me!

NAVIGATING SUCCESS
NATALIA KOBYLKINA

CONTENTS

7

<u>INTRODUCTION</u>

There is a reason why you are reading this book. It caught your attention, sure. It is a good book. Still, there is another, more significant reason. You and this book vibrate on the same frequency and pull at each other like magnets. This book attracted you, just as you attracted it.

Attracting success is not that different from allowing a piece of writing to pull you in. You should be ready for it; it must come to you in the right place, at the right time, following the right effort. Success will come your way, so long as you direct your focus correctly and take action. Reading this book, as small of a step as it may appear, is already a step in the right direction.

Allow yourself to try out different things. Opportunity lurks around every corner, and success — on every block. Your current energy, however, may not be strong enough to pull in those opportunities and successes that are waiting for you. You may not recognise your own potential. That is why this book will guide you through a plethora of exercises and meditations, all to help you awaken a higher self and begin "seeing." No longer blinded by your own insufficiencies, you will be able to spot and seize opportunities, act correctly, and propel yourself to success. Your perspective will change, and so will your way of living and doing business. You will no longer be who you were when you attracted this book. You will be more, way more than this. You will be the person who attracts success, riches, and wealth. You will have attained your higher self.

My goal is to help you become financially independent.

CHAPTER ONE
HOW DO WE POSITION OURSELVES FOR SUCCESS?

"Success is never accidental."
Jack Dorsey,
co-founder and former CEO of Twitter

HABITS OF THE RICH

This book is utterly practical. I built a million-dollar business from scratch, and experience has taught me that anyone who possesses the right qualities and adopts a wealth mindset can succeed.

I find myself surrounded by lots of rich and successful people, and I learn from them. They teach me business skills, just as they instruct me how to attain harmony and freedom. As they and I agree, everything starts with a small step in the right direction. At first, you are barely putting one foot in front of the other. You are dragging yourself forward. Then, as you grow more confident, you pick up the pace. Before you even know it, you are a long-distance runner. You are no longer treading. You are piercing ground and air with your stride, with the tempo of a winner.

Today, I can confidently say: to be rich or not to be rich, that is the decision.

Being poor is a choice; so is being wealthy.

If you are reading this book, chances are—you have matured to make the right decision.

Recently, I interviewed a successful businesswoman. She said, "I was poor and that insulted me. I dreamed I would become rich one day, just so I could buy everything. That's exactly what happened."

Just like her, I dared to dream. My family was poor. We wore the same pair of shoes throughout the frosty, freezing Russian winter. We lived frugally, but I always knew I would grow rich and succeed in this world. That's what happened. I now have the freedom to live wherever I want, to gaze at the menu and not at the price. I am not a big spender, and I treat money with love, gratitude, and respect. And I will teach you to do the same.

Having money boils down to a question of priorities. In life, we can only succeed in what we find significant, what we happily invest in, and what we pour our entire "Being" into. The right effort and the right vision help us attain mastery, regardless of the field or vocation we have chosen to pursue.

The exercises and homework assignments within this book may challenge you; do not postpone doing them. The point of working through them is to help you reach and adopt an unshakable conviction in your own capabilities. You want to amass wealth, and, to do so, you should surrender yourself to a brief, book-long apprenticeship. "I do not have time," you may note. That is wrong. If your day is busy, you've got the evening. If your evening is busy, you've got the early hours of the morning. Do it or don't do it, you will be the one to bear the consequences—or thrive because of the successes. Act now, and do not let unfinished tasks pile up on your shoulders.

ACT HERE AND NOW

"I have always found that my view of success has been iconoclastic: success to me is not about money or status or fame, it is about finding a livelihood that brings me joy and self-sufficiency and a sense of contributing to the world"
Anita Roddick,
founder of The Body Shop

Acting here and now is a habit of the rich. I, too, have internalised it; procrastination is not merely unacceptable but also unthinkable. I do everything I have to do, here, now, at this very moment. I remember when Facebook first allowed influencers to do Live Streams. I started my first live stream before knowing how live streams worked. Preparing or worrying about the "right way" to conduct a live stream would have been a waste—a loss of my most valuable resource, time. If I delegate a task to an employee, and they do not get it done by the end of the hour, I fire them. Still, I am not a hypocrite, and I do not have double standards. My team and I abide by the exact same rules and policies. We act fast. In case I must make an important decision or complete a task, I do it quickly. We've got no time to waste, and you don't either. Acting here and now is a mindset. It is a philosophy you must adopt to prevent work from piling up, to stay on top of things, to remain efficient.

Not having enough time is a symptom of a dangerous disease known as "wrong priorities."

To figure out if you are infected or not, do the following task:

HOMEWORK
HOW DO WE MANAGE OUR TIME?

Over the course of a week, you should rigorously track your time. Be obsessive — every minute matters. Find out what you do. Realise where your time goes. Most importantly, figure out whether what you do can take you to where you want to be.

I used to work a lot. Though, to the average person, "a lot" may mean seven or eight hours a day, I worked that, only doubled. I put in fifteen to sixteen hours every day. I worked 350 days per year, without a break. I developed new programs, seminars, webinars, lecture sessions, and talks. Like a madwoman losing her sanity on a keyboard, I typed away, crafting articles and emails. I brought my laptop everywhere I went.

I experienced burnout. Repeatedly. I remember the third time it happened: I used to vomit at the sight of my phone. I felt as if the next meeting (or the next seminar) would drive me to the grave. I shut my phone off for two weeks and fled to Greece with my family. For fourteen days, all I did was sleep and eat. I returned to work only after recovering. This, I knew, could not go on.

Though I love my work, it is far from easy. I encounter the human condition daily, facing grief, pain, and confusion. I speak with clients who hope that a single session with me can solve all their problems. Little do they know that no therapist—as good as she is—can solve the issues and trauma that have been "hidden in the fog" for the past forty years. Healing doesn't work that way. I always give my work—and my clients—my all.

Despite my genuine desire to help, meetings and sessions with clients wear me out. Exhausted, I read thank-you messages, hearing how much I have helped a woman find a partner or a man deal with the loss of a loved one. I hear about couples finally purchasing the home of their dreams. I see women advancing their careers. These stories keep me going, urging me to take a deep breath. I breathe. I then return to the realm of loss and pain, finding the wandering souls of my clients, taking their hand, and bringing them to light. I help them journey into the realm of love and abundance, giving them bits and pieces of myself along the way.

When I decided to work for sixteen hours per day, I asked myself the following question: "What do I dream of?"

"I have zero spare time," I said to myself. I needed more free time for myself. That was the first answer that floated to my mind—the answer that motivated me to reorganise my life. I became a mother soon after. Had it not been for my son, I doubt I would have ever made that change.

I also feared that working less meant making less. I sell my time, after all. I still decided to risk it. I had taken out a loan for my teaching centre and the reduction of my income was an unwanted consequence of my decision.

As soon as I quit working into the early hours of the night, however, a miracle occurred. Having infiltrated the internet, the American market appeared, almost as a mirage. Thanks to the internet, I could now enter the American market! I could develop my business in countries other than my own! A two-hour webinar could now make me the money I would otherwise have to spend a month earning. This made me increasingly aware of the true importance of priorities.

I schedule my days in such a way that I do not have free time. I wake up, go jogging, make breakfast, and take my kid to kindergarten. I work nine to five. I busy myself with correspondence between five and six in the afternoon. My phone is always on Silent Mode; that ensures my peace and fosters my concentration. The people I work with know they can reach me every day, between five and six p.m.

The people who are always available reach burnout. Staying on guard (at all times) will wear you out.

I am free after six. That is the time I dedicate to my family, to dinner, to conversations, to slow strolls through the park. I give myself about an hour for personal development; I read books between nine and ten in the evening. I sometimes listen to a podcast or a webinar. I reflect on my day and journal… I do not have spare time, and this is the result of good time management.

If you schedule is chaotic, you do not have time for what matters.

I also restrict the time I spend on social media. I only allow myself about half an hour every evening, just to answer messages and check the activity on my different accounts. I follow some people on Instagram, but only because they inspire me. If I feel like it, I post something. My husband and I do not have a TV—that was one of the conditions I laid out before we got married.

I strongly recommend you analyse your schedule and see where your time goes. Stop wasting time on things that don't add value to your life. Consider which responsibilities you could delegate to others. I will help you do so with the following

EXERCISE
MY PRIORITIES

Sit down and write how you would like to organise your priorities and manage your time.

How many hours per day would you like to work?

____

____

What exactly do you want to do with your life?

____

____

What do you find most important? What would you not allow anyone else to do?

____

____

What responsibilities could you delegate to someone else? We will talk more about the delegation of tasks later in this book.

____

____

____

____

FIND PEOPLE WHO INSPIRE YOU

"A mediocre person tells. A good person explains. A superior person demonstrates. A great person inspires others to see for themselves."
Harvey Mackay,
American businessman

You must colour your life with people who inspire you.

I am currently reading Marie Forleo's *Everything is Figureoutable*. I have followed her social media accounts for years; Marie inspired me to start a business! She, after all, is an American coach who founded her own multimillion-dollar business. I feel drawn by her energy, dedication to hard work, and various programs.

I also follow two Russian women—Elena and Veronika. Elena is a mother of four. When I first followed her three years ago, she was an ordinary woman from Yaroslavl. She travelled with her husband and posted pictures from her vacations to Turkey. She is now a millionaire, jet-setting to Africa, Asia, and wherever else she chooses. Together with her husband, she has different businesses and organises a wide range of courses. She inspired me to create online marathons.

I advise you find people who motivate and enliven you. Still, because you cannot follow every motivational speaker out there, try to restrict your role models to five. Having more than that becomes counterproductive.

EXERCISE

HOW CAN I FLOURISH?

Make a list of people who inspire you. Analyse what draws you to these individuals. What sort of example do they set for you? How do they help you grow? What can you learn from them?

____

____

____

____

____

____

____

____

____

____

____

The women I follow, for instance, inspired me to purchase a Bentley. "If they can do it, I can do it, too," I told myself. "Let's see what driving a Bentley feels like," I said. It felt smooth and easy, let me tell you that.

One of the qualities you must master is your ability to take risks. It is most logical to take risks up to 30%, as this probability of risk will allow you to lose within your zone of comfort, to find a way to "tame" the situation, should that become necessary.

RISK IS AN INTEGRAL PART OF BUSINESS

> *"If you are not willing to risk the unusual,*
> *you will have to settle for the ordinary"*
> **Jim Rohn**,
> *American entrepreneur*

I encourage you to take calculated risks. Prior to offering a new product or entering a new market, I always inform myself about existing businesses and barriers to entry. I also contact people who have already succeeded in the field. I ask about their experiences and request advice… and they always respond, ready to help and do good. That is, in fact, the first step of creating a new business—calculating risks, researching the competition, and learning from well-known experts.

The second step of creating a new business is all about pouring its foundation deep into the ground. You must hire a lawyer to craft essential contracts and documents.

The third step is hiring employees. The advent and popularisation of social media have facilitated this step tremendously, helping employers reach an unprecedented volume of potential employees. You should interview your job candidates. Having done fifteen to twenty interviews, you will easily distinguish the "wheat from the chaff," and hire the necessary employees faster than ever before.

Nevertheless, do not allow the hiring process to distract you from simultaneously seeking clients. Craft presentations and send them out. Set meetings. Be proactive. Assert your aspirations before the Universe.

PROMISE AND DO

The Universe always responds to my pleas for help. I tell the Universe what I need money for, and I specify how much money I need. The then Universe brings in opportunities and clients, helping me accumulate the sum I needed. When I make that money, however, I make sure to spend it on what I promised the Universe I would spend it on; I do not waste the money on unnecessary stuff. I dutifully abide by the contract I have made with the Universe.

DIFFICULTIES LEAD TO GROWTH

What doesn't kill you makes you stronger. Challenges help you grow. You ascend to a higher level by facing and combating obstacles! That is the only way to propel yourself forward and reach previously unknown horizons. Take, for instance, the process of learning a new language. If you push through in the beginning, which is the hardest part, you will be rewarded for your efforts. The same holds true for any endeavour you embark upon—whether it is taking driving courses or obtaining a master's degree, one concept always defines your experience: no pain, no gain.

New frontiers of success and abundance present themselves to you every time you overcome an internal limitation.

THREE KEY QUESTIONS & PATH TO WEALTH

"You can have everything in life you want if you will just help enough other people get what they want"
Zig Ziglar,
American author

To attain wealth, you must constantly ask yourself the following three questions:

1. What is my contribution to the world?
2. How can people learn about me?
3. How can I market myself and my product?

The entire philosophy of business stands collected within these three questions. As you can see, what matters most is your contribution to this world. What you offer people is of prime importance; make it so good and useful that they can no longer live without it. Get them hooked.

EXERCISE
I ATTRACT MONEY

Take a seat. Rest your back against the seat and fold your hands at the elbows. Open your palms, allowing your thumbs to align with your index fingers. Place your palms in front of your solar plexus. Say these affirmations out loud:

I attract money.

Money loves me.

Everything I do brings me luck.

I have so much to offer this world, and this world has so much wealth to give me in return.

I am grateful for the affluence that I possess.

I attract abundance.

Abundance is within reach.

Money grows on trees.

I deserve to have money.

People pay me with pleasure.

Feel the abundance within your life. Be grateful for it. Draw your palms together and thank the Universe. *Namaste*! Thank the Universe for this moment. Thank the Universe for allowing us to be here, growing together. I wish you prosperity! Be prosperous, rich, and happy! Walk onward and upward! Dream on! Dare! Flourish!

Keep repeating these affirmations, even if they seem unrealistic at first. Get your mind used to them. Then, if someone tells you, "That is impossible," you will say, "It's possible for me." When somebody tries to convince you that "This is difficult," you shall simply respond: "It's easy for me!"

It is crucial to ground yourself within your assertions. Align yourself with them. If you manage to do so, people's chatter will simply fade into the background.

CHAPTER TWO
THE ENERGY OF WEALTH

*"Success usually comes to those who are
too busy to be looking for it."*
Henry David Thoreau,
American naturalist

UNDERSTAND THE ENERGY OF WEALTH

You've probably heard that money is energy. I believe this to be true from the bottom of my heart. I once took a seminar that explored the essence of money. Our tutor explained there were different levels of energy—from survival to affluence. He also mentioned that every level had its own, distinctive energy. On a purely rational level, I understood his ideas. However, I could not internalise them. I did not understand them on an emotional level—at least not as I do now.

I no longer need to see someone's watch or their car to know if that person has money or not. I've realised that people's energy, like money's energy, is distinctive. People without money are air-like: they ramble a lot and never take action. They talk the talk, but do not walk the walk. People with money, in contrast, have this diamond-like vibe. It gets stronger and shinier the more money they earn. Such people are usually self-made, too.

As powerful as it is, money can be as helpful as it can be destructive. It should therefore come when we are ready for it. People who make money when they're not ready for it usually lose that money. Imagine, let's say, a middle-aged man who just won the lottery or received an inheritance. He is not prepared to bear the energy of that money. Chances are, he will either lose the money quickly or start drinking, taking drugs, and engaging in risky behaviour. The money's energy simply overpowers his own.

Let's discuss the rules of money management.

THE RULES OF MONEY MANAGEMENT

1. Do not fear talking about money

It is crucial to understand where money escapes us, and why we cannot accumulate wealth. Unfortunately, most people avoid performing this analysis. They struggle to realise their shortcomings, refusing to admit their need (and wish) for money. If you feel the same way—do not worry, this is absolutely normal.

Just take a deep breath. Now as you would, with any other problem, move on. Don't let your worries limit your progress.

2. Do not try to change your relatives

I know that—as soon as you understand how money works—you will feel the need to tell your mother her attitude towards money is incorrect. Or, possibly, you will start nagging your partner to show them what they've got wrong about their finances.

Don't do this! Focus on yourself, and let your loved ones see the result. They will approach you on their own, posing a simple question: "How did you do that?"

3. Trust the process

With the help of this book, I will teach you different practices for accumulating wealth. Do not pick and choose the tasks that I give you. Do not say: "I like this, so I will do it, but I dislike that, so I will not bother with it." Different practices work for different people. Therefore, you should do all of them! In this way, you will figure out what works for you.

I am not saying that this will be easy. On the contrary—I intend to take you out of your comfort zone! I don't care if you enjoy doing these practices. All I care about is that you become rich. This isn't that different from the process you go through at the gym. If you have a trainer, and he "tortures" you with difficult exercises, your body gets leaner and more toned. If you work out on your own, and cut yourself too much slack, your body doesn't change at all. Overcoming difficulty fosters progress.

4. Be ruthless with yourself

One of the biggest "money-killers" is self-pity. Forget the following excuses: *This makes me uncomfortable—I don't want to bother others; What will people say?; I do not have the strength or energy to do this.*

5. Take responsibility for your own wealth

Say this out loud: "Today, I choose to be successful. Today, I choose to become wealthy!"

Ask yourself the following question: "Why am I reading this book and how much money do I want to earn in the next month?" Answer honestly. Write your desired sum down: ....

As I already stated, money is energy. Hence, the following hold true:
1. You have as much self-love as you have energy.
2. You have as much money as you have worked for.
3. The less energy you have, the less money you have.
4. The more psychologically-mature you are, the more money you have.

THE SEVEN LEVELS OF MONEY'S ENERGY

1. Survival Level

People who fall into this level tend to make between £300 and £500 per month. They barely make the ends meet, having as much money as they need to avoid hunger. The psychological programs of these people are geared towards—and only towards—survival.

2. Poverty Level

People who fall into this level make about £1,000 per month. They manage, mostly by living frugally. Their psychological programs are nearly the same as those of the former group. The only difference between them and people who reside within the level of "survival" is that those at "Poverty" level have a certain dose of security. They always choose predictable actions and satiate themselves with the little things.

3. Level of the Middle Class

People who earn between £1,000 and £2,000 per month tend to fall into this group. They want nice clothes, just as they desire to go to nice restaurants and vacations.

When I left Russia, my home country, I was literally surviving. I lived on £350 per month. As soon as things started working out, and I began earning around £1,000 monthly, I had even less money in my pocket. Why? I had started eating out, buying clothes, and purchasing jewellery. Like most middle-class people, I spent money to obtain a dose of comfort. The middle-class spends on unnecessary clothes, shoes, and cosmetics. Just imagine how many unnecessary clothes you have in your own wardrobe. You don't even wear them. Why don't you sell them? Sell them! That's how you will only see and wear clothes you actually love.

When I visit clients, I often walk up to their wardrobes. I gaze at the tens of unworn dresses and outdated cardigans, knowing my client hasn't worn half of them in over a year. Then, I ask: "How many of these clothes do you actually wear?" Allegedly, 70% of the clothes owned by middle-class people, women especially, remain unworn. The same holds true for skincare and makeup. Middle-class people also waste quite a lot of food. They spend a lot, saying: "Let's buy and let's own. Let's be comfortable!" Middle-class individuals live beyond their means; they spend, they give away, never managing to save what they've earned.

When it comes to money, there really are two types of people: those who cannot attract money, and those who cannot keep money. The latter, I believe, is predominant.

4. Transitory Level: on the Path to Wealth

People who rest at this level make anywhere between £2,000 and £10,000 per month. They are above the middle class, but we cannot classify them as wealthy. When people reach this level, they decide they are rich. They begin taking out loans to purchase expensive cars. They go on luxurious vacations and believe life can only get better from then on. Such people should limit spending and focus on saving and investing. If they forgo splurging on luxuries and begin investing, these people can become truly rich.

5. Level of the Somewhat-Wealthy

People who fall into this level make between £20,000 and £30,000 per month. They successfully manage their money; they also invest. These people own apartments, houses, and nice cars. They go on expensive vacations. At this level, people usually own a business and manage their employees.

6. Level of the Affluent

People who belong to this category make between £50,000 and £100,000 per month. Their quality of life isn't much different from that of the former group. The only differences are, perhaps, that people at this level have a newer car and a bigger home. For them, as well as for millionaires, freedom and independence are leading priorities.

Personally, I strove to reach this level for two reasons. First, I wanted to be able to work from any corner of the globe. Second, I aspired to work when—and if—I wanted. At this level, excessive work is no longer necessary. The business is already established and takes care of itself. You just monitor and update it.

7. Level of the Millionaires

To reach this level, you should make more than £100,000 per month. At this level, millionaires work for the pleasure of working; they do what they love.

Realise what level you are at currently. Which level do you want to reach? Bear in mind that levels cannot be skipped, and, if they are, money can drive us insane.

I knew this woman—she was poor, a level-two type of person. She met a millionaire who fell in love with her. They got married. As counterintuitive as this may seem, marrying him was no less than a curse for her. She became jealous, did not feel worthy of her new lifestyle, and started punishing her husband for his successes. Finally, after lots of struggle, they separated, and she returned to her small, poor home. It's curious he gave her nothing in alimony, even when his ex-wife was receiving millions after divorcing the exact same man. Clearly, the ex-wife knew how to receive, and the second wife did not.

If you are at a low level, you will receive less than your colleagues.

POVERTY'S PROGRAMS

Transitioning from one level to the next is hard, mostly because we need to outgrow ourselves. Level transitions have their own characteristics. Poverty programs are coded within many of us. These poverty programs have many physical manifestations, the most common of which are undoubtedly our homes. Dirty, disorganised spaces are a sign of one's poverty program—especially if these homes are filled with piles of unnecessary stuff.

Look around. How does your apartment look? What about your office space? Are you drawers organised, or are they cluttered with things you do not need? Stand up and get a few trash bags—you will need them for this task.

HOMEWORK
TIDY UP

> *"Do not be afraid to give up the good to go for the great."*
> **John D. Rockefeller,**
> *American business magnate*

Toss everything that is broken. Stained clothes, broken decorations, torn socks—they need to go. So do the cup with the broken handle and the makeup you do not use. You will not magically fix the handle, just as you will not use that blue mascara. It is already out of date, anyway. Throw it away!

I tidy up every month. I find some things to bin, and others to give away. I am often given stuff I do not use, and I like to give it to someone who would. As someone who has been doing this exercise every month, I can assure you that there is always something you can throw away.

Still, because you are about to get rich, I want you to find thirty objects to bin. You could find more, of course. Throw away objects that don't make you happy. Trash clothes, shoes, and accessories that don't match your new status. Bin the things you have outgrown. The only things you should allow to stay are those that delight you. Only keep the things that inspire awe and appreciation with their beauty and functionality.

I insist you throw all thirty objects away, as gifting or selling them would make you forget what this process was about in the first place. The unnecessary stuff would otherwise stay there for years, accumulating energy and hindering your progress. Throw. These. Things. Away. Trust me, people who need that stuff will find it in the trash bins. Still, if you are so bent on giving it away, put collect it big bags and give it to a charity organisation. Do it today. If you have something of extraordinary value, but it does not delight you, you can sell it. You can also sell those objects that bring you bad memories. Do it now. Post a little note on Facebook Marketplace. Get rid of that object. It is vital you declutter your surroundings.

This process can be harder if you live with your parents. I remember trying to clean my parents' house once. Mind you—each of them is a bit of an objectophile. They let stuff pile up. Wanting to clear out our space, I binned receipts and long-expired cleaning products. My father panicked; he had me take everything out of the trash bin. I had to put it back in its place. "Return everything to where you got it from!" he screamed. Then, as I was putting everything into "its place," he yelled: "Do not touch my things." I promised I wouldn't. I also realised this was their way of thinking, a way I could never change.

If you attempt to change your parents, they get the unwanted feeling they have been living in the wrong way. Their smart and grown kid is not here to change their worldview. They won't let that happen. They can't stomach making such a drastic change, especially when their kid was the one to initiate it. Your parents, like mine, came of age in an entirely different time. They lived differently. They don't understand a lot of the things we do today; they find them redundant. Our values are different. Let your parents live the way they are used to, and do not bother trying to change them.

We only work on ourselves, and we respect other people's right to be poor and to suffer.

The second part of this homework requires you to declutter your phone and computer. I am certain you have thousands of photos that you don't like. Delete them! Deinstall the apps you don't use. Leave groups that don't further your progress. Unfollow people. End that subscriptions you don't need. Delete old emails. Make sure you don't receive any spam. I know this is a long, tedious process. But it must be done.

Years ago, I wanted to sell my car. There weren't any buyers, though, and my car was pretty specific. It was Italian. I tried everything I could to find a buyer, but nothing worked. Out of desperation, I decided I needed to tidy up. I deleted all insignificant emails. I also went through old documents and flipped through binders full of contracts. I got rid of everything I no longer needed. My room brightened up. My computer worked faster! And, within an hour, I had someone wanting to purchase my car. Within a couple of hours, he came and paid cash, buying a car that had remained unused—and unbought—for over a year!

A client of mine experienced a similar problem. She also wanted to sell her car. Following my advice, she cleaned her entire house. She stayed up until five a.m. that evening, diligently decluttering cabinets, and drawers, throwing all clothes away, and opening up space for the good to come. She found a buyer for her car the day after she did that.

I know so many stories like these ones. When something drags on, when you are not getting your documents on time, when you are not making the desired progress, you just need to declutter your space.

Organise a drawer. I always try to have everything in perfect order. When I opened one of my cupboards yesterday, however, I found I had a few open packs of cookies. I had bought them for my son during our walks, but never managed to finish one before opening the other. As a result, I had at least three open packs of cookies, with only one or two biscuits missing. They were cluttering up my space, and I had to fix this. I immediately took the cookies out and made cheesecake. We enjoyed the delicious desert later that day.

Organise and clean your car. Wealth and cleanliness are closely related. Rich houses are always hygienic and organised. Useless objects don't take up space. Poor homes are cluttered with unnecessary stuff. The poor keep everything, including pregnancy dresses and baby clothes, just in case they have another baby. The younger kid wears the clothes of the older one, developing unwanted psychological complexes. I have personally experienced this. I have a sister who is four years my senior. My mother dressed me in her clothes, making me wear what no longer fit my sister. And, worse, my younger sister had to wear the clothes both my older sister and I had worn for years. Even today, she still talks about the way this made her feel. It troubled her greatly, making her feel insecure and unhappy. **Keeping old things for the sake of an unlikely event, passing down clothing from one child to the next, and cluttering one's space are all indicative of a psychology of poverty.** Give away, trash, let go. You can always go shopping when the next baby arrives.

The rich live in the present. They use whichever objects they like and wear whichever clothes suit them best. The rich understand that the thrill that we get from material possessions wears off quickly, and they therefore enjoy what they have here and now.

I give my books away—even when I like them very much. I know that I will not re-read the novels I own, so it is most logical that I give them to someone I know. I only keep the most important –those that I will return to, re-read, and reference, again and again.

READING LIST

There are a few books you need to read in order to make more money.

The first book is *The Richest Man in Babylon*. Written by George S. Clason in 1926, this book has influenced millions, encouraging them to save. It is an easy read, too, so get to it as soon as possible!

The second book is *Karmic Management* by Geshe Michael Roach, Lama Christie McNally, and Michael Gordon. This book had a profound impact on me and forever transformed the way I viewed money. I first read it a decade ago. I had just established my website; however, I didn't conduct regular webinars. Instead, I led my seminars at different venues, mostly hotels and conference halls. This was very expensive. I worked a lot, and barely made any money—just because most of my earnings were spent on covering the daily rent fees.

Helped by fate, I suppose, I met two brothers. One of them, Miroslav, suggested he do some karmic management. He had examined my website and quickly noticed its shortcomings.

He encouraged me to start leading webinars. He instructed me to change my payment system, just so people could purchase event tickets and webinar spots more easily. Miroslav also crafted a work plan. He advised me to market my services more broadly. Yet, despite the genius of his ideas, I rejected them a couple of times. I wasn't ready to make the changes he wanted me to make. I was afraid to change my website, worrying I would lose the unsubstantial sum of money it made me at that time. My business had just started making about £1,000 per month, and I was happy. Back then, I did not realize this attitude had tied my hands, binding me to the Poverty Level.

Miroslav suggested that I shouldn't pay him right away. "Try these things out for a few months," he said, "and pay me if they work." This helped with some of my worries and I was encouraged to try. We created a website from scratch. It was a long month of hard work and effort. Once he had optimised the payment system, Miroslav also made me record a webinar, as people could now sign up and pay via PayPal. I checked the new system out in late December. It turned out to be the best Christmas Present I had ever received! My PayPal account contained a sum equal to my annual income! I cried from happiness. This new system made me as much money as travelling around the country and speaking at different venues would have in an entire year.

I (obviously) continued working with Miroslav and his brother. We tweaked the website a bit, created new programs, and installed new systems. I was paying them a lot more than I had paid them initially, and, thanks to my new business approach, this did not impose a financial burden on me. Things worked out, both for me and for them. Miroslav founded his own business a while after. He became successful.

You gain something valuable each time you help others develop and expand their businesses. This is a rule that the book *Karmic Management* confidently asserts: Help others with what you have failed at! You struggle to establish a business—help someone else establish theirs! You are incapable of accumulating wealth—help someone else make money! You have as much money as you contribute to the world.

ASCENSION TO THE NEXT LEVEL

"Opportunities do not happen. You create them."
Chris Grosser,
*Founded and Launched a company at age
18 while completing undergraduate studies.*

Let me ask you one thing: do you feel stuck? Are you obsessed with something, are you wanting to take action but cannot find the strength to do so?

Which of the seven levels of money are you at? At which level do you want to be?

Yet again, I caution you: levels cannot be skipped. Even when fate has you skip a level—by marrying a millionaire, let's say—, you usually return to the level you came from quite quickly.

Remember this one thing: the energetic levels of money need to be ascended step by step. Jumping to skip levels is futile and therefore strictly forbidden. Hence, you must know which level you are currently at, just as you should know which level you would like to reach in the future. Reflect on your situation. Plan carefully.

Let's do an exercise.

EXERCISE
MY ATTITUDE TOWARDS MONEY

Play some relaxing music in the background. Close your eyes. Take a deep breath. Now, remember your childhood, especially your first seven years of life. Who were the people around you? Try to think of seven people with whom you grew up. Your mother, your father, your grandparents… Your siblings, your teachers, your neighbours… What did they have to say about money? What did they believe to be true about money? How did they spend their money? How did they give money away, if at all? Did they save? Did they argue about money? What was their attitude towards money? What did you know about wealth and abundance?

Open your eyes and describe the people from your childhood. Note their attitude towards money, realise what they spent their money on, and decide which of the seven levels of money they were at.

1.____

2.____

3.____

4.____

5.____

6.____

7.____

For good or bad, these people passed their own attitudes down to you. If they were poor and barely made the ends meet, you might still live with the feeling that you have little money, that the money you have is insufficient and limited. Your brain is probably programmed to believe it will forever function with Poverty's Programs.

If your parents only spent money on food, bills, and necessities, this means you have lived in "survival" regime. You haven't considered spending on pleasurable activities, making investments, or purchasing a home. You haven't developed ambitions to one day establish a business, just as you haven't gotten used to giving away and donating to charity.

Money comes to you depending on your needs.

If you live on the Survival level, the money that comes to you is only enough to cover your bills. However, if you have greater charitable needs, then the money you attract will also be far greater. If your needs include building a hospital, equipping a factory with machinery, investing in stocks, jewellery, education, or your personal growth, then you will attract a whole lot more money than you would if you simply wanted to cover this month's electric bill.

Now, please consider what you'd buy yourself once you ascend to the next level. Allow your mind to imagine specific objects—or experiences—that you would purchase. Write them down. If you would want a trip, then make sure to write down a specific destination. How will you travel? If you wish to take a road trip, then write down the brand of the car you will travel in. Will you do some sightseeing? If yes, describe which places—or monuments—you would like to see. What food will you eat on your trip? What will you buy? Describe everything as specifically as you can.

If you desire to buy something new, write down what this thing would be. Will it be a new purse? Or a washing machine, perhaps? Let that thing be something you could possess within a month. Will you book yourself a massage? That does not seem too bad—for people at the Poverty level, anyway. But you must do this for yourself. A manicure, a new blazer, a pair of heels, a new piece of jewellery... find something you want to have for yourself! Whatever it is that you choose, make sure that your desired purchase is outside of your comfort zone. You should feel a slight discomfort as you think about it, as you work towards it. Wealth is always accompanied by that inner discomfort, a pain of sorts, as it is the price you pay to proceed to the next level.

Write down your goal.

____

____

It is crucial you do this. This is a step—albeit a painful one—you must take to move forward.

I recall my stomach churning the first time I bought myself a luxury bag. It was over £1,000, as most luxury bags are. I also remember buying business-class tickets to Bali for my entire family. They were about £8,000. It wasn't easy to spend so much money on plane tickets, but I knew it was necessary. Those tickets turned out to be one of my best investments. Shortly after, my family and I moved to London.

The more I spend on "luxuries," the more money I make. If I start belittling myself, worrying about finances, and hoarding money, the wealth disappears. Money comes because I constantly create a certain hunger for it, when I tell myself: "I need an expensive bag. I want to fly Business Class!" The pain for making these "luxury" purchases should be there, and all rich people learn to cope with it.

I am not saying you should be like me. Do what works for you. If getting a massage is good enough, then do that! The same goes for getting a manicure, eating out, and purchasing a new necklace. You know which purchases will cause "pain" for you. Enjoy those purchases in spite of the pain. This practice, as peculiar as it may sound, works like magic. Every time I do it, money comes to me. I spend with pain and fear, but I then jump with joy. Making these purchases hurts me, but the idea of making them fills me with satisfaction. I now dream about making these painful purchases. I think about that nice bag I saw at a window shop, and I imagine holding a First-Class ticket to the Maldives, and, once I have taken a step towards these purchases, I feel happy. I am working towards my goals!

The sensation that you can afford whatever you want is crucial in this case. That is how you awaken your potential for wealth. On one hand, you declutter your home and rid yourself of unwanted—and unneeded—stuff. On the other hand, you open space for things that you can associate with affluence, things that bring you pleasure and satisfaction, things that are slightly above your level.

Making uncomfortable purchases forces you to make money. After all, once you get used to the "good stuff," you do not want to have anything but that. Motivated, you strive to make even more money.

I remember this client of mine, a vegan, who dreamed of an expensive juicer. An expensive juicer was hyper-valuable to her. The second she spent all her savings on the juicer she wanted, her company gave her an unexpected annual bonus. Then, an old roommate paid for long-missed rent! Her investment returned to her in just a few days, and she became happier than she had been before making the purchase.

The people that surround us as we grow financially are of crucial significance. Their presence—and success—impacts our ability to make money and accumulate wealth.

WHO IS CURRENTLY INFLUENCING YOU?

Think of the seven people you spend most time with—the people you talk with, the people you follow, the people who surround you most frequently. Think of each of them individually. Which level of money are they at? What do they spend on? Answer these questions here.

1.____
2.____
3.____
4.____
5.____
6.____
7.____

These are people who influence you. Surrounding yourself with the right people is essential for your success. Consider which friends and family members hold you back. Realise who is constantly whining and complaining, who is always dissatisfied and dishonest. Notice who is jobless and poor. If you do have people who are any of those things, then have a conversation with them. Share your worries and admit you want to grow. If it is your family members—your mother, your father, a sibling—that hold you back, be courageous and let them know. Also, spend more time with people who inspire you. Surround yourself with individuals who motivate you to be better and be more creative. Surround yourself with people who give you joy.

EXCHANGE & COMBINE VALUABLE QUALITIES

I have two good friends in London who lift me up. When our energies interact, we all do better. It isn't sufficient to communicate with people you like. You should communicate with people with whom you can create, grow, and succeed. You should communicate with people who make you better, and whom you make better. These people should be successful in their own right. Adopt their good qualities. Help them learn from you. Find a way to unite your best skills and collaborate with them!

How can you encounter such people?

I, for instance, make a list. I meet people at events. I meet people online. I also find them amongst my own pool of clients. Recently, I had to receive a package but, due to COVID and the national lockdowns, the package wasn't delivered. I posted about my problem on Facebook. A woman saw my post, contacted me, and, with her help, I managed to get my package in spite of the hard, unfavourable circumstances. Not long after, she and I met. She had offered me something of value, thus starting a partnership which then turned into a friendship.

Acknowledge what you've got to offer. Consider the fascinating people you would like to meet—or work with—and offer them something that can improve their life. Check their websites. Is there anyone specific you would like to partner with? Contact them and share your ideas! People who are smarter, richer, and more successful than you will appreciate your ability to foster improvement. That is how my friends come to me: they contact me in an effort to help me, to offer something of value. Then, we become close. They begin receiving, too. Exchange is crucial.

Another friend of mine, a woman who helped me settle in London, now lives at my apartment in Bulgaria for free. I am genuinely happy I can help her, give her something in return for all the help she offered me. I appreciate everything people give me, and I always give back. You should believe in reciprocity. Give. If you do that, others will show their gratitude and feel motivated to give back.

That is how we get to our next homework.

HOMEWORK
OFFER AND GIVE

Consider what you will give and whom you will give it to.

Money doesn't grow on trees. However, when you're active and willing to help, others notice you. This is not about helping the poor. It is about giving something valuable to the rich.

Though the rich appear to have everything, they do not. You can offer them something they don't even know they need! You can update their website, improve their payment system, or share some valuable parenting advice. What you do doesn't really matter; what matters is that you enrich the lives of those around you. Help the rich improve their lives! If you manage to do so successfully, you will be invited into their circles. If you fail, you must simply try again. Failing is a sign that you haven't tried hard enough.

Money comes from unexpected sources. A friend of mine used to matchmake the singles she knew. Extroverted as she was, she did so with pleasure. Soon enough, there were about seven couples in serious relationships, simply due to her ability to matchmake. She (jokingly) decided to turn this into a business. She crafted a price list. Women did not have to pay. Men paid symbolic fees. Now, my friend operates a very successful matchmaking agency and makes good money. Her clients are happy.

Another friend of mine has this cute puppy that she takes on walks around town. She started attending dog shows with the puppy. As it turned out, puppies can make more than models! Ironically, my friend's puppy turned out to be her gold mine.

When you do different things, money starts flowing in from different directions. Just allow yourself to try.

INTERNALISE YOUR CONVICTIONS
AND BELIEFS

What is the human brain? It is an organ, obviously. It is also millions of neural connections—relationships between ideas, memories, and desires. Our life is hence what we believe it is. When we live with the assumption that everything is difficult, we stay poor. When we live with the assumption that success is within reach, we become wealthy. Having money is a matter of beliefs. To figure out what your beliefs are, complete the following exercise.

EXERCISE
ENOUGH IS ENOUGH

How much money do you want to have? Pick a specific sum, even if it seems too big. Take, for example, £1,000,000. This is the money you do not have but would like to have. We will do a meditation to help you realize your current level, your dream level, and the obstacles that have prevented you from reaching the dream level.

Meditations allow us to unconsciously create new models of behaviour. They also enable us to register already existing but poorly functioning models of behaviour. It is the unconscious mind—not the conscious one—that stands at the root of both problems and successes. I've treated clients with all sorts of issues, including unsuccessful relationships, poor money management, and fertility problems. As soon as we clear out their unconscious minds, the problems vanish, and their wishes materialise. They find a partner, conceive, complete projects, and receive bonuses. They allow money, and other positive experiences, to flow into their lives.

I once worked with a female client. We focused on examining and decluttering her unconscious mind. A day after our therapy session, her boss called her to his office. She thought he'd fire her. That wasn't the case. On the contrary, he praised her for her work and raised her salary. She received a bonus, even though she had never received one before. Meditation worked well for her, just as it does for many of my other clients.

Turn on some relaxing music. I like to do this meditation with a song composed by Ennio Morricone—The Mission—playing in the background.

Sit down comfortably. Don't to cross your hands or legs. Relax. Close your eyes. Take a deep breath. Breathe out. Feel your gut. Control your breathing. Repeat. Breathe in; breathe out. Sense the ease of your breath.

Remember when you attracted money and opportunities like a magnet. Remember how they flowed into your life without you doing anything special. You've always had food on the table, clothes on your back, and a roof above your head. You've been a magnet for money since birth.

Now, imagine that something wonderful happens in your life. Big changes come your way. All of the sudden, you're twenty years in the future. The calendar shows the same day, the same month even, but twenty years have passed. So many changes have happened over these twenty years. How do you see yourself in two decades? Where are you? Who are you? What do you see yourself doing, given that everything is possible? Your manifestations become reality.

What continent—which country—do you call home in twenty years? Who is with you? Where do you wake up in the mornings? What is your home like? Who wakes up next to you? What have you built over the past twenty years? What luxuries do you have in your life? How much money do you have in your bank account? What do you own? Which luxurious possessions do you now find merely normal? Imagine you wake up and there is a stack of cash next to you. You open your nightstand, and it is full of money. You then get up, walk up to the bathroom, and the drawers there are also full of money. You go to the kitchen—there is so much money inside the cupboards! There is so much money in your closet, too. Wherever you go, whatever you do, you always have money. You are rich. You feel safe. You feel calm.

How do you spend your days once you are financially free? What is your morning routine? What do you see through the window above your kitchen sink? What do you do during the day? Everything is allowed! How are you feeling? How do like to finish your days? Do you work out? What is your wardrobe like? Do you wear expensive clothes, shoes, and accessories? How do you get to work? Do you drive a car, or do you ride a bicycle? Do you walk there? Everything is allowed! What is your emotional state? How do you feel?

This is you at the level of your dreams.

Now, ask yourself the following question: "If I want this life, why don't I have it already?"

What are the internal limitations, fears, and doubts that prevent you from leaving the life of your dreams? Why don't you allow yourself that abundance? What stops you? What hinders you? Why don't you have what you desire?

Breathe and allow the answers to come to you. You may think you don't deserve this life. You may say you're too young—or too old. Is it your gender that is stopping you? Or your lack of qualifications and professional experiences? Maybe you can't get rich with the job you have. Maybe you're shy, insecure, and indecisive. Maybe your home country is at fault. Realise your fears and limitations.

Slowly, breathe in and breathe out. Return to this day, to your body, to your rhythm. Open your eyes.

Note down at least five reasons you do not have what you desire.

1.____
2.____
3.____
4.____
5.____
6.____
7.____
8.____
9.____
10. ____

I assure you—none of what you've written down is true. These are nothing more than your own limiting beliefs. They are not true. However, if you believe them to be true, they become true. It is therefore crucial that you realise what holds you back and change your personal convictions.

Now, return to each of these convictions and note who you inherited it from. Was it your mom or you dad? Your grandparents, perhaps? It could have been anyone, really. People have impacted and shaped your convictions. Inspect what you wrote down and connect each conviction to the person you inhered it from.

You should also realise believing you are lazy and unmotivated makes you lazy and unmotivated. Your beliefs shape your reality. So do your affirmations. Someone "gives" you a limiting belief, and you internalise it. You often find it somewhat convenient and choose to live with it. But this conviction isn't yours. Children do not come into this world with a set of convictions; rather, they develop one as they grow. My son believes he's allowed everything. For him, everything is possible.

You may not know where your convictions came from, but they surely came from somewhere. Someone installed them in you. Both positive and self-limiting convictions are a learned language that you need to disassociate yourself from. Such convictions are like a perfume you dislike—a perfume someone gave you for your birthday. It's right you admit to disliking the perfume. You should admit you won't use it. If you wear this perfume, you will be doing yourself a disservice.

Take a few separate pieces of paper. Rewrite the convictions you described above. Rewrite the convictions that came from your mother on one piece of paper. Note the convictions that came from your father on another piece of paper. Continue distinguishing where your convictions came from and write them all down. Assign each conviction to a person. Give each person a separate page. These convictions may have seemed true to the people that gave them to you; however, you have the right to decide whether these convictions are true for you or not. Your mother may have believed you to be dumb, lazy, and unable to make money. That is, however, untrue. No one is inherently lazy. Someone convinced you that you were lazy. They taught you that, planting the roots of laziness deep within you. Over the years, laziness became a part of your character. But this should not be—and is not—true. The authentic individual can realise and acknowledge their convictions. Hence, to the notion of inherent laziness, a mature man can simply say: "That's not me. That is my parents' conviction, and it has nothing to do with me." That's when you will be able to finally choose your own set of convictions and beliefs.

Now, I'm asking you to re-read the list you made. Imagine the people who gave you these convictions.

Stand up. Imagine those people standing nearby and turn to them. Say this out loud: Dear (mom, dad, grandmother,… mention them all), I have something that does not belong to me. These are your beliefs. You gave them to me. Out of love, I took them. Now, however, I see they do not serve me. I do not like them. I no longer wish to carry them. That is enough. I've had enough! I want to return them to you. These are your convictions, your beliefs. Thanks for lending them to me, but I no longer want them.

Breathe in.
Breathe out.

Put your palms on top of each other and raise them high above your head. As briskly and sharply as you can, take them down three times. Every time you do this, make sure to make a brusque noise: "Ha!"

This is how you can slice the unwanted relationships you have with other people. This is how you can forget the wrongful beliefs others have pushed down onto you. Imagine how those people take the pieces of paper you wrote on, how they leave with their convictions. Meanwhile, you stay in your own space, alone with yourself. What you noted down on those pages no longer matters. It is no longer your story.

Take a deep breathe in. Breathe out.
Put the pieces of paper on the floor. See how little those convictions

are, especially compared to you. Say this out loud: "They are small, and I am big! They are tiny, and I am significant!"

Now, step over those pages. Trample them. More! Crush them! Be brave! You no longer need them. This is your past. You carried these beliefs with you for so long, and all they did was burden you. They trampled you; it is only fair you trample them now. It is your time to do so. Trample them! Tread on them violently. Crush them. Feel them small and insignificant beneath your feet. You want to be an independent person! You want to be an authentic individual! Enough is enough! These convictions are no longer yours! Destroy them, crush them once and for all! You poured so much energy into them, but you no longer need them. They are untruths, fed to you by others. They are not yours! They are the fabrications of people who have an obsolete understanding of life and the world. You are a modern person. You have access to technology; opportunities are within reach. Carpe diem.

Can you sense other people's convictions—the ones you noted down—leaving you? They channel down your body to bleed onto the paper. You no longer need them. Enough! Let them go. Forever rid yourself of them.

Take deep breaths through your mouth. Feel the processes. Move your body, do everything you need. Dance! Shout! Stretch your arms! Jump!

Can you spread your wings now? Are you ready to do so? Can you fly? Do you feel free? It is time to live your life, to achieve your dreams.

Say this out loud: *I do not owe anything to anyone. Enough is enough! That is enough!*

Breathe out…. Slowly regain your composure.

Look at the crumpled pages on the floor. Bend down and take them in your hand. Tear them apart, as violently as you can! These pages contain something old, something unnecessary, something that does not serve you. You live in a new time and things happen differently in your life.

Find a safe way to burn the torn pages. As you watch the flame, release what you wrote into space. It is not yours! It does not belong to you. You grew up in poverty, troubled by your parents' problems. This is not your story. This is their story. Today, there are so many opportunities for growth and business development. It is time to begin anew.

Can you sense the relief? Remember this feeling! You are free and the world stands at your feet. You are already better than your parents, than your relatives, than the friends that chained you with their wrongful convictions. And you will keep getting better.

Stay on guard in the next one month. Observe yourself. The unwanted convictions will keep returning to you, trying to capture you, attempting to bind you with their chains. Stand your ground and push them away. Remember—you can do this. You have the qualities you need, and you deserve to live however you'd like. Do not ever allow untruths to crush you! You are a free individual.

I know you may be afraid. If you willingly jump into the new, into the unknown, you will overcome your fears. You will grow as an individual. You will become so much better than you ever dared imagine.

WHAT DO YOU LACK COURAGE FOR?

Please consider this question: Is there anything you lack courage for? It can be a new dressing style, a long vacation, or a career change. Maybe you would like to move to a new city or purchase an expensive car. Maybe you have a business idea but are afraid of change. Perhaps you've got a talent, like singing, which you are afraid to develop. Write what you're afraid to do below:

____

____

____

____

I grew up in poverty. Our home was in a poor neighbourhood. We had rats and cockroaches. They often hid under our fridge—a cheap, old Russian fridge. The fridge was older than I was. Our flat was horrible! Utter mystery. As I was living there, I often thought of France and the French literary cannon. I wished to learn French. I still don't understand the roots of this dream; French, after all, was never related to my life. Dreams are hardly ever rational. My dream to speak French and read the French classics was as irrational as it was enchanting.

I thought I had fled the misery when I left Russia. Yet, even when I moved to a new country to live with my new husband, nothing had changed. Our apartment was hideous. The white paint had been scrapped off the walls to reveal the old wall covering that my husband's grandparents had hung decades ago. The furniture was old and dirty. Rust coloured the pipes in our bathroom. Worse, the apartment had the exact same fridge my parents' flat had back in Russia. I felt haunted by the misery of my past. I couldn't escape it.

That was when I asked myself the following question: is there a dream of mine that I've always wanted to fulfil but never have? Of course, my dream to learn French was the first answer that floated to my mind. "What a stupid dream," I thought. I was already learning English and Bulgarian; adding another language to the list wasn't the smartest move I could make. I also did not have the money to pay for French lessons. My husband and I were very poor. I still promised myself to pay for the French course if I somehow gathered the money I needed.

Shortly after, a friend of mine contacted me, asking me to craft some compatibility tests for a dating website. Though I had never done this before, I decided to take on the challenge and put my psychology degree to use. I chose to base the compatibility tests on psychological archetypes! I charged my friend the exact amount I'd need for my French lessons. I paid the course fee immediately, dedicating myself to the fulfilment of a dream.

At the same time, I also met a colleague online. He led virtual seminars for men. I suggested we organise some seminars for women in Moldova, and he agreed. The issue was—I couldn't afford the flight there.

Another friend of mine reached out to me on the same day, inviting me over for dinner. She was hosting a cosy dinner for her friend and his guest, who happened to be French. She thought I could help entertain him. The French guy and I hit it off quickly, conversing in French about our lives, careers, and future goals. I mentioned I wanted to lead seminars in Moldova but couldn't afford the plane ticket.

He just laughed when I shared this with him. "Give me your bank account details," he said, "and I will send you the money."

"Why would you do this?" I questioned.

"Because people helped me when I had no money."

The French man kept his promise. I flew to Moldova, led my first seminars, and earned some money. I registered my new business, paid both the deposit and the rent for my new office, and bought chairs. As peculiar as it may sound, that's how I started my business. None of this would have been possible had I not confided in this man, in the privacy of a language only the two of us spoke.

If you have a dream, as crazy as it may be, try to pursue it. Crazy, initially incomprehensible dreams often lead us to discover hidden reservoirs of money. Regardless of the essence of your dream—it could as well be to start belly dancing or attend a culinary course—, going after this dream will further your success journey. It will lead you to encounter people and opportunities that can propel your business forward, just as it will give you new, potentially life-changing ideas.

You unlock a ginormous reservoir of energy every time you do something "crazy."

What did you write up there? Whatever it is, you should know those are your money reservoirs. The Universe has hidden them in the most unexpected places. I have repeatedly seen how people encounter opportunities by doing "crazy" stuff. Allow yourself to go after that "crazy" dream, to learn that language, to take that class. Doing so will help you transform yourself. I can guide you on your journey, but it is you who needs to take the first step. If you truly plan to build the dream life you wish to have in twenty years, you should start now. You will never have that life you keep on doing what you've always done.

I have an untraditional way of hiring employees. Employees usually come to me, offering their help, and suggesting ideas. When I first rented an office, right after I had gotten back from Moldova, I had no money to pay employee salaries. I led some courses, making a paltry sum of money. During one of these courses, however, I met a young woman.

She came up to me, saying she'd love to work for me. "Great," I responded, "but I have no money. I cannot pay you a salary. I hope that the business will continue growing, but, until it reaches a certain level, you will have to work for free. Would you be up for this?"

"Of course," she answered. "I work eight to five, but I am free after six in the afternoon. I can work for you until ten."

That's how I "hired" my first employee. Together, she and I managed to make a profit in the first month. I gradually increased her salary. She has been working for me for over fifteen years.

When making steps like this one, honesty is crucial. If your idea is good, and you know you can implement it, you will encounter people who believe in you. Money will come, too. But, before that happens, you need to take action. Do something that is atypical for you.

Here is one of my favourite homework exercises.

HOMEWORK
EARN THE MONEY YOU SPENT ON THIS BOOK

You have 24 hours to earn the money you spent on this book. Find an unusual way to do so.

Use your imagination. A client of mine, for example, walked up to her boss. She suggested she'd show him her abs—only if he paid her, of course. He agreed. She raised her shirt a bit and said: "That was it!"

Another one of my clients, who lives in in the United States, found a website that connects women with lonely men. As suggested by the website, women go for dinners with lonely men, listen to their problems, keep them company, and get paid for it. Any form of physical touch is strictly prohibited. My client connected with two men on this website. She went out with both of them, earning $120 for talking with them and listening to their issues.

I can also think of this other woman who managed to make money by telling other people's fortunes. She read their palms. I've also done this. I once sat at a café and told people's fortunes with the help of my Angel Cards. Each person paid me £12.

The value of what you sell is simultaneously determined by you, the seller or service provider, and by your customers. You can offer people a basic pen, which wouldn't be so "basic" if you managed to convince them it's a "lucky" pen. Use storytelling to add value to your products and services.

You can babysit your neighbour's children for an evening, you can ask someone to give you the money, you could even sell something or walk your friend's dogs. The list goes on. You could do a woman's makeup, read her astrological chart, or give her a dancing lesson. There are so many different things you could do to make that money. What matters is that you earn the money you spent on this very book within the next 24 hours.

Don't make excuses. Lockdowns don't impact your ability to earn money. You will stay poor if you make excuses. The point of this homework is to encourage you to go beyond your habits, to move past your usual way of doing things and find new means of making money. This homework should shake you up a bit. It's time you let go of your money-making stereotypes and conceive unconventional ways to earn money. You must allow yourself to find a new source of income. Submerge yourself in your consciousness and think. Seek new horizons.

I know this is uncomfortable. Still, if you manage to overcome the discomfort, you will make yourself proud.

You choose whether to be poor and shy or rich and confident.

You should overcome any resistance that comes your way. Do you remember trampling on the pieces of paper and your old convictions? Remember doing it again. Breathe. The resistance, challenges, and self-limiting beliefs are not a part of your story. Trample on them. Breathe. Crush them to pieces and move on. Acknowledge your feelings. Recall the sensations and call them to mind every time you need some support.

I give myself 30 seconds every time I feel shy or anxious. I close my eyes, remembering how I felt when I liberated myself from such old convictions. I then tell myself: "Natalia… one, two, three, four…. Move on!" And I do; I let go, moving on to a better future.

SOURCES OF MONEY

"Flaming enthusiasm, backed up by horse sense and persistence, is the quality that most frequently makes for success."
Dale Carnegie,
American writer

When it comes to your sources of income, the following holds true: "the more, the merrier." More sources of income—more money.

How do you earn your money? Are you earning a salary, or are you receiving government benefits? Are you on a scholarship? Whatever it is, you should know it is hardly enough.

You should have at least twenty sources of income, though you could do a whole lot better if you manage to establish one hundred sources of income.

You can make money from freelancing; you could also start a side hustle or establish a business. You could take commissions from connecting people with each other and helping them make a deal. You can earn money from stocks and dividends. You could rent out your property. You could even rent out your stuff. In London, for example, women loan their bags and get paid. They do the same with shoes, dresses, coats, and jewellery. I'm thinking of renting out some of the luxury bags that I own, as they've been gathering dust for too long. I could have never imagined that having those bags could make me thirty pounds per day. Crazy, right?! That aside, you could also make money by taking tourists around the city you live in. You could charge them an hourly rate. You could also get involved with a multi-level marketing (MLM) business. It really doesn't matter how you make your money. You should simply find a way to make money in ways other than receiving your usual monthly salary and annual bonuses.

Seek to develop your current business. A friend of mine, for example, has a fashion line and owns her own store. A one point, she felt the need to do something completely different: she wanted to paint. I encouraged her to display some of her paintings in her store and price them highly. "Don't overthink it," I said to her, "just try and see what happens." So, she did. She hung a painting on one of her store's walls. A client noticed it soon after.

"That is a wonderful painting," the client said.

"It costs £2,000," my friend replied.

"Oh, that is pricey!" noted the client.

"That is true, yes," agreed my friend. Then, she went on to explain: "The painting is expensive only because it is charged with a strong, positive energy. It brings luck and joy. I painted it!"

"Awesome, I will buy it," said the client.

My friend sold the clothes in her store for no more than £100 or £150. She didn't make that much. She phoned me as soon as she sold that painting. "Natalia," she squealed excitedly, "I just made as much as I usually do in a month. "You're awesome! Thank you for encouraging me!"

Together with her husband, she tried to display and sell paintings of other artists. No one bought them. The only paintings that kept selling were her own. Her energy, it seems, pulled clients in. It influenced them.

You could cook homemade meals as catering for people you know. If you are a good baker, you could also take orders for homemade cakes and other baked goods. Whatever you chose to do, just bear this in mind: "where there's a will, there's a way." If you wish to increase your monthly income, you could find a way to do so. Personally, I have about 25 sources of income at this very moment, and that never stops me from looking for more. Every time I think of a new way to make money, I feel a certain dose of anxiety, an unpleasant tickling in my gut. Knowing this sensation is a part of the process, I overcome it. Doing so has become a habit. So has looking for new sources of income.

In Russia, they sell little bags with beautiful ribbon ties. On the bags, it says: "Air from Saint Petersburg." A bag like this costs £12. It is literally an empty paper bag with air, but tourists keep buying them.

Do not seek excuses. It doesn't matter if you live in a small town or a rural village. If you have access to the Internet, you can search for ideas online. Notice people's demand for online workouts; film a short full body workout tutorial. Record dancing lessons. Organise virtual dancing classes and invite people to join. Charge them, of course. A few weeks ago, I joined a Zoom dance class. An American woman led it, saying her dance moves could help anyone unlock their feminine power. She charged $20. We danced together and I only heard her voice once, at the end of class, when she thanked us all for attending her virtual dance session. This woman had literally made a few thousand dollars, just from teaching others some dance practices online. Profits aside—what matters is that she had considered the idea of organising and leading these sessions to gain some additional income. She had also convinced herself that she deserved the money she made. I plan to join her Zoom dance class again. I enjoyed dancing with others from the comfort of my own home. It was a cool experience.

This woman is one of the many reasons I think anyone can create a successful business, even from a remote town in the United States or a village in the Bulgarian mountains. A stable WiFi connection makes your location insignificant.

Another friend of mine, an astrologer, lives in the Bulgarian mountains. She speaks English and charges £1000 per hour. She managed to create a website that gained international recognition. She works mostly with Americans, taking about three clients per day. She enjoys her life. Of course, to keep her business popular, she accepts invitations to TV shows and radio interviews.

Develop your talents. Study languages and accumulate knowledge. Learn things that will be useful in the long term—even when they may appear futile in the present.

If you are a talented comic, find a way to make your colleagues laugh. Put on a show and charge them for tickets. Make the money you spent on this book. If you manage to make more than you spent on this book, good for you! Do this exercise and overcome your current financial limitations.

I believe you can, and so should you. Prohibit yourself from making excuses. Hold yourself accountable for your own success. Crush your self-limiting convictions. Allow yourself to make more money. Doubts, procrastination, and excuses will keep you poor. I will never take away your right to poverty.

THE CHANNEL OF MONEY

The channel of money is connected to our fathers. They gave us the best they could. It is up to us to decide whether to fall as their victims or love them, in spite of everything they might have done.

This is a personal choice. No one can take this choice away from us. I was furious with my father because he drank a lot, abused my mother, and cheated on her. We were also very poor. I will never forget the moment I realised I was judging my father. I had no right to judge him! I phoned him and asked for his forgiveness. A while later, he apologised to me. What mattered most to me, however, was that I finally accepted him. I started loving him with all my heart. Just a week later, I received a phone call from a popular TV Show. They asked if I would like to join their show and host parts of it. I accepted. This was the start of my TV career.

I directly relate this achievement of mine with my love towards my father. Something else happened, too. A doctor had found cysts in my ovaries and wanted to surgically remove them. Two months after I stopped blaming my father, the cysts vanished on their own. My body had healed itself.

Feeling insulted and hurt by our parents only leads us to suffer. Our love towards our parents stands at the root of our health, success, and wealth. We should crush the self-limiting convictions, not the people who gave them to us. We do not crush our parents; we crush their beliefs.

If you have problems with you father, do this:

EXERCISE
WRITE AN ESSAY: MY FATHER'S CHILDHOOD

Describe your father's childhood. Note any challenges he may have experienced. In this way, you will realise he gave you a lot more than his parents ever gave him.

I've always loved my father, but I often felt angry at him. When I overcame the anger and forgave him for all the insults he had thrown at me, he stopped drinking. He hasn't had anything to drink for years. He's now an amazing husband, father, and grandfather. He adores my mother.

If you have issues with your mother, write a little essay about her childhood.

If you cannot stomach the anger you feel towards your parents, write each of them a letter. Express your emotions. Do not spare them the details. Admit whatever has been bugging you, whatever continues to scare you, and whatever dissatisfies you. Finish the letter. Now, burn it. There is no point in your parents reading it, as this is your anger and your point of view. Yes, you have the right to be angry. If your father once told you, "You only deserve bread and onions," you can buy yourself some champagne and caviar. That's what a friend of mine did. Say this to your father: "Yes, you may have struggled. That is how things were done in your childhood. But I am different, and I choose to do things differently." This will uproot your anger and foster your growth.

RICH AND POOR —
MAIN CHARACTERISTICS

"Try not to become a man of success, but rather a man of value. Look around at how people want to get more out of life than they put in. A man of value will give more than he receives. Be creative, but make sure that what you create is not a curse for mankind."

Albert Einstein,
theoretical physicist

Let's move onto our next exercise.

EXERCISE
RICH AND POOR

Note down the qualities that characterise both rich people and poor people. How do we distinguish the former from the latter? What qualities make them stand out? Also, remember that when we say "rich," we mean wealthy. We mean people who have money, families, health, beauty, and enough leisure time.

RICH	*POOR*

Here are the main characteristics of both rich and poor people:

1. The rich see opportunities. The poor see problems. The tendency to find excuses is a leading characteristic of the poor. The rich, on the other hand, are positive and ready to act, here and now. They take new ideas well. Consider what opportunities lurk around you. Why are you missing them? What are your talents? How could you develop them?

2. The rich have goals and a plan. The poor lead purposeless life. The rich plan for both the short-term and the long-term. They craft plans for the day, the week, the month, the year. They craft plans for the upcoming five or ten years. Do you write down your goals? Goals are necessary for success. To me, goals are essential. I cannot fathom how some people live without clear goals. Goals must be specific and feasible. You need to outline a time frame throughout which you will achieve your goals. Specify your dreams to turn them into goals; then, come up with a clear course of action that will allow you to achieve those goals.

3. The rich see the big picture and dare to dream. The poor are petty and stress over small things. Think about the monetary sum you wish to accumulate. Imagine how you would spend it. Now, add an additional zero, and find a way to spend this new, bigger sum. How can you make that money? How could you attract it into your life? How can you achieve that goal?

4. The rich are confident and positive; they take lemons and make lemonade. The poor remain negative and always complain. Do you spend time with people who whine? If yes, you better run. Quickly, too. I recently spoke with a man who runs in the same circles as me. It was all good until he began complaining. He whined on and on about the lockdowns, the economic crisis, and his troubled financial state. He was very unreceptive to my attempts to cheer him up and show him how many of my acquaintances have done pretty well during the pandemic. "I can't believe this," he repeated about ten times. So, I stopped convincing him. I didn't want to waste my energy on him. If someone wants to be poor, do not take that right away from them. Let them rot in their little version of hell—poor, destitute, and miserable. That is all they're capable of for now, anyway.

5. The rich delegate the tasks that they're not naturally good at. The poor do everything on their own. Delegating tasks helped me grow, both as an individual and a professional. If we do not delegate tasks, we will never ascend to a higher level. We'll talk about this later on in the book.

6. The rich love and value themselves. The poor underestimate and criticise themselves. The rich know their strengths and weaknesses. They use their strengths, honing them, fashioning them into talents. They recognise their weaknesses and hire others to perform the tasks they would not do well themselves. I know I can influence people through my words; that is a strength of mine. However, I also realise my grammar isn't excellent; that is my weakness. This is why I write however I can, and then hire people to edit my books. You don't have to be great at everything. You should simply recognise your talent and develop your strengths.

7. The rich know how to save. What percentage of your earnings do you save? Write it down here: .... If you aren't saving anything, you automatically fall into the category of the poor. But if you save 40%-50% of your earnings, then you are saving too much. You should invest instead. It is ideal that you save somewhere between 10% and 20% of your monthly earnings.

I own my ability to save to my mother. I used to splurge, buying everything I wanted. One day, my mother phoned me.

"Natalia," she said wearily, "are you putting any money aside?"

"Mom, how could I do this? I only make £1,000 per month, and I can barely make the ends meet."

"Natalia, this is not right. You should start saving money."

My mother had a point. I thought about what my mother had said. I really did splurge on stuff I did not need. I prohibited myself from going to the mall, visiting the supermarket, or shopping online. I only shopped at small grocery shops, purchasing pure necessities: meat, bread, fruit, vegetables, and water. Big supermarkets offer a lot of products that you do not need; the snack aisles are also tempting. Over the course of three months, I saved a decent amount, about 10% of my income. My savings kept growing, attracting more money. Knowing I had money saved up in the bank, I built up more confidence. I also invested the money in my new website, which helped me develop my business.

Now, I only buy the things I like. I do not buy anything that I cannot be "wowed" by. This has helped me decrease my spending. As a result, I have more money in the bank and less unnecessary stuff cluttering my home.

Save 10% of your income. This is a rule you must follow. Do not make excuses—you will save 10%, even if that means not smoking cigarettes for a week or not going out for coffee.

8. The rich have a 6-month emergency fund. Lockdown was a great financial literacy test. You should know how much money you spend every month. This also holds true for your business—you should know how much you need to keep your business running for six months, even without making profit. You should have enough money in the bank to keep both your household and your business running. This money is your security blanket. It is the money that will keep you afloat as you switch career paths and move to a new country. It is the money that will help you combat unforeseen situations and consequences. The pandemic—and concomitant lockdowns—did not frighten people who had 6-month emergency funds. It did, however, test the limits of those who had not saved up in advance.

We all have something we do not need. It could be a habit that we've adopted, like smoking. It could also be all the clothes that are hanging in your closet, or the shoes that are gathering dust in your corridor. You could sell those things. You don't have anything unnecessary, you may say. You can't sell anything to make money.

"You have your two hands," I will say to you. "Clean other people's houses, and you will make money by selling your labour."

Once, a woman contacted me. "Natalia," she said, "send me £150—I really need it." I gave her the contact information of a friend who needed a cleaner. I suggested she contact my friend.

"How dare you say this?" that woman yelled. "I asked you to send me money, not to make me clean someone else's house."

I do not give money to people who refuse to work. I help those who ask me for help by providing them with opportunities. Cleaning other people's homes is, of course, a bit of an extreme case. You could also walk dogs, babysit, do someone's makeup and nails. We all have salable skills. Use them to make money. Sure, you may not be a doctor or a surgeon, but you could still find a valuable job. I wholeheartedly believe that people who are always unable to find a job simply refuse to develop the skills they need to do that job. Plus, no job, whether working as a janitor or a cashier, is ever a reason for shame. I'd much rather become a cleaner or a waitress than be poor and destitute. As long as you live, you can find a way to contribute to society and make money through that contribution. You can read young children fairy tales. You could read seniors war stories. Do it, and make sure you get paid for it.

There is one simple way to save: decrease spending, increase your sources of income, work more, and make more. You cannot save much without working.

9. The rich keep their promises. The poor lie and cannot be relied upon. Sure, rich people omit truths and utter lies. Still, they know they'll always be punished for the lies they speak. Therefore, the rich usually try to avoid lying at all costs; they attempt to be as honest as possible with themselves, their families, and their clients.

10. The rich pay attention to detail. The devil is in the details, as you may have heard. The rich understand that the most important things are usually typed up in small font, or said briefly, amid a conversation. The poor, on the other hand, do not pay attention to detail. They frequently sign contracts without reading them. That is how some of their problems start. They create those problems themselves, only to complain about them later. I've travelled quite a bit in my life, and there is something that I have frequently noticed on airports. Many airports promote travel spending, encouraging travelers to spend a small sum here and a small sum there. Though most sums may seem paltry, when combined, they lead to millions of pounds in revenue. A tiny detail — such as a billboard encouraging travelers to spend 5 pounds on something — can have a profound effect.

11. The rich take responsibility for their life and their money. The rich never complain about being tired. They don't go off about their personal and professional duties, telling you "how little time" they have. Instead, they do everything they can to get things done, to ensure their own well-being. **The poor consistently blame others for their lack of success; the country and society at large are at fault. The poor are blameless.** You are at fault for your poverty. It's no one else's responsibility to make you rich. Change your convictions. Internalise the knowledge I teach in this book and take action. Become rich!

12. The rich value personal growth. The rich are always taking different courses. A friend of mine, who is a multimillionaire, runs a successful business in 18 countries. He is 52 and has a wonderful family. Still, this does not stop him from seeking personal growth. He's never stopped enriching his knowledge or gaining new skills. He now takes saxophone lessons. The rich are curious and seek sources of new information. **The poor don't do anything new.** They lack curiosity and do not have productive hobbies. Nothing fascinates them and everything seems impossible. But, because you are reading this book, chances are—you are not one of them.

13. The rich live in the present. The poor live either in the past or in the future. The poor frequently recall past achievements and declare their desire to do something great—in the future. You should always live in the present. The present matters most! What we do here and now is what matters. What we do here and now is what you should think about to succeed.

14. The rich contribute to the world. The more you contribute to the world, the more money you make. If someone manufactured a pen and helped people write with it, then that is their contribution to the world. If someone else created a new computer program to help children with ADD learn faster, that, too, would be their contribution to society. The world gives it back, usually in the form of money. **The poor only consume and are never satisfied.** Start giving the people around you the things they'd find meaningful.

15. The rich are persistent. The rich never give up. They follow their goals; they push until they make those goals happen. Yes! If you were to ask me about the secret to my success, I'd simply say: "I'm very persistent. If something does not work out, I will simply keep on trying until it does. I don't take 'no' for an answer. To me, 'no' means 'not now.' I try again, soon after. And I succeed."

I remember one of my conversations with the multimillionaire I mentioned above. I had just started my business and I was very afraid. I shared my fears with him. "Will it work out?" I asked.

"Natalia," he laughed, "if it does not work out, you will try again."

"How many times will I have to try again?"

"As many as you will need to make it work."

His words were as simple as they were logical. I began experimenting with my first seminars, changing prices, ideas, and even my logo. I managed to see what worked and what did not. Even today, I keep altering the topics of my courses. I also switch up instruction formats. I always strive to improve my business. Even when you don't succeed the first time, you will find success the second, third, fourth, or even twelfth time you try. There are times when selling a painting that you should change the frame. The same holds true for your product or service: test things out, switch them up a bit, play with the design of the packaging, and alter your pricing. Do not (ever) give up.

16. The rich take risks and invest. Let's imagine you had £100. How much of that money would you risk? The poor will either not risk at all or risk it all. The rich would risk 20-30% of that money. When they do that, they will be able to take the hit, even if they lose the money they risked. Losing the money will be unpleasant, sure, but it will not be unexpected. Risk is a crucial part of personal and professional growth.

I am always finding ways to improve both my business and my

personal life. A while ago, for instance, I invested over £12,000 into my website. We had needed to make some serious changes to my website, as it was frequently overloaded and crashed all the time. I ended up investing more than I had initially planned, even when doing so made me largely uncomfortable. I knew I had to improve the platform my business was built upon. Right after I did that, right after we fixed the website, making it the best it had ever been, the pandemic began. I was then conducting all my seminars online. I remember the first seminar I led at the beginning of the pandemic. Seven thousand people had joined—a number of people whose participation would have overloaded the old website. Recognising how fruitful my investment had been, I never regretted the large sum of money I spent to improve my website. Never. I even readily invested more money to improve my other website, even when I wasn't sure if the money I had invested would return as profit or not. Well, of course it did! I am now developing a Russian website…

In business, risks come one after the other. **Risk-taking is a never-ending process.** I risk 30% of what I earn, not knowing if the money I invest will return to me—doubled—or if I will lose it all. In either case, I am not too bothered. I have made taking calculated risks—with roughly 30% of my earnings—a part of my lifestyle.

You can invest in your education, equipment, and anything else that would stimulate your progression in life. You could perhaps purchase a stock and sell it for a higher price to make a profit. **But you must invest.** Sometimes, you may not even make monetary investments; maybe you invest your time instead. You could, for instance, invest your most valuable resource, time, to improve your social media profiles. You could also invest in yourself, especially if you are a woman wanting to marry a rich and successful man. In this case, the investments you make for beauty treatments, flattering clothes, and etiquette courses will return to you in the form of the desired marriage.

17. The rich establish well-functioning teams and hire the best.
Hoping to save some money on employee compensation, I used to work with incompetent people. Yes, I was saving money. But at what cost? The people I had hired never carried out tasks successfully. I had to micromanage, and that took away from the little free time I had back then. Because of these experiences, I became very careful when hiring people. I don't hire incompetent people. I now have the best team I could have ever hoped for. They really are an awesome, strong, and competent bunch! They're all beautiful, too. I tend to think that if someone looks good—that is, they have a clean and pleasant appearance—, then they must be doing well in their lives. If the person is unkempt and unhygienic, however, I tend to assume there is something wrong going on in their life. A bad hairstyle, unmaintained nails, and dull-looking skin are manifestations of much more than a person's hygiene—they also speak of the order of things in their personal life. Chances are, you will not be a great employee if you cannot keep your hair tamed.

I once hired an employee through an employment agency. The agency had set up and conducted the interview with her; she and I hadn't formally corresponded. On her first day, she came to work with a chipped manicure. Some of her nails were longer than others. Her hair was messy, and her skin looked dull and dry. She wore no makeup. She was hired to be one of my company's managers and, as such, she would often represent us when meeting with important sponsors.

I walked up to her. "Are you healthy?" I asked, "Are you well?"

"Yes, I am very well, thank you," she replied.

"Do you get your nails done?"

"I didn't have the time," she said. She began looking at her nails, examining them as if she had never done so before.

"Fix yourself up a bit," I suggested. "We have a meeting soon."

"I am ready." She did not even brush—or run her fingers through—her messy hair.

I realised I couldn't possibly bring her to the meeting. I fired her two days later. To me, your appearance matters. I am very critical of the appearances of the people that I work with. If you look good, then that means you have a strong energy: you find the time to take care of yourself. The rich surround themselves with healthy, classy, and beautiful people.

18. The rich are debt-free. The poor have accumulated sizable debt; they're also always indebted to someone else. Find a way to pay off your debt—if you have any. We're not only talking about financial debt. If you promised your mother to take her out for lunch, do it. If you have a call to return, do it. If you've ever borrowed a book from somebody else, give it back. It is crucial you eliminate any debt you may have accumulated over the years. Pay your taxes, your fines, your speeding tickets. Do this to allow yourself a peaceful sleep. Do this to allow yourself a successful life.

I will help you do this with the following exercise:

EXERCISE

DEBT

Debt You Owe to Yourself	Debt You Owe to Others	Debt You are Owed
Note down what types of debt you may have.		

The unsolved problems that weigh you down constitute the debt you owe to yourself. If you wish to start working out, clean your house, speak with someone, or learn a new language, but you don't do it, this begins to drain your energy. Your inaction also lowers your vibration. As soon as you begin doing the things you owe to yourself, your energy becomes stronger. **I am very careful with my words.** A few years ago, my friend and I were in Italy. We met a few Argentinians there. We talked a bit and they invited us to Argentina. "Come visit us," they said. "We will come," I answered. My issue is that I always keep my word. I began thinking of visiting Argentina, all so I could keep my promise. I got in touch with a travel agency and, not much later, I was on a plane to Buenos Aires. This was a big obligation for me. I had so much work and—despite that—I kept my word. I landed. I went out with the Argentinians I had met in Italy. We had coffee together. They couldn't believe their eyes. "You actually came," they admitted in surprise. I had come. I had kept a promise I had made eight months before. My energy increased as soon as I did that.

Unkept promises lead to trouble.

A client of mine once promised herself a vacation to the Italian Alps. She had the money for it—roughly £2,500. However, she was hesitant to make a booking. "Is it too expensive?" she continually asked herself. "Why should I go there? I could always ski in the Bulgarian mountains." She tried to reason with herself, convincing herself not to go. A day after she told her friends she wasn't going with them, she got into a car accident. She wasn't hurt. However, as she did not have insurance, she did now have to spend £2,500 to fix her car. She ended up spending the same amount of money she would have if she had gone skiing—only in the most unpleasant of ways.

If you've promised someone—even yourself—something important, you must keep that promise.

If you own others anything, you must give it back. Your debt to others can be ethical, moral, emotional, but you have to pay it back. If you cannot afford to pay it in its entirety, then start by paying a fraction of your debt. This will stimulate the flow of money in your life.

If someone owes you something, give them a call and say: "You owe me money. You owe me this particular sum of money, and I want it back." Say it as assertively as you can. Then continue: "Here are my bank account details. I expect the money by noon." When people hear this and sense the conviction in your voice, they will return the money. This has happened to many clients of mine. I've seen this work hundreds of times.

You should first clear off the debt you owe to yourself. **Someone owing you a debt is a sign that you owe something to yourself.** If the person who owes you a debt refuses to pay it off, you should forget about it. Wipe it from your memory; forget it ever existed. Uproot it from your consciousness. Breathe in. Hold your breath. Breathe out. Imagine memories of that debt inhibiting your breath and exiting your body as you breathe out. This is hard, I know. It is even harder is the debt is big. You should do it anyways. You could also contact that person and send them the following message: "I forget the money you owed me. You no longer owe me anything."

This is the inflection point of abundance. My first husband and I had saved a good amount when we first moved to Bulgaria. A friend of his called and asked for a loan. He wanted to invest. He suggested he give us a percent of his earnings each month. I was twenty. Naïve as I was, I gave him all our money: the money we had saved up while working in Kazakhstan, some other savings, and the money my parents had given us as a wedding present. The sum I gave him would have been enough for us to purchase a flat. My first husband's friend, whom I can no longer call a friend, gave us a percentage of his monthly earnings for a while. Then, he vanished into thin air. I worried, I phoned him, I begged him… nothing helped me get the money back. I learned he had bought himself a new car, a Porsche SUV. He was just living his life, and his attitude—his deed—was eating me from the inside. It was killing me. I couldn't let this go on for long. I decided to let go. I gifted that money to him. I forgot about it. It was an expensive life lesson; I now know not to give anyone money without a contract, not to trust too much. I moved on. Things began working out for me, I came up with a business idea, and I filled up with energy.

You should do this yourself. If you want to stay poor, of course, you can forget about all that debt; you have the right to poverty.

If you have a debt and offer to give it back, and the person will not hear of it, then simply thank them, and accept the gift. You could give a part of the money to someone in need, doing a little good yourself.

I don't lend people money. If my friends and family ask for money, I simply gift them a sum of money that they can take as a present. They take it, and we never speak of it again.

Loans are a different topic. Though I am not a fan of accumulating loans in the bank, I've taken out loans in the past. I have a golden rule when it comes to loans: I will only take as much money as I have saved up. This allows me to pay back the loan at any time, should I need to do so. I also use the money I get from loans for a very specific purpose. If you take out a loan for a good apartment, and then you fail to pay the monthly loan contributions, you could always sell that flat. Still, if the money you need to pay every month to pay off your loan worries you, do not take out loans. I know of people who got sick and committed suicide because of the weight of their loans.

Are you ready to ascend to the level of the rich?

EXERCISE

<u>*MY POTENTIAL FOR WEALTH*</u>

Read the aforementioned eighteen characteristics of the rich and the poor. Add three more. Analyse how many of these characteristics you have. Do most of your qualities characterise the rich or the poor? Use this chapter's discussion of "rich" and "poor" qualities to determine which <u>category your per</u>sonality traits fall int<u>o. Give each q</u>uality one point. Add the points up and write the score down below:

Poor: points.   Rich: points.

Which qualifies are predominant in your character—those of the rich or those of the poor?

____

Choose one characteristic of the rich you do not yet have. Choose, for instance, planning or risk-taking. Write it down:

You should find a way to develop this characteristic. If you do not have a plan, make one! If you do not love yourself, do something that will make you happy! Then, once you have adopted and developed the quality you wrote down, move onto the next! Strive to develop all of them, one by one. Personally, I couldn't delegate tasks well. As soon as I learned how to do so, I began making more money! When I forgot and forgave the debt people owed me, I attracted more money. You can adopt many of the qualities of the rich for a short period of time. Two months should be long enough for you to learn those qualities, to allow them to shape your new lifestyle.

Read the biography of someone rich. Examine the personality traits of that person. Realise which traits and behaviours made them successful. Feel inspired by that person's story. Allow yourself to learn from it, to adopt the traits and behaviours that made it possible. There are some truly great things we can learn from successful individuals.

Here are three movies—all based on true stories—that can motivate you and increase both your energy and your vibration.

"The Founder" This film tells the inspirational story of the founder of McDonald's.

"Joy" This movie follows the life of a middle-aged woman and four generations of her family. She successfully overcomes poverty to become a millionaire.

"The Pursuit of Happiness" This film tracks the lives of a father, played by Will Smith, and his young son, who become homeless after their lives take an unexpected turn.

I am certain that my book is not the first book you've ever read. You've probably read a ton of helpful books, gaining knowledge about both business and psychology. My book, however, has already helped you unleash the flow of powerful energy. It has already helped stimulate the neural connections in your brain. It has urged you to make new ones by considering things from a different perspective. It has helped you move forward.

People thank me quite often. They say I've helped them somehow. **Beware of the word "help." I strongly dislike it. I prefer the word "partnership." I help when I have something unnecessary by giving it to someone else.** The friend who helped me settle in London—the same one I already mentioned in this book—is still living in my apartment. She recently shared she wants to work with television networks. I got her an invitation to a popular TV show. To me, this isn't help. I did not really put too much effort into it. On the contrary, I quite enjoyed doing that! I both support and believe in my friend. To me, such actions are common in partnerships. It's not the same as help. It's partnership. I give them a hand whenever I can, as a part of our partnership. Another friend of mine was sick, in critical condition. I managed to book her an appointment with an outstanding doctor. He saved her. I help whenever I can. Still, I am not one of those people who dedicate their entire lives to the sick, the poor, and the oppressed. I give whenever I sense the need to do so. I recently gave some money to a single mother—not because I felt pity for her, but because I felt like I wanted to give. **I did not want her gratitude; I did it for myself.** But I will never give because of a sense of obligation. I don't believe in giving simply because I have, and others do not. Predicated on guilt, this would not be a good reason to do good. One of the biggest advantages to being rich and successful is that you can give—whenever you feel like it.

Charity is crucial. My business donates a certain percent of its revenue to different non-profit organisations. We recently donated 10% of the revenues from my "Money Marathon" to the improvement of school classrooms in Bulgaria. I never do charity for publicity; never.

I do it as it has become a part of my lifestyle. **To me, charity is a normal, regular practice.** I often donate clothes and useful objects. I give stuff away. I also lead free seminars—this is yet another aspect of charity. Charity should come to you as something natural, something that is inherent to your nature. When that happens, you should try to donate as much as you feel is necessary. **Giving will enhance your energy.** There will come a point when you have money you do not need and can give to strangers.

People come into this world with different energy reservoirs. I, for example, have so much energy. I jog a lot. I run for miles. I also work for 14 hours a day. I came into this world with so much energy; it is something I've always had within me. If you feel a lack of energy, you should analyse how big your energy reservoirs are. Consider what charges your energy and what drains it. Notice the foods that charge your energy and the foods that deplete it. I've tried different food regimens: vegetarianism, raw veganism, and the ketogenic diet. After some trial and error, I found what worked for me: I need meat, primarily chicken, some fish, and a bit of seafood. **Everyone chooses what works for them. There isn't a one-size-fits-all approach here.** Also, think about your sleeping schedule. How much sleep do you need? At what time should you go to bed? When should you wake up?

Sleep aside, there are other ways you can gain energy. Regular exercise is one of them. Exercise tends to charge people with energy. Still, there is a catch: you should pick your form of exercise. I, for instance, become frustrated while doing yoga. I find that intensive training works better for me. I adore jogging, fitness, and any other dynamic form of exercise. Some people enjoy the same forms of exercise as I do. Others prefer dancing, swimming, ballet, and so on. Your hobbies allow you to charge yourself with powerful energy.

Knitting, painting, and singing are hobbies some of you may have. Others may be into meditation, reading, or walking. Intellectual discussions may be your type of thing, too. Analyse your day-to-day activities and figure out what charges you with energy and what drains your energy. I am very extroverted, and I love social gatherings—events where I can be around large groups of people. Unlike me, introverted people prefer to stay home. Though staying home would drain my energy (and drive me insane), it makes those people feel good. They love being alone; communicating with others depletes their energy. Some love warm weather while others adore the cold. Notice your behaviours and observe your reactions to different events. Notice which exact activities charge you with positive energy.

If you do not have much energy, you will probably have someone with high energy around. According to my Human Design charts, I am a powerful Manifestation Generator. My husband, on the other hand, is a Projector—energetically-speaking, he feeds on me. I give him energy and he does the rest. He works, he finds a direction to aim towards, he knows where we are headed as a family. Human Design can help you realise your inherent qualities, just as it can allow you to understand what types of people you should have in your life. I even consider Human Design charts when building my business teams. Recognising my own strengths and weaknesses, I find people who excel where I fail. Partner up with the people who complete you.

HOW CAN YOU HOLD ONTO MONEY?

"Money is power, and rare are the heads that can withstand the possession of great power."
Benjamin Disraeli,
Prime Minister of the U.K.

Only your willpower can help you hold onto the money you earn. Start by saving. Only buy necessities. Pick a month throughout which you will stop spending and just purchase necessities—like food and medicine. Notice what happens to you.

The exercise "plank" strengthens the will. As you hold yourself, parallel to the ground, you should imagine money pouring into your life. Imagine yourself saving that money. Saving is natural for you. When you strengthen your willpower, you can more easily forgo immediate gratification to receive something of value—like a new flat—in the future.

HOW CAN YOU OVERCOME PETTINESS?

Generosity is the only way to combat pettiness. You should give, expecting nothing in return. You should become generous. You should treat your colleges and friends, give something to your family members, and give whatever you can to those in need. Step by step, you develop your ability to give. You become more generous, even despite the pain that often comes with giving.

You should also keep your promises. Keeping a promise is directly related to the strength of your willpower. Start with something small. You can, for example, come up with a schedule for tomorrow, and stick with it. Leave yourself some extra time—you're just beginning, after all. Over time, you will learn how to manage your time more effectively. You will gain self-discipline.

In my "Academy for Winners," I follow the golden rule to never allow late attendees into the room. If the same people show up late again, I eliminate them from the course. The Academy, after all, includes seven days of hard work, and I make zero compromises with the material I teach or the people that I work with. I remember two women who came late to my seminar. I did not let them in until the end of the day. They did not take my decision well but learned to come on time. We met again three months later. They told me a miracle had occurred in their lives. The first lady, who had been trying to conceive for years, was now pregnant. Her friend had finally managed to become a partner in her company. Both events, they said, had happened only because they learned to be punctual.

Each year, I only work with thirty-five people at my "Academy for Winners." I spend time with each one of them individually, trying to pinpoint and uproot bad habits. It's a difficult thing to do, and not everyone can cope with it. Whoever manages, however, transforms themselves for the better.

You, too, can learn to be punctual. You can learn to stick to a daily schedule. Once you do, you will feel your life changing for the better.

HOW CAN YOU COPE WITH EMOTIONAL DEBT?

As you already know, I grew up in poverty. When I was eighteen, my mother started her own business, but failed to manage her money effectively. I once found a stack of cash in the dustbin. I felt tempted to take the money for myself; after all, the food we had was never enough and I dreamed of new clothes. I hesitated. After a lot of thinking, I took the money out of the trash and bought myself some sweets. I also got a new dress. My mother never learned this happened. She did not look for the money; she had forgotten about it.

Unlike her, I kept thinking about that day. I could not forgive myself.

That was my emotional debt, and I was riddled with guilt because of it. About three years after it happened, I had saved up enough to return the money with some interest. I walked up to my mother and told her what had happened. I gave her the money. She did not want my money and kept repeating: "You've lost your mind. The money was at home, so it's the family's money. It belonged to all of us." I insisted she take the money. The second she did, I felt relieved. I made a whole lot more money after that. I even took her on a vacation.

The flow of abundance becomes stronger every time you pay off old debts.

If you have ever taken anything that did not belong to you, you should give it back. That's how you will clear both your conscience and your karma. It might have been a purely innocent or unintentional act, I know. You could have, for example, taken somebody's book. If there is no way you could give it back to them, you should give a book—or many books—to a local library. The debts of your partners, parents, and friends should not concern you. They are a part of their story, and they should burden their conscience—not yours.

HOW CAN YOU COMBAT INCONSISTENCY?

Inconsistency is often a distinct characteristic of women who fall under the archetype of the "girl." Develop your willpower, make a decision, and carry it out regardless of the cost. It's good that you overcome all your addictions. Stop smoking. Stop drinking. Cut out sugar.

Money and willpower go hand in hand. Some may say: "He drinks, and he is rich!" Let me tell you this: I know a lot of people with addictions. They look wealthy, sure, but they have accumulated a substantial debt. Such people often do not have cash.

I fully believe in leading a life that is addiction-free. You can take charge of your life only when you've freed yourself from any addictions that are currently controlling you.

Consider your addictions. If you smoke, quit smoking for thirty days. If you consume too much sugar, do not eat any in the next month. Start by attempting to overcome whatever addiction you have in thirty days. If you can, make it one hundred. Do this for the sake of your personal growth and professional development.

I was addicted to both coffee and chocolate. I quit consuming both cold turkey. I had decided on a sum I wanted to save and invest, and the money came to me as soon as I overcame my addictions. However, even though I was truly suffering without coffee and chocolate, I extended my "cleanse" to one hundred days. Even better things began happening in my life!

I also cut out meat, rice, alcohol, cake, and bread. I quit midnight snacking. As hard as that was, good things just kept on happening in my life. Try to overcome your addictions! You can do it.

CHAPTER THREE
PLAN FOR WEALTH

"Don't tell me where your priorities are. Show me where you spend your money and I'll tell you what they are."
James W. Frick,
Former Vice President for Public Relations
at Notre Dame University

DESIRE AND ASPIRE!

DO NOT CONCERN YOURSELF WITH THE FEASIBILITY OF YOUR DESIRES

You must craft a concrete, detailed plan.

We will begin this chapter with a brief, yet effective meditation. A few years ago, I held a seminar in a small town in Eastern Europe. I did not know any of the seminar participants, and I didn't remember any of them once the day had ended. Two years later, I led another seminar in Austria. A woman took me aside and gave me a hug. Surprised, I asked: "Have we met before?"

"Yes," she said. "I attended a seminar of yours two years ago. You helped me so much. I had just lost my mother to illness, and my father committed suicide shortly after her death. He couldn't take it. It was a very rough period for me, but you helped tremendously."

We continued talking for a bit. She shared that she used her last savings to purchase a ticket for my seminar. Despite the rough circumstances, she knew she deserved a better life. The meditations we had done together had strengthened her desire to be better. She was convinced she wanted to marry within a year. She therefore began imagining herself happy, speeding along in a red coverable on a smooth German highway. She visualised her ideal life. Within a year, she fell in love with a German man. "Big love," she exclaimed to me. They got married and, for her birthday, he gave her a red convertible. She drove herself to my seminar with her new car! She showed it to us, stressing the feasibility of dreams: "Ladies, everything is possible! If someone had told me I would find a loving husband and live happily just a year ago, I would have probably laughed in their face. But look at where I am now!"

I am using this example to show you that your dreams are not impossible. Nothing is impossible for the universe. Desire, even when you think what you wish for is too big. Desire, even when you think doing so is foolish. Dare to dream.

MEDITATION
MY DREAM LIFE

"The problems of the world cannot possibly be solved by skeptics or cynics whose horizons are limited by the obvious realities. We need men who can dream of things that never were."
John F. Kennedy,
President of the United States

Turn on some peaceful music. Sit down. Straighten your back. Close your eyes. Breathe in. Breathe out.

Rewind your life. Remember how many times you've succeeded.

Remember how many times you've achieved amazing things, even when they initially seemed impossible. Recall how those successes and achievements made you feel. Heed the emotions that pass through your body. Focus on the joy, the love, the ease of achievement. Imagine falling asleep tonight, surrounded by angels. These creatures are your guardian angels. They've come to Earth to show you your future, the path of your higher self. Feel your body warmly wrapped up in your blankets. Sense your back resting against the mattress. Feel your soul leaving your body and flying up to the ceiling, to the roof of the building, to the sky.

You can feel the cool air caressing your skin as you ascend higher, floating through the night sky to grasp your life's plan. You spread your wings, too. Your wings are white, strong, big, and beautiful. They serve you. You feel so good when you fly with them. You are so happy! You are happy! You give love to everyone you encounter on your way. You sense the light emanating from your heart. You detect yourself charging your entire body—and everyone else's—with light. You have enough for everyone. You have enough to give to yourself, to your friends and family, to your clients and colleagues. The more love and light you give, the more love and light you gain.

You see yourself reaching the life you will lead in a year. Your guardian angel smiles. "Look at it," he says to you calmly.

You also notice your sleeping body, resting peacefully on your cosy bed. You slowly return to it, becoming one with it again. Where are you? Where did the angelic path take you? Which country do you live in? What neighbourhood do you live in? What does your bed look like? Is there anybody sleeping next to you? Everything is allowed. Keep your body relaxed.

What does your home smell like? Vanilla, perhaps? Can you detect any smells around? Can you sense the energy of your home? How long does it take you to wake up in the mornings? Do you jump out of bed? What do you see through the windows as you walk to the bathroom? What is your morning routine like? Do you eat breakfast? If so, do you do it with someone else? How do you dress yourself? What are the brands of your clothes? How are you feeling?

You open your calendar to check your schedule for the day. What errands do you have to run today? Do you have any important meetings coming up? Are you more focused on your career or on your education? Do you have a family that you take care of?

What do you wear to your dream job? How do you contribute to society, and what do you get in return? What comes next in your day? How do you get to your job? Do you bike to work? Do you take the train? Do you drive? If yes, what kind of car do you drive? How do the seats feel against your back and lower body? What does your car smell like?

What do you do during the day? Where do you eat lunch? What do you have for lunch? What's the view there? What can you see? What do you do for living, and does it bring you joy? Are you satisfied with your career? Can you sense your inner strength?

Where do you go once you're done with work? Do you work out? What sport do you enjoy? Do you return straight home to your family? What are they like? Do you prepare supper? Do you get ready to go out for dinner? What do you do after dinner? Do you attend a concert, or do you read a book? What do you feel as you fall asleep?

Say this out loud: *This is my life! I deserve it. I am building the life of my dreams. This is my life. This is my reality. I create it, and I deserve it. Amen.*

Breathe in. Hold it. Breathe out. Remember what this feels like. What do you have in your dream life that you lack in your current reality? Notice your surroundings. Little details matter, too. Engrave the design of your house into your mind. Remember what living there feels like. Transport that feeling into the current.

Slowly return to the present, to your current house, to your current rhythm.

You are here. You exist here and now.

You are still relaxed, enjoying what you just lived through.

It is time to write it down. Be concrete. Allow yourself to include as many details as possible. Recall all that you saw and experienced. Write this by hand!

THE LIFE OF MY DREAMS

I live in ____

Now, here comes something crucial: how can you internalise everything you wrote?

Retell what you wrote from someone else's perspective. You live in

____

____

Copy this again, imagining someone else talking about you with others. He/She lives in _______________________________

____

In psychology, this is usually called association and dissociation. For some, it is far easier to comprehend—and internalise—an idea if they zoom out and observe themselves from a distance. Such people can either imagine someone else explaining the idea to them or go a step further and visualise someone else introducing to others.

Take your phone. Turn on the Voice Recorder. Read what you wrote out loud, and record yourself. Make sure to play those recordings every morning. Play them in the evenings, too. I love falling asleep while listening to such recordings. I sometimes listen to them as I walk around the park.

This works in a very peculiar way. I've noticed that some clients feel significant resistance when listening to these recordings, especially if their dream life is vastly different from their current reality. I've worked with people who lose their jobs and become desperate. Then, they unexpectedly find a much better job—the job of their dreams. I've had some other clients who separate from their current partner and then find someone else—someone that makes them truly happy. This practice will free you of the aspects of your life that are simply not fit for your higher purpose. Don't worry about it. It's all a part of the journey you've embarked upon. You're redesigning your brain to reshape your life. You may feel some physical discomfort while doing so. Expect it—it is normal, and it will pass. It is a part of the journey. Don't let it discourage you; don't use it as an excuse. If you desire to make your dreams a reality, you must do this. Remain persistent.

Remember the miserable apartment my first husband and I used to live in? Well, that is a practice I would frequently do during that period of my life. On a small piece of paper, I had written the following: "I live in the centre of the city. I walk everywhere. I walk to work. I have a car with white leather seats. The car is small, and I park easily. I have a spacious apartment with a beautiful kitchen. The carpet I have in my bedroom is pink. The space smells like freshly-baked croissants."

To attract my dream life, I did what I could afford to do: I bought frozen croissants and baked a few every morning. It smelled of my dreams!

I also purchased a new set of bedding. I had bought it at an outlet, on sale. It was a luxurious set and sleeping in it felt amazing. My bed began looking like the bed of my dreams.

It was through these two things that I began to provoke the future. More and more projects were coming my way. I woke up one morning, and I knew I could no longer live like I had been living. I walked to the building that is now my retreat centre. I had noticed it while walking around town, and I liked it a lot. I saw some of the apartments were out for rent. I called. There weren't any available apartments in that building, but the agency suggested a few flats nearby.

I booked a viewing. I was shell-shocked—the bedroom had a pink carpet! Spacious, beautiful, and clean, this apartment was a five-minute walk away from my job. It was the apartment of my dreams!

The rent was low, too, as the landlords needed to let the flat quickly. I rented it, and my then-husband and I moved. We lived there until I bought my first home.

The better you describe your future life, the more easily you will attract it. Find a way to connect the future—your dream life—and your current life through tiny details such as aromas, clothes, and decorative ornaments. If you happened to see a coffee machine in your future home, find a machine like it and purchase it immediately. Tie the current to the future; use that thread to guide you ahead.

Listen to the recordings you made for 21 days. Do it every day. I've seen the dreams of my clients come true so many times. I do this, too, at least once a year. I used to dream that my husband would work in hospitality, just so I could lead seminars at his hotels. That's how I met my husband—I led a seminar at one of his hotels. When the lockdowns began, however, I could no longer work as I always had. I shifted my seminars to a reliable online platform, which was a positive change for both my business and my son. I also used to dream that my husband would make significant investments. My husband recently opened an investment brokerage firm in London. He had never thought about it before. He just thought of it one day, without my help, and did it soon after. He received his certification in Greece, gained clients, and we moved to the United Kingdom.

Don't worry about your dream life being in full alignment with the dream life of your partner. Your partner's dreams may change in accordance with yours. Your energy may influence his or her energy, leading your partner to align his or her path with yours without even realizing it.

I currently dream of a house. I imagine it with flowers—lots of bouquets and flowerpots—in every room, adorning the space, filling it up with beauty and energy. I frequently buy flowers—to me, they are bits of the future, portents even, that attract my dreams and slowly unfurl them into actuality. The more specific you are with your dreams, the more easily you will attract your dream life. A lack of specificity, on the other hand, will perplex the Universe, blinding it to your desires.

I sometimes do tests and realise **my desires have been wrong**. I used to dream of living on a Greek island. My husband had to work on a business project on Crete, and we lived there for a few months. I disliked it. I loved being in the city, enlivened by the crowds and noise. I also used to dream of living in the South of France. We lived in Monaco for a while, too, and I did not like it there. **But I tried**. If I desire a certain brand of car, I go to the car dealership and request a test drive. I always try. I conjure up dreams that I can somehow connect to my current reality. I feel great in London. My family and I want a bigger house. I dream of a house in California; it seems like a good fit for us. This is a dream, sure, but it isn't farfetched. Anything is possible.

Once you've specified what you want, it is time to craft

A PLAN FOR ACHIEVING YOUR DREAM LIFE

"If you were born without wings, do nothing to prevent them from growing."
Coco Chanel

Craft a ten-step plan to achieve your dream life. If you want to purchase a new house, inform yourself about the prices of real estate in the area you want to live in. Consider any loans you might need to afford this new home. Devise new sources of income. As soon as you have a concrete, specific goal in mind, new information will come to you. You will pay more attention to your surroundings. You will become more aware of opportunity. Your mind will come up with ideas. Your entire Being will attract the right people towards you, bringing them into your life to help through their impending partnerships with you. Specify your goal. Take on responsibility when opportunity strikes.

When you've found the *right* goal, your heart fills up with energy and shines with joy.

When you are working towards the *wrong* goal, you feel resistance bubbling up in your body. You don't have energy to work towards that goal. The goals others impose on you are usually *wrong, fake*. Find your own goal and aim your entire Being towards it.

1.
2.
3.
4.
5.
6.
7.
8.
9.
10.

HOW CAN I OVERCOME BAD HABITS?

One of the best ways to increase our life force energy is to overcome addiction. We create our own bad habits—such as smoking, drinking, and taking drugs. Controlled by them, we poison our minds and bodies every day.

Year ago, overcoming my own addictions gave me more strength to move along the path of abundance. I used to drink nine coffees per day. I would also eat an entire chocolate bar. When my own "coach" told me to quit both coffee and chocolate, I felt I'd rather commit suicide than let go of these addictions. I could not see how I would live without coffee or chocolate. At that time, I had a goal of making £2,500. I had no clue how I would make the money; I just knew I had to make that money. I decided to give quitting a try. Overcoming an addiction usually takes 30 days, though, in some cases, people may need around 100 days to do so. I was miserable without coffee and chocolate! What an empty life, I often whispered to myself. I stopped going out, just so I could avoid passing cafes and smelling coffee. This process, the practice of utter self-discipline, is called Ascesis. It is very useful and even necessary when you're trying to beat an addiction. I placed my entire trust—and faith—in the process and, soon after, I received an invitation to the show "Dancing with the Stars." I also made money through another TV show, only because I correctly guessed which box had £2,500 inside. My goal had been achieved.

Now, I think you should consider your own bad habits. Do you eat too much sugar? Do you go to bed too late? Do you gossip a lot? Do you procrastinate? Do you spend too much time on social media? Do you wear too much black? Do you wear trousers all the time? That could be an addiction, too, especially for women.

When we first moved to London, I decided to practice intermittent fasting. I stopped eating after six in the evening. That worked well for my body, and I lost weight. I also had more energy. After that, I stopped drinking coffee for 100 days. I cut sugar. I also stopped consuming rice for 100 days. I did the same with dairy products. Though all of these were big challenges, I believe my efforts were rewarded when my family and I finally received our U.K. visas—which the government had denied us four times already. Ascesis works extremely well. Therefore, whenever I feel something holding me back, I analyse my bad habits and find a few to overcome. At this point, I don't really know what I can go into Ascesis for; I can live without coffee, just as I can live without sugar and rice. I have no addictions. Work may be my only addiction, but, if I have a second child, I may stop working for 100 days.

Find something to overcome.
Raise your hand, like you would when making an oath.

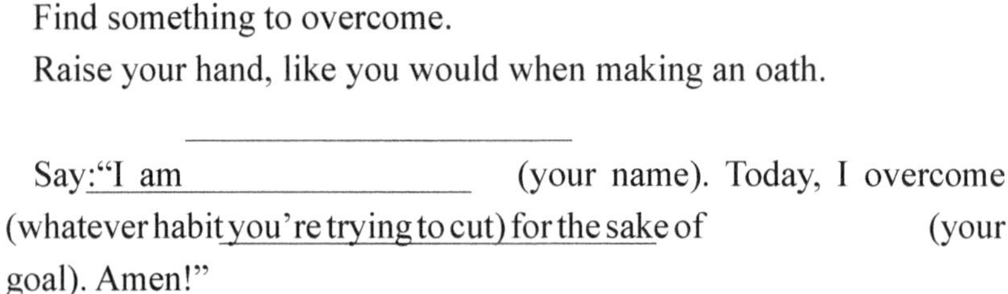

Say:"I am _______________ (your name). Today, I overcome (whatever habit you're trying to cut) for the sake of _______________ (your goal). Amen!"

Now, place your hand in front of your stomach. Your thumb should be pointing towards the ceiling. Feel the energy within your body. Feel yourself triumphing over that addiction. I, Natalia Kobylkina, am here with you. I support you. I have faith in you! Feel my trust. I know you will not betray yourself. Make a promise to yourself. If there is a critical moment when you feel like breaking that promise, get in plank position and move forward!

I cannot control you. Doing so is unnecessary. You should control yourself. That is how you can build faith in yourself.

After this practice, good things will begin happening to you. They've been in the making for a while, but you've just given them a chance to appear to the surface, to become visible to you, to materialize in the tangible world. You will make more money. You will think of more ideas and encounter more opportunities. This only happens because we are energy containers. Our addictions are the cracks in the container, the holes through which the energy disappears. When we fill in those cracks, however, the energy piles up in the container, making us stronger and helping us ascend to the next level. We also find opportunities and people who propel us forward.

Enter Ascesis with love for the sake of a meaningful goal.

It is time I give you another

EXERCISE
HOW WILL I SPEND MY MONEY

At the beginning, I asked you to write down the sum of money you'd like to make per month. Note it down below but add an additional zero at the end.

____

If you wanted to make £3,000 per month, you now want to make £30,000 per month. You should find a way to spend this money. Write it down and be as detailed as possible. If you will buy yourself some clothes, write down the brands of those clothes and how much each piece of clothing will cost. If you will purchase a new car, specify what type of car it will be and do not forget to name the brand.

____

____

____

____

____

____

Now, add an additional zero to that sum. Your £30,000 income is now £300,000. How will you manage that money? What are some of the things you will spend money on? Notice your internal monologue as you're writing. Check the prices of whatever it is that you wish to purchase. Your brain is better equipped to comprehend specific targets than it is equipped to understand theoretical abstractions.

Add another zero! The sum of my example is now £3,000,000 per month. How will you spend the three million you earn each month? Note it down below.

Examine your reactions. How specific are you? How well do you know how you will spend that money? Money comes to people with a clear vision. Fear hinders money. If you do not know what you will do with that much money, you will never have that much money. **If you decide what you want to spend on, you will have the money**

to spend on those things. Still, money will not come to you unless you have clear expectations of what you will spend it on. If you are a philanthropist, you need to know what charities you will support. If you want a big house, you need to open a real estate website and see how much money you'd need to spend on that house.

At this point, this is a mind game. Over time, however, your brain will slowly become used to these ideas. It will no longer cringe at the idea of spending thousands on clothes or donating tens of thousands to charity. Your focus will slowly shift to your dreams. When you reach the specificity that the Universe requires you to have, when you make yourself ready, the Universe will step in to support you.

You should sometimes test your dreams. I used to dream of a yacht—it was a major goal of mine. My husband bought a little boat and, as we were on it, I realised I get seasick very easily. On the level of my dreams, a yacht sounded great; in reality, it made no sense.

Go for a creative walk. Go out without your phone. Be alone. Think about your abilities.

Consider what sources of money these abilities will allow you to develop. Pray. Say, "God, give me the strength to find my abilities and talents." Stroll around town and think. Gaze at the windows of shops, notice billboards, observe people. Spend at least half a hour doing that. These types of creative walks are extraordinarily useful, especially if you're feeling stuck and confused. Every time I get stuck with work, or cannot solve a problem that plagues my mind, I simply go out for a stroll. Sometimes, I come back with a clear plan to tackle that problem. Other times, I come back tired and fall asleep... only to wake up with a new idea.

ESTABLISHING NEW CONVICTIONS

Let's begin with an

EXERCISE
I HAVE AS MUCH MONEY AS I WANT

Note the sum you wish to have in your bank account:

Ask yourself: "If I want this sum, why don't I have it already?" Write your thoughts—excuses—below.

Do you realise you just don't want that much money? I am saying this because I know you would have already tried to make that much money if you actually wanted it. **If you don't have the sum you wish you had, it simply means you have restricted yourself and hindered the flow of money.** Everyone has as much money as they want. **The amount of money you currently have is the amount for which you can take responsibility.**

Say this out loud: "I have as much money as I want."
That is an honest start. It works the same way as admitting to an addiction does: until the alcoholic admits his own addiction, no one is able to help them.

It is crucial to crush your limiting beliefs and take unprecedented action.

People always tell me: "I have an amazing job, but I do not make enough." In cases like this one, I think that these people actually want this job—they enjoy it, even when it doesn't pay as well as they'd like. You can always change jobs or even switch career paths; the question is, will that make you happier? You can grow your social media accounts, learn a new language, attend an acupuncture course, learn how to do hair and makeup professionally. My sister is a doctor. She loves her job—its well-paid and respectable. She used to work at a hospital and earn a meagre salary; she could barely make the ends meet. She has a child, too, and that further complicated things. My sister then decided to attend courses in osteopathy, a form of natural, holistic medicine. My mother helped her pay for her studies; so, my sister dedicated herself to the study of this new field. Today, she is among the best osteopaths in our hometown; she charges as much for an appointment as she would have made in a month working at the hospital. She hasn't stopped educating herself either. She keeps learning about osteopathy. She is also about to graduate with a degree in psychology. She takes care of her child all on her own, and this does not prevent her from pursuing her dreams.

You should carefully consider the following: **is it that you cannot make money or that you do not want to make money?** Yes, you will probably need additional skills and qualifications to make more money, but, as far as I am concerned, nothing stops you from obtaining them.

I was young and still living with my parents when my mother—who was taking care of the house and her three children—got involved with multi-level marketing. As I've mentioned, our home was old, cold, not well-maintained, and small. The only "free" space we had was the tiny bathroom—which wasn't heated. In the winters, the temperature in our bathroom would fall to about twenty degrees below zero. This never stopped my mother. She used to put on her thick winter sweater and a jacket. She'd layer a few pairs of socks on top of her tiny feet, put shoes on, and go sit in the bathroom, just so she could listen to seminars about sales and marketing at peace. That's how she studied to earn her qualification. She worked during the day, took care of us in the evenings, and studied at night—all so she could make some more money for her family.

My mother's story is why I laugh at complaints about the lack of opportunities. Not only is such a lack non-existent but the people making the excuse are also committed to staying poor. Avoiding change is convenient for them.

If your job is not well paid in a given country, you could always move to another nation. My profession is, for instance, far better paid in the United States. I want to work there, in California, perhaps, as I could make ten times more. I've already taken a step towards this goal; I sent in a visa application.

Don't expect things to sort themselves out of their own accord. Don't expect money to grow on trees. Put in some effort. Work. Money has its own zone of turbulence. When poor, most of us become helpless. Still, we deal with this "helplessness" in two ways. The first group of people find a way out; these people analyse their circumstances, prepare themselves for action, and seize opportunities when they arise. The second group never finds a way out. They do not even try to get out of the situation they're in; they simply grow destitute and let misery consume them from within. Unfortunately, most people belong to the latter category. I want you to realise where your troubles stem from. Let's use me as an example.

I used to make about £400 per month, **mostly because I had chosen** to speak English and Bulgarian poorly and seek jobs that were prestigious but badly paid. I had also chosen to attend parties and other social gatherings after work when I could have been working on myself instead. I wasn't preoccupied with the future; in fact, I wasn't thinking about it at all. I had chosen to spend all my money instead of saving for something better. I had chosen to borrow clothes from my female friends and to seduce men who could support me financially. That's why I made £400 per month.

When I decided to change the situation, however, things began to shift. The first thing I did was to enroll myself in language courses; I was learning both English and Bulgarian. I prohibited myself from speaking Russian. I stopped communicating with "party-animals" and casual acquaintances; I ignored their party invitations. I followed different YouTube channels dedicated to self-growth. I developed new habits. I found a second job. I also signed up for NLP courses, which took up the little free time I had allowed myself. I contacted a Russian man online, only to say how much he inspired me. This man helped me establish a Facebook group that would later become instrumental for the development of my business. **I made new, better choices and my income began to grow.**

Consider your situation. Put your hand on your heart. Now, say the following:

This is where I am. I work as a ________________ I earn ________________ per month, all because ____

I intend to change the situation in the following way:

____

____

____

____

If your intentions are honest, if your motivations are clear and honorable, the circumstances will change to facilitate your success.

HOW TO FASHION YOURSELF FOR BUSINESS

"Cherish your visions and your dreams, as they are the children of your soul; the blueprints of your ultimate achievements"
Napoleon Hill,
American self-help author

Your personal style is crucial in business. I insist you purchase enough clothes. Men should get lots of high-quality shirts, suits, and ties. Women should buy elegant skirts, dresses, blouses, and blazers. These clothes are your new dress code. If you want to position yourself like a successful businessman—or businesswoman—you must dress like this. Don't forget to spray perfume every morning, too. **Dress like this even if you work from home.** This is your new lifestyle.

If you want to have the job of your dreams, you should dress as if you already have it.

You will feel the difference immediately.

You should watch a cartoon called "Ballerina." Directed by Eric Warin and Eric Summer, it premiered in 2016. It is a great movie. The cartoon poses one question, which is of crucial significance: why do you want to dance?

And I ask you now:

WHY DO YOU WANT TO DO BUSINESS?

You should first accept the following as true: I am a businessman. I am a businesswoman.

If you resist this little statement, you will never become rich.

Even the best (and highest) salary cannot measure up to owning your own business.

Straighten your back, breathe in and out, and repeat this a few times: I am a businessman / I am a businesswoman.

Now, let's say this instead: I am a successful businessman / I am a successful businesswoman.

Notice how your body reacts to these words, to this practice. What about your conscience—how is it feeling? What's up with your internal dialogue? Can you internalise this assertion? Repeat it and sense how it feels.

What are the first associations that come to your mind when you hear the words businessman and businesswoman?

When I first established my business, I could not dare utter this word. I worried it would somehow 'jinx' me. I could not describe myself with it, and I could not describe my business as a business. I kept telling my therapist, "This isn't a business. This is a hobby!" It was a protective mechanism, I now know, which hurt me more than it helped me.

My therapist had something to say about it: "Natalia," she cautioned, "it is time you take your work seriously and stop perceiving it as a joke."

Her words were a slap against my cheek. I finally realised the resistance I had against the word "business." I realized I was a businesswoman.

WHAT DISTINGUISHES A BUSINESS FROM A HOBBY?

Businesses make you money. I like writing books but, if they do not make me money, then writing them is a hobby. I like taking care of children but—unless I build a private kindergarten—this is also a hobby.

People often ask me if everyone can build a business. Probably not, I answer. Only 20-30% of people manage to establish a successful business. Most people have the potential, sure, but they either do not allow themselves to start or do not have the necessary skills and expertise.

What do you think stands at the foundation of any successful business? A good idea, of course. What makes an idea good? Good ideas have the potential to change lives; they give people

something they've needed for a long time.

Have you had any business ideas? Have any of these been crazy? Have you noticed a lack of something in the market? That's how the idea for the dishwasher was born—a woman was frustrated she could not keep up with the dirty dishes. That's how kindergartens and day-care centres were created, too. The same goes for Facebook and a thousand other inventions. **Ideas arise when there is something that we, as a society, lack.**

THE POWER OF YOUR MISSION

Let's examine the questions that can unleash your inner potential.

1. What talents do your relatives have? What are your parents and your grandparents good at?

My experiences have led me to conclude that 99% of your mission comes from your family. This can't be true, you may say. A young woman I know loves cooking. She moved to London, and started a catering firm. When we began seeking the reason for her success, she mentioned her aunt, a passionate cook, had raised her. She was now turning her aunt's unfulfilled career into a successful business.

My mother always dreamed of writing books. She had tons of notes scattered around the house, some in notebooks, others on sticky notes. She never wrote a book, and she regrets this deeply. She is brilliant. Like her, my grandfather had a silver tongue. He kept diaries his entire life. I surpassed them, in my own way, when I wrote and published a couple of books.

Some people are incapable of succeeding on their own. They find someone to take care of them instead.

Your ancestors may have known how to have fun. Perhaps they had the talent of befriending the right people. My grandmother, for example, was a doctor. Like me, she was a great saleswoman—she used to buy clothes and re-sell them in Moscow. **You have everything your kin has had**. Like many other traits, talents often skip a generation. Consider the talents of your ancestors and see which ones you've inherited.

2. Which people do you admire? What skills of theirs do you value?

Do you admire people who dance well or dress well? Do you look up to people who cook delicious meals and serve them beautifully? Do you idolise people who are masters at making sales? Admiration is a sign that you and the people you admire may have some qualities in common, the difference being that they've developed these skills and you have not.

3. What will you do if you have a ginormous financial reservoir?

Let's skip the part where you buy clothes, jewellery, real estate, cars, and plane tickets. You've already satiated your needs and cravings for luxury. How will you spend the spare millions you have? What will you invest in? Why?

Perhaps you'd like to feed the poor. I congratulate you for this idea, but I also caution you that, sooner or later, you will run out of millions to give. Think of ideas that will bring you money. Money flows in circles; there is a reason why economic theory is often presented in circles, why we speak of the circular economy. You should give 10% to charity. People and businesses that give more usually go bankrupt within months. Your idea to feed the poor is just not going to work. How will you make more? That's where the next question comes in.

4. What do you love so much you'd pay to do it?

You might love baking. Maybe making cakes is your passion—something that you will keep on doing even if you have to spend your own money on food ingredients. Maybe this is something to which you willingly dedicate your time. Or, perhaps, you love children and enjoy organizing parties for them. You love planning birthday parties, even when doing so can be a pain. Maybe you love writing. You love writing so much you cannot stop thinking of plots and narratives that you wish to put into words. You might also love dancing, singing, cooking, painting, socializing… so much more. What do you love to do? Write it down:

A while back, one of my friends shared she loved drinking wine. She asked me if she could write this down. "Of course," I proclaimed happily. I encouraged my friend to explore her hobby; she came around and signed up for a sommelier course. She was talented, too, naturally recognizing smells and distinguishing tastes. She attended a wine conference in Germany, where she met an Englishman who had just inherited a vineyard. She is now a renowned sommelier! She organizes wine tastings throughout England. She has a second talent, too. For as long as I've known her, she's been a good writer. She writes articles about the wine tours she leads and publishes them on her own blog.

Everyone has a talent that they can turn into a successful business.

I know someone who turned smoking into a lucrative business; he trades cigars.

5. What drives you to get up early in the mornings, just so you can get more done?

What type of work gives you pleasure and joy? What makes you happy. Write it here:

I wake up early. I feel charged with energy at the beginning of each seminar. I love my work. Do you feel happy when doing someone's nails? Perhaps you like to style people's hair. This is a sign that you can turn your hobby into a business. If you have a knack for cleanliness and order, you may establish a cleaning company. You could also lead seminars that teach people to organize their homes and keep them clean. Don't underestimate yourself. You've got a talent.

6. How would you spend your days if you knew you'd find £1,000 beneath your pillow every morning?

Write your answer below:

If you tell yourself you'd continue doing what you are already doing, it means you have already found your mission. If you imagine an entirely different lifestyle, however, you should change your daily habits and routines. Transform them entirely. Substitute them with the actions that can turn your dream life into an actuality.

We already have business ideas. Let's now ask our unconscious minds for help. The following meditation will allow us to do so.

MEDITATION
WHAT DO I NEED?

Close your eyes. Relax.

Breathe in. Breathe out. Scan your body. Get in tune with your senses. Register what you are feeling. Imagine that a miracle occurs in your life. You are a businessman/businesswoman. Having your own business is now completely normal for you. You wake up happy, knowing how joyful your work makes you. Working pleases you. What is your business like? Imagine it. Consider every detail. What does your office look like? How big is it? Is there a waiting area? Is there a reception desk? Do you work in a corner office? Do you work at home? Do you manage a team? Do you own factories? What do you sell? What services do you offer to your clients? How much did you invest to start your business? How many clients do you have? How many clients do you gain each month? How many employees work for you? What do you earn in terms of revenues? How much do you make in profits? How much do you spend on expenses? How much money do you make? What does having a business feel like? Note that feeling. Embrace that feeling!

Slowly open your eyes.

Describe your dream business.

When I first started my business, I worked with a business consultant, who was also my friend's father. He asked me to describe my business. "I cannot," I said to him.

"Describe it," he insisted.

"Well, I wish to have my own personal development centre. I want to have a big, spacious office. I also want to have some other space where I can lead seminars."

Nodding, he asked: "How many seminar participants do you wish to attract?"

"20-30 people. I also want to conduct one-on-one therapy sessions with clients."

"How many employees do you want to have?"

"Two, three… maybe four," I said.

That was my vision and, at first, that was exactly what happened. The business expanded over time.

You already wrote what you need to start a business.

Talents unlock after your thirtieth or even your fortieth year.

Can you sense anything scaring you? What about anything holding you back? Let's analyse the limits that might control your behaviour.

The thoughts that can hinder you from establishing a business are the following:

1. I have an amazing idea, but I will not work on it until I make enough money.

I suggest you watch a film I mentioned in Chapter Two: "The Founder."

2. If I take out a loan to start a business, I might not be able to pay it back. I will always have this loan.

I know a crazy story. This young family moved to London a few years ago. At first, they made a living from putting posters up. One day, they went into a store and the cashier, who turned out to be the store owner, asked them if they wanted to purchase the space.

Surprised, the man asked: "What do you mean… buy this store?"

"Yes, this store. I need to leave this country, so I am selling the store.

I'd like to offer it to you guys," responded the store owner.

Though somewhat financially unstable, this couple took out a loan and bought the space. Their friends helped them with the renovation, even gave them some money to start a business. Now, the couple, long married, have a successful chain of stores. They also help a lot of people in need.

Yes, we sometimes need to take out a loan to start a business. But, before we do so, we have to be 100% certain in our business idea.

3. I am sick of other people using me. I want to establish my own business, but I am afraid to do so.

Don't allow fear to hold you back. If other people managed to overcome it, then you can do so, too. Of course, I am not telling you to compare yourself to others. You are you, unique and special in your own way. That is why I am telling you—dare to start. Believe you were born for this, born to create a business. You have the potential deep within you. People need your product or your service. You will start small, and allow your business to grow over time.

Young entrepreneurs underestimate the significance of small steps; they seek immediate success, which is unlikely.

At the beginning, you need to concentrate on the wants and desires of your clients… Find things that you can improve. Your business is like a baby—you have to raise it with lots of care and love. Get to know all the little details that comprise your business and keep improving on them even when you aren't making that much money. Some of the greatest businesses have a slow start. Also, it is normal that you have another job during the first year of your business; this will allow you to earn a stable income while working to develop your own company.

Don't worry about not having enough energy.

Energy comes when you do something you love; passion and enthusiasm always find a way to push your forward.

My sister gave birth to her second child soon after opening her own kindergarten, "Montessori." She did not sleep at night. She cooked in the mornings, took the food to the kindergarten, and worked all day. The little money she earned was spent on salaries and rent. She was working out of pure altruism. She simply loved what she did, and this pushed her forward. It charged her with strength and energy. She managed everything, too, all on her own.

Many people make mistakes and lose their businesses; success is not guaranteed.

There are many myths about business that are rooted in fear. Let's discuss these myths.

1. You need lots of money and connections.

This is not true.

All you need to start a business are an idea, a business plan, motivation, and passion. As long as you have those, you can attract investors and convince others to support your idea.

The most important one of them is passion. Here, I ask you to think about the cartoon "Ballerina." When you are passionate about your business, you often ask yourself "How do people live without my product?" **And you want to give it to them.**

2. Someone will steal your business or your business idea.

Many people worry about someone—a fraudulent politician, a mob member, a dishonest employee—stealing their business from right under their nose. In such cases, I advise you to calm yourself with the following words: "I live in a peaceful time. Sure, I may encounter problems, but I will always overcome them. If I face big problems, I will move to another country, and everything will be fine."

3. Taxes are unbearable.

I know many people who fear taxes. They want to avoid them at any cost, even if that cost is never starting a business. England, thankfully, had a flat tax of 19%, which is not nearly as "discouraging" as taxes in France would be.

4. There is too much competition.

I hear this quite often. Yes, many things have been invented already! So what? Nike has this popular experiment; the company sent its marketing expert to Africa. He believed Nike should not enter the African market because people there walk barefoot. Just a few years later, one of Nike's new managers proclaimed, "The African market is full of potential. We must clothe those people!"

Competition is great; it shows the need for a given product or service.

I will share a little trick with you. If you are a personal development coach, for instance, you often follow your competitors on Facebook. This creates an information bubble, which leads you to think that everyone has now become a coach. "Why am I headed in this direction?" you wonder. The same will happen regardless of the product or service that you're offering. You follow your competitors and, the more you monitor them, the more you grow to believe that there is far more competition than there actually is. You internalise an illusion, believing it is reality. It isn't!

The competition should not stop you from establishing a business. On the contrary, it should push you forward, motivating you to do better, to perform better.

5. You need entrepreneurial talent to establish a business.

This is wrong, too. There are different types of entrepreneurs. Some are calmer than others. Some are more introverted and establish businesses that make millions but do not become mainstream.

6. People will mock me for failing.

In this case, we should consider your fear of failure. Remember the following:

Not trying is failing.

As long as you begin to act, to do, you can actually succeed. Test out your ideas. See what works. Don't get discouraged even when you make mistakes: you can always change your approach.

Note the fears that hold you back from starting a business:

Rewrite the following sentence: This is only true in my own incorrect fantasies.

When you hear you fears calling out to you, speak to them in this way:

"There is competition." Yes, there is, and my business is better than theirs.

"People will mock me." Oh, and I am currently mocking myself by not working on my business.

"I need entrepreneurial talent." I already have it, just as I have so many of the other qualities I need to succeed. I was born to do business. It is a part of my life's mission to give people whatever product or service they need.

THE PSYCHOLOGY OF WEALTH

"One must still have chaos in oneself to be able to give birth to a

dancing star."
Friedrich Nietzsche,
Philosopher

It is vital that you understand the qualities of money and realise what types of people have money.

The following exercise will help you do so.

EXERCISE
FOR ME, MONEY IS

Turn on some relaxing music. Sit down comfortably. Close your eyes.

Take a deep breath in.

Breathe out.

Think about some successful people you know. Conjure up the images of individuals whom you associate with affluence and abundance. Call to mind the people you admire, the people you would like to befriend. Who are some individuals that impact you even when you do not know them in real life? Who has helped you grow over the years? Why are you so fascinated by these people? Which actions of theirs inspire awe in you? Which actions compel you? Which actions do you mimic? Remember how you aspired to be like these people. Recall the times when you followed in their footsteps.

Allow your imagination to bring these people to life in your mind. Allow yourself to see them.

Notice their strengths.

What qualities do these people have? Why do they inspire you?

What do you feel when you think about money? What is money? What do you associate with money? Do you come up with nouns or adjectives? Do you think of verbs? Finish this sentence: In my opinion, money is

What, if anything, leads you to avoid money? Does money scare you? If yes, what aspect of money frightens you?

Breathe in.

Breathe out. Open your eyes.

Complete the sentences and answer the questions:

Wealthy people are

Which actions of theirs—good or bad—captivated your attention? (You could have first heard of those people from a friend or read about them in the newspaper; just try to remember what drew your attention to them.)

Why are they role models to you? What aspects of their characters could you adopt? What actions could you emulate?

How do they treat you?

If you were to ever meet them in real life, how do you think they would treat you?

How does comparing yourself to them make you feel? Are you on the same level? Are they levels ahead of you? Are you ahead of them? How would you interact and behave with each other?

Stand up and close your eyes. Imagine a rich, successful, and formidable person is now standing before you. How do you feel? Will you stand up straight with your shoulders back? Will you hunch? How will you look at that person? How will you shake their hand? Will your handshake be strong and firm? Will you extend your hand horizontally as you shake their hand? Trust the process—your body knows all the right answers.

Regardless of your gender, imagine you are facing a very successful woman. She manages an empire, so to speak, making million-dollar decisions every minute of the day. Feel what your body wants to do. Does your body want to pull back, to clear her path? Does your body feel a need to extend its hand and shake hers? Does your body feel the need to take up space, to position itself as a worthy competitor? Maybe your body doesn't want to do any of these things—maybe it would just like to hunch and hide from the danger it senses. Do you feel anything else? Stay standing and heed the reactions of your body. Bring them to the surface. Acknowledge them.

Now, feel what you would like those reactions to be.

You can start off by saying: "You and I are equals! I might not have all that you do but I surely have the potential to achieve it in the future. I can do it, too! I will succeed. I am your equal. I have the potential for growth, abundance, and affluence!"

Now, extend your hand halfway to this lady. Make sure your right thumb is pointed upwards and your remaining fingers are pressed together. Shake her hand. Firmly. Feel her handshake. Imagine her speaking to you: "You are my equal. You have the potential; you have the talent. I am honoured to collaborate with you, to establish a new partnership and succeed!"

Remember your time at school. Remember the older students. You were younger than some of them were but, once you grew up, you became equals. Relive this again. You grow and turn into an equal of the best. Sense that you deserve the best; it has always been that way.

Remember this exercise. Relive the feelings it gave you every time you feel unworthy, every time you feel the need to hunch back and hide. Remember the strength you hold deep within.

Say this out loud: "Yes, I am equal to all rich and successful women."

Take a breath in. Breathe out. Open your eyes.

Take a step to the right. Close your eyes. Breathe in. Breathe out.

Imagine there is a successful man standing in front of you. He, too, runs an empire. He is strong. Breathe and observe him. What do you feel? What sensations are passing through your body? Do you want to bow to that man? Do you want to punch him in the face, punishing him for his selfishness and cruelty? Do you want to loom over him, as if to prove your ego is bigger than his?

Channel your emotions through your body. If you want to shake that man's hand, do it. If you want to swing your arm at him, do it. Figure out what stands at the root of your emotions.

Feel yourself growing out of this situation. You can stand up against this rich, successful, powerful man. Stand up. Breathe and feel. Standing up against a formidable man is always a big challenge. It is hard, I know. Say this out loud: "I am your equal. I deserve my success. I have the right to a good life. I am your equal."

Feel the joy. Understand you were meant to be as rich and successful as the man you imagined. If you are a woman, feel the fear escaping your body. Women are often afraid of men—a phenomenon that we refer to as the "glass ceiling." Women simply don't allow themselves the right to be as rich, strong, and successful as their male counterparts. They fear the development of a successful business will rob them of their femininity. Women, however, are not the only ones that may feel intimidated in the presence of powerful men. Men who have been abused by dominant male figures also feel threatened when surrounded by successful men. These men hardly ever succeed in life, primarily because they think: "I am insignificant, unworthy, and weak. The big "daddy" can crush me to pieces."

Scan your body. Feel the potential that runs in your veins. Growth and opportunity characterize you. You're allowing yourself to grow. Say this out loud: "I allow myself to become an equal to rich and successful men. I am their equal. I have the strength, skills, and knowledge I need to become as wealthy as they are."

Now, let your body language reflect your new convictions. Extend your arm. Shake that man's hand. Do it firmly. Look him in the eyes as you're doing it. You are equals now. You can sense the respect he has for you; you can hear him saying: "Good, you are doing an excellent job!"

You now know that—regardless of your age, gender, or nationality—you have the right to be successful. You have the right to speak with wealthy people as equals. You have the right to cooperate with them, to form professional partnerships, and to succeed in business. You have a right to do all of this.

Put your hands in front of your solar plexus. Stay like this for a while. Feel the warmth beneath your hands. Feel your strength. Know you can succeed. You have the potential to become an equal to the rich. Many of us came of age in abusive families; we were insulted and held back until we broke the chains of the past and moved forward. Like the ugly duckling, we grew into beautiful white swans. This was only possible because we recognised our potential and lived up to it—despite the hardship. More importantly, we found people—the rich, the successful—who accepted us, noting: "You are one of us." Feel yourself become one of them: join the elite men and women who worked their way to the top. You may not acknowledge it, but you are one of them.

Once you realise you belong to their group, you can officially become one of them. You are one of them! But your membership in their community wouldn't have been possible without your belief in yourself.

Remember this feeling: "I am one of them; I am an equal to the rich and successful."

Imagine yourself attending a business meeting. You are dressed elegantly. Your clothes have been tailored specifically for you. You look well; you feel well. You are also received well. People perceive you as their equal. They value your opinion. They appreciate your mind, consider your ideas, and support your decisions. You are their equal.

Put your hands down. Breathe out slowly. Return to the current moment. Open your eyes and take a seat.

 Rewrite the following with capital letters: *I allow myself to be an equal to rich and successful people. I am on their level.*

In case you yawned during this practice, there is something you should know: yawning is a sign that your brain no longer has a sufficient volume of oxygen due to the formation of new neuron connections. Yawning speaks of your body's resistance. It is something you must overcome in order to adopt new convictions, increase your confidence, and grow.

This practice yields incredible results. I use it quite often. Just like you, I am trying to improve my own life, and improving the way I approach wealthy people is a step I have already taken. Years ago, however, I wasn't who—or how—I am today. I used to view every woman as competition. Men, on the other hand, I idealised; I wanted to bow down to them, to fall to my knees. As a poor young girl, I viewed men as gods, primarily because they would pay my bills. **I now realise there is no need to idealise successful men. They are not bigger or better than I am. I no longer exaggerate their power. I also know there is no need to dumb myself down, to make myself small, or to underestimate my abilities.**

If you weren't the "smart kid" at school, you might have an unpleasant thought coded deep into your mind: "I am not one of the best. Good things happen to the best, but do not happen to me. I am not among the chosen ones." People who have this conviction engrained deep into their unconscious often fail to notice opportunities. Limited by the "glass ceiling," they struggle to communicate their wishes and dreams. It is therefore crucial that you overcome any internal limitations you have. Say this to yourself: "Yes! I can do this too! I am interesting. I am worthy. I deserve to be the class valedictorian." You can even do this little practice where you imagine yourself as the popular kid at school. Everyone wants to take photos with you. Everybody likes you.

I also recommend adults to read the fairy tales of Hans Christian Andersen. I rediscovered them about two years ago! Though frequently viewed as children's tales, those stories are grounded in archetypes and patterns that characterize adult life. The ugly duckling, for instance, is a behavioural pattern; many of us remain stuck in the ugly duckling phase even if we were supposed to grow out of it years ago.

Move beyond the ugly duckling phase! Think of yourself as a swan. Realise that people's opinions of you are reflections of your own self-worth. Recognize that people tend to buy products from companies and salespeople they respect. A business product—or a service—is ultimately an extension of the person who has created it. Once you begin viewing yourself as a swan, you will become a better salesperson. People will gravitate towards your energy, noticing bits of that energy in your products. They will purchase your products just so they could obtain a bit of your glory for themselves. However, none of this would be possible if you do not treasure yourself first.

Your relationship with your parents matters, too. **If your mother is dominant and controlling, you are probably afraid of women. If your father is dominant, you tend to feel fear and intimidation in the presence of men. Your goal is to become your parents' equal, to interpret things in your own favour.**

What am I trying to say? I know this woman here, in England. She is very successful; she even has her own jet. I once noticed she had made her Instagram account private. I wasn't among her followers, and I had no access to her feed. This didn't feel great. "Am I not on her level?" I thought. I decided to text her, to check my hypothesis. She quickly approved my follow request, and we began talking.

"Oh, you are on vacation," I exclaimed.

"Yes, I am. That is why I made my profile private; I didn't want others talking behind my back. This wasn't anything aimed at you, Natalia. Don't take it personally!"

I use this example to illustrate how quickly we project our own assumptions onto others; we jump to conclusions. We conjure up untrue scenarios that are often far from the truth. Always test your hypothesis.

Inspired by this woman's feed, I felt the need to travel. Three of my friends had flown to exotic destinations and I, too, wanted to enjoy the sun and the warm weather. "I want to do it" I said to myself, "so we can be equals." I caught a flight. **It's best when the wealthy people you admire also inspire you.** This happens quite frequently in my life. I often see someone doing something, only to decide I want to do it, too. **That thing simply resonates with me: its vibration aligns and harmonizes with my own. We begin pulling at each other, like the north and south poles of magnets.**

That's how miracles happen. When I truly want something, I imagine myself as a ball of energy, rotating around my axis. I imagine spinning so quickly that it makes me dizzy at times. I am so fast, so powerful that nothing can touch or stop me. I am like a potent tornado that sweeps everything it touches.

I needed to update my ID card during lockdown. You can imagine how difficult that was. My ID was supposed to be ready in June but, somehow, arrived in my mail earlier—and exactly when I needed it! It was delivered right on the day of an upcoming trip. It was as if the universe had sent me a special present. My lawyer was shocked. "I've never seen such a thing happen," he said, "and I have done my job for more than twenty years." I just smiled knowingly. I know that nothing can stop me when my desires resonate with me. Nothing can hold me back. I fulfill my dreams through my elevated vibrations.

That's also how I felt when I brought Lise Bourbeau, an author and the founder of an international school focused on personal growth, to Bulgaria. She never really planned on coming to Europe, even after many of my colleagues had tried to invite her to their homelands and lead seminars with her. She always turned down their invitations. She turned down two of mine, and finally accepted the third. That third invitation, however, was sent during a time when I had harnessed all my energy, when I had it engulf me in its power and lead me to my goals. Desire drives me forward. When I desire something, I cannot eat, sleep, or rest until I get that thing.

When I decided to travel, I could not eat for nearly three days; adrenaline kept me satiated. I felt myself vibrating, pulsing with energy. I felt the first trace of hunger a few hours after we settled into the hotel. When I am in such high-energy, high-adrenaline states, I can do everything. I can accomplish goals that seem impossible. I could even lift a mountain.

You could learn to enter such states. If you manage to do so successfully, you will not face a single "no." Don't be scared. Remember the game Super Mario? All kids had it. The avatar had to jump over holes, as falling into one meant death. It also had to climb hills. "Catching" food made it unstoppable, strengthened its aura, and allowed it to pass through all hurdles unhurt—for fifteen seconds. Once that short time was over, the avatar returned to its normal state. Just like it, we have times when we face obstacles, jump through hoops, and conquer hills, not allowing anything or anyone to stop us. We are on a roll. For a little while, each of us becomes Super Mario. **You can maintain your motivation by visualizing your goal and reminding yourself you deserve to obtain that goal.**

Now, such Super-Mario states are entangled in both fear and risk. These seemingly negative qualities stimulate the adrenaline that leads you to move to a different country, invest a large sum of money, and hire more employees. You need adrenaline to grow.

MALE AND FEMALE MODELS OF BUSINESS BEHAVIOR

> *"I learned to always take on things I'd never done before.*
> *Growth and comfort do not coexist."*
> **Ginni Rometty**,
> *CEO of IBM*

Risk is a crucial component of business. Men and women approach risk differently. Women are often risk averse. Men, on the other hand, are more inclined to take risks. Competition motivates them, leading them to enter an "alpha state" where they can willingly take on anything that crosses their paths.

Women could be motivated by competition. However, they are more often influenced by inner dilemmas, as manifested in the question: *Will I succeed, or will I fail?* This question impacts all behaviours of women: from their ability to attract clients, through their desire to tackle problems, to their efforts to pay off loans. Truthfully, this constant struggle leads many women to adopt masculine behaviours and enter masculine vibrations; adrenaline, after all, is characteristic of male nature. Led by adrenaline, men are usually better at creating start-ups and handling the initial stages of business development—which women tend to find too stressful. Women are therefore more likely to become managers than entrepreneurs. Once men have established a business, women take over, developing existing ideas and bringing the business forward. Women, unlike men, are more inclined to be stimulated by serotonin; that is, they are more likely to seek and foster harmony at the workplace. They are better at sustaining businesses, not at establishing them. Doing so is a part of their nature, especially if they reside in their feminine energy. Hence, these innate differences between male and female models of business behaviour are the very reason we need teams. Women are typically calm, accepting, and keep teams going. Men are the conquerors; they organize mergers, swallow up companies, and lead teams.

In fact, many families have successful businesses structured upon this very model. Two friends of mine, a couple, have a real estate business. The man finds new properties, negotiates with sellers, makes impossible deals, and sells. The woman keeps her husband's projects running. She is responsible for the financial side of their business: she does their accounting, finds new markets, and evaluates financial risks. Her husband supports her as she does that. If a woman does not have a man by her side, it is usually her team that fills his role. **Reflect on your character. Figure out what your role is based on the things you are naturally good at**. If you run on adrenaline, you must stay active. Pursue your goals. Get up and do.

In a business team, it is best to have a combination of adrenaline-dominant people and serotonin-dominant people. These people will inspire each other, propelling the team to success. They will notice the different strengths that they have and exclaim: "I can do it, too!" Just like them, you should recognize your potential and self-worth. That is the only way you can get used to the idea that success is possible and within reach. Success is a matter of time. Still, to succeed, you should first believe in yourself.

I recommend you watch the film "Queen of Katwe." Based on a true story, it follows the life of a young (and poor) girl from Uganda. She is illiterate and incapable of doing anything but raising corn crops. However, as it turns out, she has a talent. She is an excellent chess player. The movie makes many noteworthy statements, including the following: "In chess, the small one can become the big one. That's why I like it." Referring to the fact that a pawn can turn into a queen if it successfully crosses the entire chess board, Gloria shows viewers that in chess—and in life—anything is possible if we put in the work. Unfortunately, Gloria's mother never recognizes her daughter's dreams. "We were born poor," the mother says, "we are poor, and we will stay poor until we die." Gloria does not let her mother's hopelessness get to her. If anything, she manages to infect her family with her own desire to succeed. As a result, her mother makes an incredible sacrifice—she sleeps with a man—so she can buy Gloria new clothes. As hard as it may be on your emotions, this movie is a must-watch. It portrays a poor, little girl coming of age, educating herself, and becoming the chess champion of Uganda. Now world famous, she has managed to buy her mother a house, pay for the education of her siblings, and help many children in her home nation. This movie made me cry! It also reinforced a belief of mine: if you have a clear goal, you can yourself get out of misery. You can allow your dream to guide you, crossing the entire chess board to become a queen.

I am not saying this is easy. Being rich isn't easy; it requires a lot of risk-taking. Each one of us chooses whether to let our dreams die or if we should fight for them. Only the strongest make it out of misery; the weak stay stuck in destitution. You can call this the survival of the fittest if you wish. You do not have the right to spend your entire day on your bed, simply "going with the flow."

Personally, I felt motivated by Gloria's story. She went from sleeping on the hard dirty floor of her home to being recognized as a gifted chess player! If she made it, why can't you? Why are people like you (or your team) not progressing in life? Unlike Gloria, you've been handed a chance to normal life and higher education. What is stopping you? Do not look for excuses. You have so much strength, so many skills, so much potential. Put in the effort and seek the path to success. Recall the things you did not excel at and give them another try. Consider what else you could do to improve. Start now.

I remember organizing a course once. It was quite important for me, as I needed the revenues to pay my team's salaries for the next two months. The course fee was about £1,000, which, for most people, is a sizable sum. Only ten participants had signed up for my course. I needed at least twenty to make the money I wanted. I couldn't give up. I took my phone and began calling all my friends and acquaintances. "You will not put that phone down, Natalia," I said to myself, "until you find more participants. You can die on this chair if you wish, but you will find more people to attend your course." Certainly, many people turned down my invitation to attend the course. However, many also accepted. By the end of the day, thirty-two people had signed up for my course. Once the seminars were over, each one of these people was happy that he or she had participated. **What this experience taught me is that I—just like you—should be always prepared to hear the word "no." People won't accept all your offers. They will not always agree with you**. Still, their "no" usually means "not now."

You should try, again and again. You don't have another choice. You must do the impossible in order to survive.

Find a way to motivate yourself, especially when a point of your business development scares you. You can motivate yourself with a long-desired vacation. You can incentivise yourself by gathering the sum you need to pay for your children's education. You could also stimulate your success by purchasing a new piece of clothing. Find the "carrot" that will urge you forward.

You must know what your "carrot" is. What is the pleasure you allow yourself after achieving something greater? Do you go shopping? Do you attend a concert? What do you do?

I, for example, feel motivated by travelling. I am ready to put immense effort into my job—to pull all-nighters, skip meals, and make personal sacrifices—as long as I know I will reward myself with a vacation once my goal has been achieved. I also feel motivated by providing the best for my family. This is what constitutes my "carrot."

In business, you must keep fighting—regardless the cost. You cannot achieve everything by meditating and visualizing your dream future. You must put in the work. Meditations surely facilitate the process; they stimulate your right hemisphere and foster the mindset you need to succeed. Pure work, however, expands your left hemisphere, which is responsible for skills, talents, and knowledge. Find a way to improve both sides of your brain—the right by convincing yourself that you are an equal to the rich and powerful, and the left by doing the work you need to succeed.

If you are simultaneously working on many different ideas, focus on the product/idea that makes you the most money.

Learn to postpone certain projects. Focus on what is most important—and most lucrative—in the present. Concentrate on what matters—the nucleus of your business, so to speak, and delegate the remaining tasks to your employees.

MAKE BRAVE DECISIONS

Allow yourself to be creative. If you want to take a risk—with a probability for failure up to 30%—you could always increase the prices of your products. You could also introduce a new product, hire an employee, or collaborate with a successful individual who works in the same field as you.

We can allow short-term losses for the sake of long-term profits.

If your number of clients is decreasing, you should try to find new markets. How did one of my clients manage to find new markets? She travelled a lot! She used to sell flats on the Bulgarian Black Sea Coast at a time when everyone was selling real estate there. Smart as she was, my friend would catch a flight to Moscow and then a train to Vladivostok, Siberia. She'd buy first-class train tickets, as she knew all the rich Russian women would be there. After all, there weren't any planes that connected Moscow and Vladivostok. My friend would then introduce herself, find shared interests, and befriend those women, all before making her pitch—she was a real estate agent, offering beautiful properties in one of the most charming places on earth. That's what she would tell them, in her broken Russian. Not only would these wealthy women find my friend (and the way she spoke) captivating, but they would often invite her over to their houses, introducing her to their husbands and other rich Russians. My friend sold flats like freshly baked bread.

Debit and credit cards were not common when my friend was finding her rich Russian clients. She accepted deposits in cash and would often return to Bulgaria with suitcases full of money. She used to sell about twenty apartments—an entire apartment building—during a single trip. And, when everyone else asked her how she managed to do so, she'd say to them, "Well, I went to Siberia. Did you go to Siberia?"

Of course, her trips to the Russian East were risky. She was a woman alone who did not speak the local language. She also carried suitcases full of cash. But she did it all because she knew she was discovering markets no one else wanted to approach. Even today, my friend keeps on finding markets that most people would never consider.

When you lack clients, you should consider all the places you've never been to. That is where you will find more customers.

Another friend of mine, a millionaire, found a way to sell SIM cards in Africa. He travelled there on his own—which was a risk in itself—and managed to meet a local businessman, who then popularised his product in Benin. My friend now makes millions of pounds every year. He still works with Africa, too. He never gave up on it. As he likes to tell me, Africa—and taking the risk to go there—took him out of poverty, out of his job as a bartender, and gave him a better life. The least he could do, he notes, is continue to work.

Not everyone goes to Benin or Siberia; most people are afraid to look beyond their immediate surroundings. That's why most people never grow rich. Success happens when you get out of your comfort zone and seek opportunity where others refuse to look.

Money is everywhere, but you will often find it in the most unexpected places.

A colleague of mine recently shared she makes the majority of her book sales in Mongolia. "How is this possible?" I wondered. She explained the Mongolian market is small, lacks a sufficient offering of services and products, and there is relatively little competition. That's why her books sell so well in the Mongolian market—and have relatively little success on the American or British markets. Small markets often offer the best opportunity for success, especially when the competition is weak.

You must know how to sell yourself. Prepare yourself to go under the spotlight and face criticism.

Criticism is always present, regardless of the field you work in. There will always be those people who criticize you for your age, gender, appearance, accent, etc.

You must strive for fame and be ready to pay the price to receive it.

You must be ready to publicly market and defend your product. Your name and face must stand behind that product, assuring clients of its use and applicability. No one will buy or recommend your product unless you have faith in it—and you put yourself on the line—first.

A client of mine asked me to promote her product. "No problem," I responded. "Just let me see your Instagram feed first."

"I don't use Instagram," she said to me.

"What about Facebook?"

"No."

"Why not?"

"Well," she muttered, "I don't like having my face all over the Internet."

"So, let me get this straight—you want me to show myself with your product while you hide in the privacy of your personal life? Why should I do this for you if you don't put in any effort yourself?" I was livid. "I won't promote your product," I concluded.

Clients can sense your dedication to a business. If you are all in, they will have faith in your products, too. If you are having doubts about your products, they will feel that hesitancy and buy from someone else. You need to find a way to sell. If you need to grab everyone's attention through something scandalous, then go for it! The media will eat it up. There is no such thing as bad publicity. People must know who you are.

I, like many others, have a persona, a mask. I eat bananas and ice creams. I talk about blowjobs… because that sells. I am well-aware of the way PR works, and, from time to time, I do something a little scandalous to maintain my persona. Scandal has allowed me to attract followers who can then learn about all the other courses I offer. I use salaciousness to sell.

Consider any double standards you may have. Many (unsuccessful) businessmen and businesswomen share the following double standard: they wish to sell their product or service, but, at the same time, they want to do so without associating the product or service with themselves. This never works. You cannot expect others to like and purchase your products if you refuse to associate yourself with those very products. **Do not allow yourself to have double standards: they are a major obstacle to the success of your business.**

When you analyse which business tasks are outside your comfort zone, you can learn what areas of your life—and your business—you should develop. If you do not like conversing with clients, you should do exactly that, as it will help you grow. If you do not like showing your personal life, then that is exactly what you must do—your personal life is the hidden reservoir you've been hoping to find.

Your biggest strength and your biggest fear often reside in the same place.

PREDISPOSITIONS FOR AFFLUENCE

I suggest you take the following test:

1. How much money would you like to have in five years?
a. £100,000 – £200,000
b. £250,000 – £500,000
c. £500,000 – £5,000,000
d. £5,000,000 or more
e.   (some other sum)

2. What are your financial dreams?
a. I want to win the lottery.
b. I want to find a job with a generous salary, employee benefits package, and decent vacation time.
c. I want to own a home.

d. ~~I want to have an unlimited income from my business; I want to~~ make money through different passive streams of income.

e.

3. Which sentence describes your current financial situation?

a. I am satisfied with my current financial situation.

b. I am generally "okay" with my finances.

c. I am unhappy with my financial situation, but I don't see how I could improve it.

d. I am dissatisfied with my financial situation; I want to make more money.

4. How much time do you spend per day on improving your financial situation?

a. Less than 30 minutes.

b. Between 30 and 60 minutes.

c. Two hours.

d. More than two hours.

5. How much money do you invest in your own financial literacy? How much do you spend on the things that would improve the efficiency of your business and increase your income?

a. Less than £50.

b. Between £50 and £250.

c. Between £250 and £600.

d. More than £600.

6. What do you do when you are faced with an important issue?

a. I ignore it and hope it goes away.

b. I complain to my friends and family.

c. I place the problems on someone else's shoulders and let them worry about it.

d. I brainstorm until I find an appropriate solution.

7. What's your attitude towards your current job?

a. It's not great, but I can stand it.

b. It is not my dream job at all; I would like to do something else.

c. It is okay; it pays well.

d. I love my job; it delights me and charges me with energy.

8. What would you do if you lose your current source of income?

a. I would apply for government benefits.

b. I would attend a course and obtain a qualification in a field of interest.

c. I would look for another job.

d. I would establish my own business.

9. Which sentence best describes your energy levels throughout the day?

a. I have energy throughout the entire day.

b. I feel energetic in the mornings, but I become tired around noon. By the time the evening comes, I am exhausted.

c. I can work for eight hours a day.

d. I am a fountain of energy; I never get tired, and work makes me happy.

10. How do you react when someone says, "This is impossible"?

a. I internalise their words and feel like a victim.

b. I feel hysterical. I throw a tantrum. I am angry. I yell.

c. I try again.

d. This arouses me. It fills me up with energy and motivates me to work until I get what I want.

11. How do you react when you must take an important decision but do not know what to do?

a. I watch TV for hours.

b. I speak with my friends and ask them for advice.

c. I analyse the situation and do what is most logical.

d. I follow my instincts and make that decision.

12. What is your attitude towards people?

a. I trust they will not lie to me or steal from me.

b. I surround myself with people who admire me.

c. I hire the best, knowing they will do their work well.

d. I hire the best, but I do not trust them. I micromanage them.

13. How do you react when someone harms your reputation?

a. I feel depressed and wonder why nobody loves me.

b. I ignore them and do not bother to react.

c. I try to understand why they are trying to harm my reputation.

d. I punish them.

14. What would you be doing if your life were going "great"?

a. I would take time off.

b. I would try to maintain what I already have.

c. I would think of a new business and possibly a new career path.

d. I would concentrate on my business to yield better results.

15. What is your attitude towards marriage?

a. I am married and I would never get divorced.

b. I believe my partner loves me. The love between us will remain, even if we separate.

c. We can always separate, but that is not something I like thinking about.

d. I love my partner, but I would like to sign a prenuptial agreement before marrying him or her.

The answers to these questions reveal your attitude towards abundance. Your dreams are of primal importance. The statement "you are only as big as your dreams" holds true here. How did you answer the first question? How much money would you like to have in five years?

I first did this test years ago. Having so much money felt impossible back then. I worked hard to earn that money, but despite my efforts, I never could. That was when I added another 0. The £5,000 became

£50,000. I now dreamed of making £50,000, even though I couldn't even make £5,000. This worked like magic! New people entered my life. Opportunities manifested themselves. My team and I began working on a new project and, within two months, I made £50,000.

Money doesn't come when the sum you're working towards is too small. Find a sum that truly motivates you.

Rich people dream big. Talking about millions of pounds is normal for them—that is a part of both their mindset and their lifestyle. We often grow up in environments where people are always trying to save money, focusing on the little coins rather than thinking about the big banknotes. If you believe that making money is hard, you are probably limiting your own income and opportunities.

The first thing you need to do is grapple with the idea of being rich and making lots of money. _______________________

Stand in front of the mirror and look yourself in the eyes. Say this out loud: "I am currently making   (say the amount of money you make every year). In five years, I will have
             " (say the amount of money you wish to have).

Did you feel your breath halt for a moment? Breathe in. Breathe out. Move your body. Relax your muscles. Say this out loud, using a different, bigger sum this time: "In five years, I will have

This should be the first thing you do in the mornings when you pass by a mirror. Do this every morning! Then, as you are brushing your teeth, look at yourself in the mirror and say: "Good morning, millionaire! In five years, you will have

Set a clear goal. Motivate yourself to earn the exact sum you are thinking about right now. Give yourself a deadline. This works very well for me. I, for instance, set a goal to make a certain sum by the time I was 35. I made that sum a while before I turned 35. What's important is that you select your sum according to your life. My friend, the multimillionaire I mentioned a few times, was born in a poor family. He once told me: "I've always known I'd be a multimillionaire by the time I turned 35. I used to walk to the city centre, which was far from the house my family and I lived in. I'd always look at a house there. I knew I'd own it one day. At that time, I worked as a bartender, and this seemed impossible. But I made it happen. I bought that very house when I turned 35. I had programmed that success into the ridges of my brain, convinced myself I was worthy and deserving of it. I also frequently told my wife—a children's teacher—that we would be rich one day, living in the city centre. She would just laugh. Then, she would say: "You are insane, but I love you."

You must know where and how you would like to live. I wanted to live in London. If you know where and how you would want to live, things will happen to facilitate your success. You may not live in your dream city today, but you will live there in five years.

There is one quality you need to get rid of in case you wish to make lots of money. That is why we are going to do a constellation right now.

A COVERT CONSTELLATION

Take three pieces of paper. It is best if they are A4 size. On the first piece of paper, write the number 1. Write 2 on the second piece of paper, and 3 on the third. This will be a hidden, covert constellation. You will not know what is happening until its very end. It will allow you to enter your unconscious mind and check what is going on there, to figure out how your unconscious works.

Place the first piece of paper wherever you choose.

Do the same with the second and third pieces of paper.

Now, touch the first piece of paper and close your eyes. What is your attitude towards the second and third pieces of paper? What about the first?

Piece of paper 2 makes me feel

Piece of paper 3 makes me feel

Now, touch the second piece of paper. Close your eyes. What do you sense? What is your attitude towards this piece of paper?

I sense

Touch the third piece of paper. What is your attitude towards the first and second pieces of paper?

Piece of paper 1 makes me feel ___________________________

____

____

Piece of paper 2 makes me feel

Let's analyse this constellation. Where did you place the three pieces of paper? How did the first piece of paper relate to the second and the third?

The first piece of paper represents you – your personality, your Jungian self.

The second piece of paper embodies the challenges that hold you back. These challenges include your fears, limitations, incorrect attitudes, and problems—all the negative things that diminish your financial success and prevent abundance from flowing into your life.

The third piece of paper symbolizes money.

Notice where you placed the three pieces of paper. Is the third one close to you? Is there direct contact between you and the money? It is best if papers 1 and 3 are close to you and paper 2 is far away. If paper 2 stands to the right of paper 1, then your challenges are related to the partnerships and relationships you have—or lack—in your life. Your partner may be afraid and his/her fear may be holding you back. It is also possible that the lack of a partner is draining your energy.

Now, consider the placement of paper 3 relative to paper 1. If the two pieces of paper are far apart, this shows your unwillingness to connect with money. You do not allow yourself to become one with it. If paper 3 is behind you, you have your family's support; chances are, you finances come from your marriage, partnerships, family, inheritances, etc. In this case, you probably grew up in a family that paid for your education and taught you how to approach and make money. If paper 3 is somewhere far away, this speaks of problems. If you feel a certain connection—sympathy even—for paper 2, this means you wouldn't mind living the way you are right now.

Poverty is often a matter of convenience: it does not require people to leave their comfort zone.

Now, place paper 1 on top of paper 3. Feel yourself become one with money. Make money a part of you. Invite money to enter your life. Place your hands in front of you and fold your elbows. Begin to draw your arms together until your palms touch. Notice how you feel when you encounter money. Sense the energy of money. Imagine your entire body is now touching money. You are engulfed in abundance. This is usual for you. You love money, and money loves you. Consider all the wonderful things that can happen if you allow money to pour into your everyday life. Visualise your cells attracting and consuming abundance. Imagine the membranes of your skin pulling in opportunities like thousands of magnets scattered all over your body. Feel that money is something natural for you, something that comes to you naturally.

What will your parents say when you become wealthy? How will they react when they learn you have ………………………………… in your bank account? How will they act knowing you are that rich?

How would your friends react if they learned this as well? What would change if they learned you have attracted abundance into your life? What about your partners? What would they say? Ask yourself: "What is holding me back? What prevents me from attracting abundance into my life?" Breathe. Scan your body. Notice what you are feeling. Acknowledge the answers your mind conjures up with when you ask the following question: "What stops me from being wealthy?"

Breathe in. Breathe out. Put your hands on your third chakra—the Solar Plexus. This is the centre of your willpower, the place where you hold your money. Feel your energy. Now, rub your hands and pat your cheeks. Exit this constellation. Write down the challenges you now know you have: ________________________________

____

OBSTACLES TO ABUNDANCE

"Success isn't measured by money or power or social rank.
Success is measured by your discipline and inner peace."
Mike Ditka,
American former football player and coach

1. You struggle to define your worth.

If you feel anxious demanding what you deserve, if you always question if you've given enough, let me tell you this:

Give what you have in excess; give what you do with ease.

Personally, I couldn't take care of children before giving birth to my son. I preferred to work for 100 hours per week; that made me happy. I find it easy to offer people ideas; when someone asks for an idea, I offer one quickly, with pleasure. When a friend and I are having coffee, and that friend is telling me about his or her problems, I come up with solutions immediately. I have an excess of ideas, which is why I offer them. The rich have an excess of money; they therefore give money away quite often. The rich, however, lack time. **If you cannot demand what you deserve, you simply do not trust people**. Your position puts you at a disadvantage, as you have assumed the following to be true: "I am at loss, and you are winning." However, if you attempt to analyse this assumption more deeply, you will soon realise it stands for: "You guys are so dumb and incapable that you are failing to pay me for my service." **When you underestimate your own efforts and labour, you also underestimate your clients**. In this case, the people who purchase your products often feel as if they've bought something of low quality. Don't ask me why that's the case. Stop rationalising. If you walk on the street without gazing at your feet, you may fall into a hole. If that happens, you will not ask yourself how you fell. You've fallen already. It would be wise if you ask yourself: "What could I do to never fall into a hole ever again?"

When examining your problems, you should consider solutions—not causes.

The question "why" will not lead you to the solution of a problem; on the contrary, it will reveal the root of that problem. Problems are caused due to multiple reasons, and we can hardly ever pin the exact cause. As a clinical therapist, I struggled to stop asking "why?" Sure, this question is necessary at times, but substituting it with "how can I solve this?" is far more fruitful in the long term.

Substitute the word "problem" with the word "task."

Say this out loud: "I have a task to charge the full price for my product and/or service."

Don't ever underestimate your efforts.

I usually divide the prices of my products into different groups: **free** (I always give something for free), **cheap** (I offer commercial goods/ services every time I lead big groups), **elite** (small groups of 20 or 30 people with the possibility for individual interactions with clients), and **VIP** (these are my personal consultations with people, the price of which I keep raising; I simply pour so much of my energy into these consultations). **I allow my clients to choose, and they decide what is comfortable for them**. If I consult people for a lower price, I will become angry and suffer. I will also not help my clients as much. Personal consultations require a lot of energy, hard work, and patience on my behalf. Hence, not charging as much as my labour is worth would be a disservice to myself.

It is crucial that you and the price of your product/service vibrate on the same frequency. You should feel good charging that sum of money.

The price will not pose a problem to your clients. There are all sorts of clients out there! If anything, your higher prices may motivate your clients to work more, just so they can afford your services. I, for example, want to purchase a property in London. Because real estate here is very expensive, I am now working three times harder than I was before to afford my dream home. I feel inspired and motivated to work. **Your high prices can inspire others to develop an idea; they can even start a business just so they can afford your products and services. Have faith in people and their potential**! Your higher prices will challenge many to work and earn money.

"Expensive" is a subjective term. £100 can be expensive for some, and a joke for others.

Prices should be a concern of the client, not of the seller.

If a client does not like the price of a product, then they must simply look for another product. Diamonds are expensive, and yet many people buy them. If, as a consumer, you happen to like a product you cannot afford, simply pass by it. Someone else will appreciate it soon enough.

If you find that your product has a downside, you tend to fixate on that downside, leading your clients to notice it. If you are ashamed that your products are made in China, every client of yours will suddenly become concerned with the origin of your products.

2. You cannot manage your money.

You need to know how to manage your money. You need to know what you will use your money for. If you use that money correctly, you can grow. Learn how to use money so that you can then make more money.

3. You don't allow yourself to think beyond your salary and start

a business.

Many years ago, as a business coach, I was making the most anyone in my sphere could make. However, I was still unable to afford a nice car and the vacations I wanted. I feared losing my salary. I also doubted that I, a young woman, could succeed in business. I had no money set aside, and I had no startup capital. I started my own business anyway! The rich take risks. People who receive monthly salaries, on the other hand, seek security. **In business, there is no such thing as security; this frightens most people**. Starting your own business is a matter of choice. If you are so worried about being left without a salary, you could always start a side hustle. One of my employees does multi-level marketing (MLM) sales on the side, earning twice as much as I pay her. Another one of my employees started a YouTube channel; she makes money by publishing makeup tutorials. Both of these women find enough time to both work for me and develop their side businesses. I had most of my employees take my "Academy for Coaches," just so they could learn to seek additional streams of income. If you have initiative, you can always find more ways to make money. My employees often suggest business ideas that they develop in their free time; I, of course, pay them for it. You can always think of suggestions you could pitch to your boss to make more money. **You should overcome your fears and seize any opportunity that comes your way**. Seek opportunities. It doesn't matter if you are walking dogs or teaching people on Zoom… what matters is that you find a way to make more money.

4. You doubt your ability to sell.

Overcome personal convictions like: "I am not that type of person. I don't sell well." With the help of the right courses and education, you can do anything! Trust me—I wasn't a good saleswoman. "Selling is below me," I used to tell myself. I felt insulted by those who stressed the importance of sales. I didn't want to be a salesperson.

"I am a psychologist!" I exclaimed once, "I did not wander hospital hallways for five years to become a salesperson. I am a clinical psychologist."

Patient, as always, my coach asked me a question: "Natalia, do you want to be a rich psychologist or a poor psychologist?"

"A rich one," I answered. "But how can I be rich?"

"Learn to sell."

"But I can't do that. I can't. My mother is the 'business' person in our family. I hate business. I don't want to get involved with sales. I won't bother with it. That is not the type of person I am."

"Change your mindset," he responded quietly.

I began considering my limitations. As much as I did not want to, I started leading seminars about sales. This helped me realise how much I value selling well! **Rich people are excellent at making sales**! You will not become successful if you are a bad salesperson. The way you sell doesn't matter all that much. If you are a good salesperson, you can sell anything! People will be grateful, too. Many of us have money we do not know how to use. If not you, someone else will sell people something—and it may be of lower value. You should therefore offer people something valuable, something that could change their lives.

Once I understood the importance of my products and services, I felt a compulsive need to sell. I wholeheartedly believe my products can change lives. This leads me to market and sell my products to as many people as possible.

I suggest you take courses about sales and marketing. Learn how to be a better salesperson. This will help you tremendously in business—and in life.

WHAT IF YOU ARE CURRENTLY UNEMPLOYED?

First, **stop perceiving your temporary unemployment as a problem**. Eradicate that word from your dictionary and substitute with the word "task." You now have the task of finding a job! "I have a task to find work" sounds a whole lot better than "I have an issue; I have to find myself a job."

Second, learn to view the situation as **a stroke of luck**. Think this way: "I am lucky to be unemployed." You can find an interesting job, start a business, and find useful partners.

Put your hobbies aside. Everything that brings you pleasure but not money is a hobby. **Your brain must learn to calculate necessary investments and potential profits**. Compare yourself—and your business—to your competitors. Research their revenues. Consider your skills and figure out how they could help you make money. Monetize your talents. How can you contribute to society?

To become rich, you must have an idea and sell that idea.

People should learn they cannot live without your idea. It should be vital for them to obtain your product. The product itself may be utterly useless. Even then, you must popularize it and motivate others to buy it. Present that product as a matter of prestige.

Focus on opportunities—not problems.

If you do not yet have a website or a payment system, you could still find ways to present and sell your product. A Russian woman I know invited 1,300 people to a call on Instagram; she refused to pay for Zoom! The fee for her event was £60, and that woman made £78,000 without spending a single cent. Even today, she keeps selling seminars on Instagram, charging up to £2,000 per class.

If you encounter an obstacle—find a way around it. Do not think about your lack of abilities; focus on your capabilities. Strive to find solutions. There is a solution to every problem.

DREAM OF ABUNDANCE

1. Dream big.

2. Face and overcome adversity.

3. Develop your habits for sales.

4. Stay "hungry." Keep raising your standards.

Food satiates us, making us lazy and relaxed. Hunger is what motivates us to act. Personally, I grow rich when I find new goals. I want to purchase a home here, in London, and my brain is always preoccupied with finding new ways to make money. I keep thinking of business strategies I can apply to enter the American market. I had maxed out in Bulgaria. I had already achieved all I could, and I was bored and unchallenged. That's why I moved to the U.K. **Every time I notice I am comfortable and bored, I take myself out of my comfort zone. This stimulates growth**. I make myself uncomfortable when my life becomes too comfortable. That is a rule of the rich.

I used to have a small office. I paid its rent easily. One day, however, I decided to challenge myself and purchase a bigger office. The first loan instalment was four times as much as the rent. Too busy finding ways to make that much money, I was no longer bored! My revenues increased, and so did my team. The cleaning fees were raised, too. This motivated me to work harder, and **ascend to the next level**. My family and I moved to Greece shortly thereafter. I expanded my business there. Once I'd done that, I moved on to the American market. I never stop growing—as a person or as a business owner! **Being "hungry" is important for me; I seek discomfort and even a tiny hint of fear**. That motivates me to grow. When you don't have any money left, you should get up from the couch and find a job! You should learn the tricks of the trade, begin selling new products, or produce something… activate your brain. If you complain about a lack of money, but do not do anything to make money, you are simply comfortable being poor.

A friend and I went for a run in the park one day. My friend, a wonderful man, has been jogging for over twenty years. I lack that type of training. I struggled to keep up with his pace. Unlike me, that man runs 20 kilometers—quite quickly, too! As we were jogging around the alleys, I convinced myself of **the importance of comparing yourself to the best**. I tend to run with my husband—who is far from an athlete—and I feel like an excellent runner when I am around him. However, running with this man showed me my actual running abilities. Even though he had me break all my records, I also noticed that I am not that good of a runner.

Run with the best. Find people who are better than you. **Surround yourself with those who have achieved more than you have**—both in business and in your personal life.

How can you make yourself uncomfortable? You can buy yourself an expensive car, a watch, or a property. You can take yourself on an expensive vacation. I took three groups of people to Bali in 2019. To do that, I had to pay £100,000 in advance. This was a huge challenge, mostly because I hadn't formed those groups yet. I, of course, found a way to fill all the spaces in those groups. If anything, I exceeded my expectations. I even began speaking English! I formed two American groups! I sold retreats for about £5000 per person. So many people were interested in my retreats that I had to send some of them back! I had booked three entire hotels! I spoke a bit of Chinese, too! I had Chinese people attend my seminars in Bali! This was a powerful challenge! **When you challenge yourself, you can raise both your prices and your standards**.

You may wonder what motivated me to do this. There is this American woman who organizes retreats for £100,000 per person. She only takes 10 people and makes a million dollars. Not bad at all, eh? I cannot assimilate that sum. I therefore raised my former price—£2,000—to £5,000. It was a major jump for me! **Everything is possible if you just keep competing with yourself**.

Learn how to make yourself uncomfortable.

5. Live life to the fullest.

The rich value their time. They are present in every second! If they speak—they speak. If they have sex—they have sex! They do everything as well as they can. They act here and now, **rather than then and in the future**. If a rich person is working out, he or she knows this will help them have a better body. Working out also makes them better at sales. If a rich person is learning a new language, he or she knows he or she will be able to speak that language after discovering a new market.

Act here and now. Concentrate. Don't allow yourself to become distracted. Don't check your phone, don't think about the past. Make a schedule for each day and stick to it! Notice how that makes you feel.

There are three types of people: losers, champions, and people who live in flow. Losers don't make plans; they live for the day. Prohibit yourself the life of a loser! Plan and do. Carry out your tasks. Google Calendar is available to everyone; use it!

Champions constantly set impossible goals, do not have time for themselves, and are not in touch with "the flow of life." These people frequently fail to "sharpen the saw." There is this wonderful Stephen Covey book: *The Seven Habits of Highly Effective People*. One of these seven habits is "sharpening the saw." What does that mean? Covey uses an example of two loggers who work under the same conditions. One of them rests from time to time, and the other keeps does not. The one that rests is far more efficient. As that person points out, rest sharpened his saw. You should take a break if you feel tired. Rest after meetings, between workdays, and on weekends.

I used to be champion. I was very proud of working 24/7. I used to start working at 9 a.m. I had meetings and personal appointments until 7 p.m. Once the evenings came, I began working on webinars, which frequently lasted until 11 at night. I then checked my email and answered my messages. I worked 49 weekends per year; I only took three weekends off. Back then, I never asked myself "What would be convenient for me? Why should I work in the evenings and on weekends?" I was shocked when I realised I had put myself in a bad spot to make things convenient for others. I also surprised myself when I figured out I was postponing a trip to Germany only because I had to leave my newborn son to my husband for a few days. I also did not like the hotel I had been booked once I got to Germany, and I didn't like the early time of my flight. I love my job, so I obviously still led the seminar. However, I got sick as soon as I returned home. Putting others first had to come to an end. I am now ashamed I allowed this to happen.

I've therefore put in lots of effort to become a person who lives in flow. I now strive to make things convenient for me. I lead webinars at times that are convenient for me, and I do not compromise. As it turned out, these new times are often far more convenient for others, too.

Make things convenient for you, and this will improve your business. If it is not convenient for you, then you have either not found the right business or the first solution. Perhaps you haven't delegated tasks to others; perhaps you've failed to do something effectively. Question yourself and conceive of solutions. Pour your entire self into your work. Focus. You're playing a long-term game.

6. Track your expenses.

An airline used to put three olives in each salad they made. That is, for every 200-300-person flight, that company used 600-900 olives. Their flights were sometimes as short as thirty minutes. When the company calculated how much these olives cost them per year, they figured adding olives to salads cost them about half a million pounds per annum! Knowing their passengers hardly noticed those three olives, the company decided to cut that expense and invest it somewhere else.

My webinars used to be indefinite; that is, people could watch them at any time. My team and I researched the American market and figured that Americans only allowed their clients a day—or a week—to watch webinars. We therefore changed our policy; we now allow people to watch webinars for two to three months after they've been streamed. In case people need extra time, they can pay an additional fee. I had never considered that these long—and sometimes indefinite—streaming periods made my business lose money!

Every business loses money in a couple different ways. Understanding this to be the case, the rich focus on minimizing expenses.

Analyse: Where does your money go? Which business expenses could you save on? What small changes could you make to save a lot of money?

7. Absorb knowledge.

You must be competent in the field you work in. Stop fantasizing about hiring a manager to handle your business instead of you. That will not happen—not soon, anyway.

**Business requires your time, presence, and attention.
Business demands your control.**

You should keep track of your business. If you rent out your real estate, you must make sure all your tenants pay their rent and keep your properties pristine. Something always requires your attention. I, too, dream of a passive-income business. However, there has not been a single day when I haven't monitored my firm or communicated with my employees. It is crucial you know the nature of your business operations; this will allow you to prevent others from stealing money. **People steal when they locate your weaknesses; people steal when you allow them to.** Surveillance isn't a reliable way to prevent theft; plus, there are so many ways one can still steal while being monitored. Nothing can replace your personal involvement in a business. You should be present at every point of control. Only the owner should control money. Your employees, regardless of how much you love and value them, should not manage your money. Do not allow them to trick and seduce you.

8. Find creative solutions.

Creative thinking is a special talent of the rich.

Consider what brave ideas you may offer the world. Look around and notice opportunities.

9. Adore your business.

You should love what your do. No business can thrive if its owners and managers lack passion and energy. The rich do not believe in the word "impossible." Nothing is impossible for them. Uncertainty and the unknown captivate them, motivating them to create new inventions. "Impossibility" turns them on. Losers give in as soon as they encounter adversity. Winners, on the other hand, try again and again. Don't give up on your ideas. You will always find an opportunity and a solution.

10. Trust your gut.

The rich smell money. They use their instincts to sense opportunities and find money. People who've grown up with a dominant parent struggle to succeed in life; they've never been given a chance to consider and reflect on their goals. **You must allow yourself to choose your own wishes and goals. That is a clear manifestation of self-love**. Write down your goals and work towards them. Flee your comfort zone. Find creative solutions. Observe your competition; notice their ideas. Allow yourself to make demands. Develop your instincts and trust your intuition. **To "smell" money, you must have faith in yourself; you must allow yourself to try things out**. Work towards your goals, even when they seem impossible. If you've ever dreamed of doing something, then find a way to do it! **The path to abundance narrows every time you postpone a goal or fail to fulfill a wish**. You may think your business is not in any way related to your postponed goal to cut sugar. This is not the case. You will make more money as soon as you begin fulfilling your desires. I've seen this happen many times. The nature of money isn't exactly logical. Stop looking for logical explanations about your lack of money. You always wanted to exercise more, but somehow postponed it for months. You recently began doing it, and, all of the sudden, you found a new job. Your new job is well-paid. Money is energy. **You can attract more money by strengthening your energy**.

Moving to Greece was a difficult decision for me. I had a flat, an office, and a "life" in Bulgaria. Deciding to push me forward, my husband said: "We are moving to Greece." As soon as we moved, the opportunity to enter the American market showed up. A woman—whom I had known for five years at that time—suggested we partner up. She said she had dreamed of me. She is a very strong woman. She trusts and follows her intuition. We now have a very stable partnership.

We are both happy with it!

When you don't know what is to come, you feel like you have knots in your belly. Still, as soon as you trust yourself and follow your intuition, you enter a new beginning. That's how you raise your energy and increase your income.

11. Hire the best but don't put your entire trust in them.

Don't compromise with your personnel; don't always try to save money on salaries. I've made this mistake myself, and I lost a fair amount of time and money because of it. Many of my clients decided they no longer wanted my products due to bad customer service. What did I do? I fired all my employees. All of them! I only kept this one girl and then hired a new team according to my new, higher standards. I paid them more. My business expanded quickly. I am now very careful with the people I hire, and I never try to save money when paying salaries.

12. Don't rest on your laurels.

Regardless of your past successes, you should keep working. Strive to improve. You need to invest in your idea and make it better. Develop your business. At the same time, educate yourself, improve your health, and don't turn your back on personal progress.

13. Sign a prenup.

Your business budget and your familial budget should remain separate. To me, keeping these separate speaks of honesty and maturity in your familial relationships. A few female clients of mine built business empires; now, they cannot get divorced, only because their husbands would be entitled to a half of their businesses.

14. Like yourself.

Audrey Hepburn had a small chest. She loved herself—and her small breasts—so much that she made small breasts fashionable.

It doesn't matter who you are; what matters is that you believe in yourself. The rich mold the Universe to fit their characters.

When I noticed Bulgaria did not have proper seminars on sex and relationships, I decided to make such courses fashionable. Sarah Jessica Parker isn't a beauty. However, she managed to make both her big nose and her style fashionable. Find your individuality and bet on it. My Bulgarian isn't great, and people parody me by imitating my accent. **Turn your defects into effects. Beauty is not a sign of success; your self-worth is.** Decide if you will criticize yourself or find a way to like—and even love—yourself.

15. Having a good business is easier when you have a good marriage.

Your spouse should keep a professional attitude towards your business. They should act like a partner, helping you maintain your image and offer advice. It would be great if they take on some of your familial duties, too. My husband helps by taking care of our son when I lead webinars. I do the same when he is busy.

Your spouse should not attempt to compete with you or your business. Your spouse should not kill your ambitions or seek to discourage you.

My husband hates taking pictures. However, he agreed to have a photo session with me and our son, as I needed those pictures for my business. **Two people are always better than one**. I often ask my husband to attend some of my meetings, just so he can offer his opinion to my partners. You will suffer a great deal if you spouse makes you choose between work and family. If you do not have a partner, you will pour a lot of energy into finding one and sorting your relationship out; this will drain your business energy. You should therefore have a spouse who is also **your ally**, a person who supports your dreams and goals with their own resources. Sex may be the only thing that partner gives you but, if the sex is good, this may turn out to be a great motivator for you. Good sex charges your energy. You must find balance. Don't overwork yourself and find a way to balance your relationships and your career.

16. If you ever fail or go bankrupt, you must find a way out.

Your attitude in difficult moments depends on you. You may panic and paint yourself as a victim or you may get yourself together and find a way out. You should always do the latter. The rich take lemons and make lemonade. The poor whine about lemons' sour taste. **Program your mind to notice tasks—not problems**. Know that when one door closes, another one opens. Think outside the box. Think fast.

MALE AND FEMALE EXECUTIVE STYLES

"Our emerging workforce is not interested in command-and-control leadership. They don't want to do things because I said so; they want to do things because they want to do them"
Irene Rosenfeld,

CEO of Mondelez

1. Women enter partnerships.

2. Women take fewer risks.

3. Women enjoy the process and like what they do.

4. Women are more creative. They channel energy into their products through emotion. Men are logical; women are emotional. Notice what parts of the process excite you, what parts of the process charge you with energy and turn you on. If the product turns you on, then you will find a way to create and sell it. **For most men, everything boils down to numbers.**

5. Women adore their teams. To them, their teams are highly valuable—much like a second family. **Men do not develop a personal attitude towards their teams**; they view their team members as parts of a well-working machine. They must be there to keep the whole going.

6. Women work with people they find pleasant. If a woman has a team member whom she dislikes, her energy will be diminished, and her business will suffer as a result.

7. Women sell through seduction: they use their beauty and sexuality to market their products and services. **Men sell through aggression and manipulation.**

8. Women establish personal and collaborative relationships with clients.

9. Men are goal-oriented. They value achievement. The process doesn't matter to them.

10. Men prioritize money. If the business is not bringing in the revenues they desire, men are inclined to let it go—even when that business gives them pleasure. Masculine women act the same way.

11. Men seek competition; it challenges them—turns them on even—and motivates them to achieve results.

12. Men do not strive to build personal relationships with their

teams. To them, their teams are just people who work for them. **Therefore, the best managers are often either women or men who reside in their feminine energy**. The men with dominant masculine energies are usually horrible managers. They are only concerned with results, sales, and achievements, which is why they hire someone to manage the team.

SEVEN STEPS TO STARTING A BUSINESS

"Most people have achieved their greatest success just one step beyond their greatest failure."
Napoleon Hill,
American author

1. Choose the sphere of your business.

2. Collaborate with other businesses and people.

If you are a personal stylist, you must know that photographers, makeup artists, and hair stylists are all potential partners for you. Together, you could collaborate to attract clients for your individual business.

If you've written a book about astrology, you should find social media platforms and Facebook groups that are about astrology. Promote your book there.

If you have a restaurant, you should collaborate with local farms, businesses that produce kitchen equipment, and companies that organize events.

If you have just established an art gallery, you should get in touch with event planners and the media. You should also collaborate with painters, photographers, and art collectors. Charity organizations will do, too!

3. Research the market.

You should be well-aware of the market you are attempting to enter. What products have been created? Who are the most influential companies? What client needs are these companies attempting to meet? What is the profile of your target group?

I usually research both the market I wish to enter and the markets of other countries, including Russia and America, as they give me ideas.

If you have invented something entirely new, you are faced with both a challenge and an opportunity. You will need to popularize your product. This could be done with the help of famous people, including celebrities and influencers.

However, when looking for people to promote your products, do not immediately turn to those who have the most followers. Start small. Find someone who has about 3000 followers, for instance. Oftentimes, the audience of micro-influencers is a lot more loyal. Plus, micro-influencers are more likely to promote your product for free or in return for a small present.

You should always research the market before entering it with a new business or product.

4. Create your ACO—an Amazing Commercial Offer.

What are the strengths of your product? What distinguishes you from the competition? Why should people buy from you and not from somebody else? What additional benefits will you offer your clients? How will you motivate them to buy from you and not from your competitors?

You could steal your competitors' clients by offering them something new or something different. Your stores, for instance, could be open longer hours. Unlike your competitors, you may offer free delivery. You could also create groups on social media where you publish information, free tutorials, and success stories. You could also organize fun games and giveaways. **Find ways to add value to your products**.

You should decide whether you wish to sell normal goods or luxury goods. I suggest you sell both. Then, you could profit from selling large quantities of normal goods and smaller qualities of luxury goods. Take, for instance, Zara and Louis Vuitton. The former makes money through selling tons of clothing; the latter makes money through smaller quantities and higher pricing of products.

If you have many business ideas, start by focusing on one of them.

5. Craft a business plan.

There are two types of business plans: business plans for investors and business plans for yourself. The former allows you to seek funding while the latter helps consider the startup capital you need.

6. Come up with a plan of action.

Consider all steps you need to take. Understand the order of those steps. Take them one by one. See which one should be first, which should come second, and so on. Think about the team you need to hire, the tools you need to acquire, the negotiations you need to lead, and the contracts you need to sign. The creation of a website and the crafting of advertising materials are just as important. You must plan and prepare to execute all of these tasks.

7. Start your business. Make your first sales!

This is perhaps the most exciting part of your business development. Great emotions await you at this phase! The very first sales always make you the happiest.

It is crucial you manage your revenues and profits effectively. I've met many businessmen who make lots of money and then waste it all on unnecessary luxury goods. Therefore, you should **separate the money you need for your business and the money you need for your personal life**. Assign yourself a specific salary. Invest anything outside that salary into your business. **Not receiving a salary would be a big mistake, as you will not feel rewarded for your efforts**. At the end of the year, once you've paid your taxes, you can manage the dividends; until then, you do not consider the profits of your business as personal profits. Invest them into your business: improve your website, hire employees, and even attend some courses yourself. Don't ever spend that money on personal expenses.

ANALYSE RESULTS

Constantly analyse the financial state of your business. Figure out what your best-selling products are. See which products had the least number of sales over the last month. Why was this the case? Consider any possible reasons for the weak performance of those products. Is the packaging bad? Is the price too high? Is your advertising strategy appropriate? You may be selling the right product at the wrong time! There can be so many reasons for a product's poor performance.

Have weekly meetings with your team to discuss the performance of your business. Solve current problems.

Remember:

YOU CHOOSE YOUR CLIENTS

You may think that raising the price of your product or service will lead you to lose clients. Trust me—that is not the case.

I was shocked when I saw that all inhabitants of Bali have an iPhone. Many of these people live in utter poverty, but still carry an iPhone. How can that be? They have simply decided that iPhones are valuable; to them, iPhones are worth the money.

If you present your product as truly valuable, people will do anything they can to get it.

There might be some clients that you do not need. Personally, I don't like the people who only purchase my cheapest courses. They complain a lot. They remain unhappy regardless of the discounts I offer or the products I give for free. I've noticed that the more expensive my course is, the more satisfied my clients become. The fee for my "Academy for Winners" is about £1200, and everyone is happy with the course. My "students" internalise every word I say.

When I lead a seminar that costs £8, on the other hand, there is always someone who complains and criticizes my method of explaining things. Poor customers bargain a lot; if you offer them a pen for a pound, they will always say they could get it for 80 pence from someone else.

There is this meme going around Facebook: a beautiful woman stops by the farmer's market and bargains with one of the sellers. "£2 for a clutch of eggs? I will buy it for £1.50," she says. She bargains until the seller agrees to sell her the eggs for £1.50; for him, after all, something is always better than nothing. The woman purchases the clutch of eggs and moves on with her day. She goes on to have lunch at a fancy restaurant. There, she tips the waiter £10. However, because she is the one that decides the tip, she feels that £10 is a reasonable sum. That's some basic psychology of consumerism. The best, most-desirable customers, are the middle class. They spend money with pleasure. You can overprice the products you sell to them: because books, cosmetics, and jewellery are not necessities, you can absolutely overprice these items.

WHO ARE YOUR IDEAL CLIENTS?

"Contact with the customer is what business is all about."
Jay Leno,
TV Host

Now, you should realise who your clients are. To help you do so, I am assigning you the following:

TASK!

Consider the following characteristics of your clients:

1. Gender and Age:

2. Education and Career:

3. Income:

4. Interests and Hobbies:

5. Wants and Values:

6. Dreams:

7. Problems You May Solve:

You may not even have clients yet! Still, it is crucial you decide what sort of people you wish to work for!

Fortunately for you, there are all sorts of clients! Some seek low prices while others look for quality—especially when purchasing food products. You don't need to have all types of clients! Pick a target group. Find a way to attract it through advertising and market segmentation.

You should carefully check the terms and conditions of delivery, especially if you are offering delivery as a free service. Calculate the costs. You should not be losing money. Personally, I find only businesses with large revenues can afford to offer a free delivery service. **Small businesses, however, tend to lose money from the smallest of things, including gift bags and chocolate**. Modern businesses therefore look for bonuses that do not impose a financial strain. Such bonuses include a personalised attitude towards customers, free online activities, etc. Discounts are yet another bonus, but small businesses should only offer them when the client has already spent a sizable sum of money.

Knowing your clients is crucial. If possible, it would be great if you manage to offer them personalised products and services. A friend of mine has a catering company that recently entered the street food scene. My friend now has many food carts all over London. One of them is near a school. That specific food truck offers deals for school-aged children for just £5. Children love those deals. They come during every break and spend more money than the adults. **Don't underestimate your clients. Even children can make you money**.

If you know the interests and hobbies of your clients, you could organize meetups and send out surveys to improve your customer service.

You can only solve your clients' problems after figuring out your clients' wants.

But you must figure out what problems your clients have. If you offer housekeeping services, you may need to deal with the mold in people's bathrooms or the stains on their underwear. You should promote yourself as the person—or company—that cleans those things better than anyone else. You could even contact a cosmetics company and offer each hotel you clean cleaning products with a distinctive aroma. These are ways to accentuate your individuality and present your service as extraordinary.

You can use social media to get to know your clients. Here are some questions that can help you:

1. Why are my clients on social media? What are they trying to get out of it?

(Some social media users seek information and others look for entertainment. There are countless reasons why people are on social media.... What matters is that you figure out why your clients are on social media.)

2. When are your clients active on social media?

3. Where are they at that time (at home, at the gym, at work)?

4. What do your clients find more interesting: pictures or written content?

5. How much time do your clients spend on reading your posts?

Answer these questions. You must know these statistics, as you will craft your business plan based on them.

Describe your product/service in three words:

These three words should be present within everything you do. They should be mentioned on your website and your social media platforms. They should be easily associated with your appearance, lifestyle, and business offers. If you offer cleaning services, and you noted **fast, concrete, and precise** as your three key words, you should have a very clear business proposal, brief mission statement, and your website should be relatively simple. Everything about you and your business must mimic these three words. If you sell eco-friendly products, you should have the following on your website: "We only communicate through email. We are paper-free!" If your three words are **helpful, colourful, and fun**, all of your social media posts should give off positive vibes. If you sell with the words **"quality," "comfort," "beauty,"** you should have perfect photos that present the fabric of your products; you should also clearly describe your dedication to quality materials on your website.

If you do not have any competitors, you should begin by popularizing your brand.

Your business will become successful if you charge it with energy through:
- **Loving your product/service.**
- **Loving yourself.**
- **Loving your clients.**

Have you started buying new clothes yet? Are you building that business-appropriate wardrobe we talked about? If not, what is stopping you?

If you already have a well-established business and a reliable group of clients, you might have entered a routine. You are used to conducting things in a certain way. However you are doing things, there surely is room for growth. **Every product can be improved to attract a new group of customers**. Usually, 70-80% of a business' customers constitute the client base. The remaining customers only purchase products and services occasionally. Nevertheless, even those "occasional" customers may become a primary source of income when circumstances change. The same holds true for a company's products. Take face masks as an example. Prior to the pandemic, few companies—if any—relied on them as a leading source of revenue. Then, during the pandemic, face masks became a major source of income for many companies all over the world. Something similar happened in my own business. Online seminars were a bit of a side hustle for me. I made most money by leading events in hotels and other public spaces. During the pandemic, however, online seminars became my main source of income. They went from bringing in about 30% of my revenues to 100% of my revenues. So, if you have any "side" products that have a lot of potential, make sure to keep developing them. They could make you more revenues when the circumstances— or the markets—change. Stay informed and follow world trends and events. This will allow you to act and adapt your current products and services to unforeseen stations, should that become necessary. Rely on the distinction between "leading" and "potentially leading" products to create two groups of customers: regular customers and potential customers.

Two years ago, someone I know made an online educational platform. "Who would ever use this," I said to him many times. I even laughed at him. "Children have enough duties already; they attend school during the day!" As soon as COVID hit, my friend's company skyrocketed. "You're a fortune-teller, aren't you," I noted one day, "I applaud you."

People who struggle in business are—in one way or another—stuck. There is a wonderful movie about this topic; it is called "Why him?" This movie presents the two types of businesses—traditional businesses and modern businesses.

You must have the strength to let go. You should be able to let everything you've created go. If something isn't working out, you should let it go and move on.

PSYCHOLOGY OF SALES

"People buy emotionally, then justify logically."
Jerry Acuff,
CEO and Founder of Delta Point, Inc.

WHAT IS YOUR CONTRIBUTION TO THE WORLD?

If you want to be rich, you should always ask yourself: "What is my contribution to the world?" The Indian tradition believes that we all have our dharma—that is, we are all born to do something in this life. The size of your dharma is irrelevant.

What did one of my clients—a nail technician—do when lockdown began? She started leading online nail tutorials. At her salon, she used to charge £20 for every manicure she did. Online, she charged each of the 170 participants £20. That is, with the help of the internet, she made 170 times the money she would usually make for the same period of time. That is also how she managed to increase her income in quarantine, all whilst taking care of her newborn. She did not turn breastfeeding or sleeplessness into excuses; rather, she noticed a gap in the market and filled it with her new service. That is how she contributed to the world: she helped thousands of women learn how to do their manicures at home. She enabled those women to continue feeling beautiful even in the unusual circumstances that lockdown had created. My client now has over 50,000 followers on Instagram—all of whom she reached not through advertising but by offering free advice and selling nail tutorials. The main resource that enabled her to do this was time. She put in the time and made money later.

Another client of mine used to have a wedding agency but, as lockdown put a temporary halt on parties and weddings, she could not continue doing business as usual. She therefore created an online course called: "How to organize the perfect wedding." She sold tens of thousands of videos and became a millionaire! What's most fascinating is that—as soon as lockdowns began to lift internationally—all her viewers wanted her to organise their weddings. My client, of course, raised her fees tremendously, make more money than ever before. Over the course of a single year, her business expended drastically. She now has offices all over Russia.

Try to **grasp the gist** of these examples, to understand them as abstract models of behaviour rather than concrete examples.

Your contribution to the world rests at the root of your success. If people need your product or service, and if you offer parts of it for free, the money will come.

Your clients should be able to reach you easily. You should also find a way to somehow connect yourself with the best, regardless of the sphere you work in. If you are a photographer, you can contact a celebrity and offer them a free photo session; all you want in return will be a tiny social media mention and a tag on their picture. That is how you can gain popularity and find potential clients. Your contribution to the world can be the meal recipes you publish on your blog, the clothes you sew in your atelier, or the songs you sing on YouTube. The possibilities are endless. You can contribute to the world by taking care of children or the elderly. You can contribute to the world by giving yoga or dancing lessons. You could even offer gardening advice! What matters most is that you give something to the world. If you have a talent that you do not utilize—that is, you are a talented writer that does not write books or an excellent astrologer than nobody knows about—you will never be rich. You simply wouldn't have done the very thing that fosters success; you have not contributed to the world.

In other words, **your dharma is your life's mission. It is something that you were born with, something that you can only materialise through giving**.

HOW CAN PEOPLE FIND OUT ABOUT YOUR PRODUCT OR SERVICE?

The second question you should constantly ask yourself is the following: "How can people—as many as possible—learn about my services?"

Analyse your social media and figure out how many people you can reach through posts and stories. Calculate the number of people you can reach through other means, including a newsletter and emails. Do all these people know about your products and/or services? Do you advertise them? If not, do you fail to market them because you lack confidence? Is your shyness stopping you from advertising your products? Perhaps you are waiting to lose some weight? Or you will only begin streaming lives when you purchase new clothes? Well, you will stay poor if you keep making excuses. If you want to stay poor, feel free to admit it. Write it down: I am poor because I am insecure and allow my psychological complexes to impact my daily life.

Nothing—and no one—will make you rich unless you begin by taking action.

IS YOUR PRODUCT GOOD AT ALL?

The third question you should ask yourself is the following: "Is my product (or my service) good at all?"

It is crucial that you strive towards the best. You should pour your heart, soul, and energy—your entire Being—into whatever you've chosen to do. **You don't have to be perfect; however, you should be dedicated**.

Once people sense your dedication, they will begin to contact you. Find a way to facilitate your communication with clients. There should be different ways through which your clients can find you. They should be offered at least three different methods of payment upon checkout. You should view your social media accounts as your shop window, and your website as the store they need to enter to purchase your products.

There are certain countries that do not have much opportunity for growth. Their markets are small, and the population is poor. If you live in a country like this, you should either find a way to improve existing services or to spot a gap in the market. Take Bulgaria as an example. The Bulgarian market is far smaller than either the American or British market; therefore, entrepreneurs there must either locate a gap and fill it or cater to the demands of the international market. A friend of mine, for instance, recognised there weren't many books on manners circulating Bulgarian bookshops. She wrote a book on etiquette, which has ranked among the most-purchased books in Bulgaria for three months in a row. My friend's success is yet another proof that everyone can succeed, as long as he or she puts in the work and stays proactive.

When you pour strong, honest energy into your work, you tend to get more than you give. A photographer once gifted me a photo session, the pictures from which ended up in Playboy. To her, this was an unimaginable success. **You will have the clients and partners you deserve**; both clients and partners are merely mirrors of our own selves. If you do not like your clients and partners, look within, and spot the mistakes you are making. Set clear boundaries. Have people pay for the products or services you offer them. All business processes must have a clear structure; that is, there needs to be a goal, a deadline, and a plan.

Don't approach your business ideas with unrealistic expectations. Have a clear idea of how much your business can grow, how it can develop, and how much it could make in revenues over time. Start small. **Small steps are often more important than big ones**. Incremental progress is the best type of progress: it will transform your business from a start-up, through a sole proprietorship, into a big cooperation.

A PROPER ATTITUDE TOWARDS SALES

Let's see what associations you make when you hear the word: "sales." Write these associations here:

1.____
2.____
3.____
4.
5.

How well can you sell? Rate yourself from one to ten and note it down below:

Your attitude towards sales plays a crucial role in your success. I want you to adopt the following attitude: **"sales are my help to others."**

Let me write this with capital letters.

SALES = HELP TO OTHERS

We all like to help, as helping is encoded in our behaviour. We want to be good, liked, and appreciated.

When we sell our products of services, we contribute to society. We give people what they need and help them improve their lives.

If this value rests at the root of your attitude towards sales, you will sell your products in services very easily.

There are three important components that constitute the success of your sales:

1. Self-love

The love you feel for yourself, for your work, and for your product will transmit itself to your client. The more you love yourself, the more valuable your products and services become. The less you love yourself, the less your clients will appreciate your products. Your products—and services—reflect and transmit your personal energy.

I remember this saleswoman—she offered to sell me some skincare products. When we met, her appearance starkly contrasted with the appearance I expected her to have. Her hair was oily, and her face was full of acne. She was also quite unpleasant. I could have never imagined she sold skincare! If the products she sold you were so good, then why hadn't they cured her acne?

There was this other saleswoman who attempted to sell me a course on sexology. She was quite voluptuous and looked horrible. She dressed like my grandmother, too. I couldn't take that woman seriously, especially when she talked about sex while looking as if she had just come out of the Victorian age. What a paradox! Her energy sharply contrasted the product she was trying to sell.

Your appearance and your energy need to be congruent with the product you are trying to sell. Looking well is a sign of self-love. No client will ever like the product of someone who doesn't like themselves first. Take care of your appearance, cherish your energy, and use both to sell.

2. Love for your product

I prohibit you to sell a product you hate. If you love smoking, then go ahead and sell cigarettes. If you hate smoking, however, how could you possibly sell vapes? You will find it difficult to sell something you find unpleasant and unlikeable. Your conscience will weigh on you. If you sell things you dislike, you will begin hating your job—not because of the job itself but because of your opposition to the products you are selling. No salesman—or saleswoman—can sell large volumes of a product they dislike.

3. Love for your client

When you truly love, value, and respect your clients, you **always end up giving them more than they expect**. You are deeply concerned with the satisfaction of your clients, and you do everything you can to cater to their needs and wants. **Your honest love and interest for your clients increase sales; so does your desire to understand your clients and improve their lives**.

Now, aware of the three factors that determine the success of your sales, you should reflect on your shortcomings. You may be tired, exhausted, and dissatisfied with your life. You may be overweight. You may not have found the product you wish to sell. You may not like yourself enough, and you may allow that attitude to become reflected in your products. You may not like your body and struggle to find a partner. You may have a strong, difficult character that few people can put up with. Or, maybe, you just don't know your own clients.

To me, the love we feel for our clients comes down to understanding their client profile. Currently, you are my client, and I am selling you my knowledge with the help of this book. I also treat you like a family member—a sister, brother, child… I value your soul, your personality, and your needs. I do my best to teach you something important. **I understand your needs only because I have received feedback from thousands of clients that came before you**. I therefore pour all the love I feel for you into this book.

Can you think of anyone who sold you something in a way that you enjoyed? There is this store in the city centre that I like. Every time the owner has a shift there, I walk out of the store with at least one new piece of clothing. When someone else has a shift, however, I never find myself liking anything. What does this show you? That store owner is a talented saleswoman. She is always interested in finding out what occasion I need new clothes for, how I would like to present myself, and so on. She also knows my body quite well and always suggests clothes that fit well. She knows I have a tummy, though she wouldn't admit to that, and she always offers me clothes that can help me hide it. She shows me a piece of clothing and says: "This is for you." Her attitude saves me time and worries, just as it encourages me to buy more things. She often has me sit down and drink a cup of coffee as she walks around the store, finding clothes that will fit me. Then, she comes back to me with five outfits. I usually buy four of them. She also either offers me a discount or gives me an accessory, and I always leave her store satisfied. I like her for many reasons. She is positive. She knows me well and knows both my body and my style. She saves me time. She also prioritizes me over other clients. She always gives me a little more than I give her, which keeps me coming back again and again.

QUALITIES OF THE SUCCESSFUL SALESPERSON

Analyse the people you buy from most frequently. The products you buy don't really matter; these people can sell clothes, food, cosmetics, cars… that is irrelevant. What matters is the way they sell. Consider their approach. What do you like about it? What keeps you coming back for more? Now, note the five characteristics of a successful salesperson:

1.____
2.____
3.____
4.____
5.

Let's discuss the qualities of successful salespeople. The following qualities are based on statistical data and both qualitative and quantitative research. Analyse which of these qualities you possess. Trust that you can develop the qualities you do not yet have.

1. The ability to listen to your clients and understand them.

The ideal salesperson asks the right questions, listens to his or her clients, understands what those clients need, and offers exactly that. Communication stands at the foundation of sales.

I get annoyed when people offer me products before asking me what I need. I get irritated when I enter a store and the saleswoman proclaims "I've got the right shoes for you!" and shows me a pair of heels. I do not need heels. I want sneakers. You should always ask your clients about their needs before offering a product. **People usually come to you with a problem – they need something specific. You should therefore first figure out what that problem is before offering any product or service.**

I, for instance, check my mailbox before every live stream. I also read the messages my followers have sent me. This allows me to understand what my audience needs, thus guiding the topic of my live streams.

2. A talent to speak, simply and clearly.

I always speak simply so that others can understand me well. That has led many psychologists to resent me; I, after all, speak of complex psychological phenomena with basic, everyday terms. I say: "we have to fix our relationship with our parents and set clear boundaries." My colleagues, on the other hand, state things like: "You should assimilate the experiences you've had with your parents and interiorize them. This will allow you to then exteriorize them and complete the healing process." Influenced by the work of Jean Piaget, that's how the psychology departments in universities teach us to speak. Internalization is a process through which we assimilate the behaviours, beliefs, and attitudes of others, including our parents, into our own characters. This often leads to the establishment of limitations that we must then overcome. I refer to this process simply. "We must overcome the convictions and behaviours of our parents," I say. My seminars and books are popular science; my methods, meditations, and exercises can be understood and applied by all readers.

I remember wanting to buy myself a new car. The car salesman began explaining details I neither understood not wanted to know. Sure, these details may have been important characteristics of the cars I was looking at; however, as someone who does not know much about cars, I could not understand the majority of what this salesman was talking about. He made me felt stupid, and I just stopped listening to the things he was saying. **We push our clients away when we speak in an incomprehensible manner.**

I have a test I like to apply when speaking about my products. If a six-year-old child cannot understand me, this means I am speaking in a manner that is too complex. I suggest you converse with young children and try to explain your product to them. If the kids begin wanting your product, then congratulations! You are a good salesman/saleswoman.

Now, why does this work? As customers, we buy at the level of our reptilian brains; that is, we are led by the oldest and most primitive part of our bodies. Our inner child exclaims: "I want this!" Let by emotion, we make irrational, illogical purchases. We spend the money that we were supposed to use for electric bills. Despite the evolution our brains have gone through, our desires are still quite reptilian. They remain at the level of the reptilian brain. Therefore, when we want something, we act immaturely like six-year-olds. A good salesperson finds a way to appeal to these reptilian tendencies—we'll discuss how later in the book. The sentences you should use in these cases are short and comprehensive. This will allow the buyer to assimilate and understand what you are saying.

3. The ability to ask the right questions.

When my clients say they want something, I always ask them why they want it. I try to figure out what problems they may have in their life, just as I question their wants and goals. This allows me to cater to their needs by suggesting the most appropriate seminar for them.

Clients often purchase things they do not need. This is not our goal.

We aim to understand what our clients want.

We ask questions like "Why do you need this?" and "How will you use this?" **Such questions allow us to gain loyal clients**. Questions like these also lead to win-win situations; the clients are happy because they are getting what they need, and the salespeople are satisfied for selling more products and/or services. In cases like these, clients always keep coming back for more; they sometimes bring other people, too. **The dissatisfied customer will tell around ten people about their disappointment.** Such clients will complain about your customer service and share all the negative details with their friends and acquaintances. **That is human nature; the satisfied client will tell two people, and the dissatisfied one will tell ten**. The latter poses a danger to your business. If you have dissatisfied clients, you should find a way to respond to their needs and fulfil them.

The art of sales comes down to attracting new clients and maintaining old clients.

Maintaining clients is harder (and more effective) than attracting them. If loyal clients—that is, your customer base—constitute about 20% of all your clients, these 20% will account for 80% of your revenues. **Our biggest aim is to make our clients loyal by establishing a loving relationship with them**. This process requires your personal attention and participation. I have many friends in the hospitality business who—despite their highly qualified personnel—make an effort to be present at their hotels and restaurants. My friends meet their clients, converse with them, inform them about the menu and additional services, and offer them a drink for free. This personal attitude satisfies clients greatly, leading total revenues to quadruple. Personally, I don't support businesses whose owners are not involved in day-to-day operations. **The client should be able to reach the business owner, whether it would be through email and phone calls or through social media**. I often happen to solve some of the problems of my own clients in the middle of the night. I am happy to do so—I am happy they are contacting me personally.

Other good practices include helping to fulfil personal wishes and giving little holiday gifts.

4. Knowing your products and services.

When I was buying my phone, I could not decide between two phone models of the same brand. I asked the sales assistant and, confused, she said: "One of them is 'A' and the other is 'S'."

"Yes, that I know. How are they different? Are there any particular differences in the software or hardware?"

"Umm, google it. This information should be up on the website."

I thanked her and never entered that store again. I also cautioned all my friends. "Don't go there," I said to them, "their salespeople do not know what they are doing."

I, of course, still needed a new phone. I went to another store. There was a great salesman there! Young, kind, helpful—he was all I needed to make a decision. I even planned on taking an additional day to think about the phone, but he was so knowledgeable about the products that I ended up purchasing the most expensive phone right away! I also bought some things I had not intended to purchase, including cases and cables. I left with a couple of bags, but it was worth it. The man had even asked me some questions to figure out my needs! "Why do you need fast WiFi?" he wondered.

"I make videos and work with social media."

"How much RAM memory do you have on your devices, and how

much do you need?"

"I don't really know. The bigger, the better. What can you offer me?"

"If you take videos, then this phone will not work for you. The other one would be better."

The man kept explaining phones, and RAM memory, and cables. He knew about everything! He also convinced me to buy the most expensive products, as they truly were best suited for my type of work.

5. Charisma and self-confidence.

I seldom buy from boring, unattractive, unpleasant people. There is a series about a real estate agency, and all real estate agents are beautiful women with perfect haircuts, elegant outfits, and well-maintained nails. Like these women, car sellers are usually quite good-looking. **The more expensive the product, the more expensive the salesperson's appearance should be**. Jewellery stores require their employees to dress elegantly. Shops for sportswear, on the other hand, allow their employees to wear leggings and tracksuits. **The appearance of the salesperson is an extension of the product**.

A client of mine once asked me how I managed to keep selling my courses—at good prices, too. I suggested that she and I meet for coffee. She showed up wearing a T-Shirt—that I would only wear as a pajama top—and a regular pair of jeans. She had slippers, the type you wear to the spa. She also wore no makeup, and her hair was oily. I couldn't imagine she communicates with clients looking like this. "Have you taken the day off?" I asked her.

"No, darling, I am working. I just came to meet you for coffee," she replied.

"Darling, are those the clothes you wear to work?"

"Well, yes. Why are you asking?" she wondered.

"You're joking! You are wonderful at what you do, but you will never manage to raise the prices of your products if you look like this. You are such a beautiful woman and yet you look like an uncut diamond. Fix yourself up. Change your wardrobe. Wear perfume. Put on some makeup. Alter your lifestyle!"

She listened to me carefully. Within two months, her services doubled in price. She was grateful when more clients began to seek her services. **Like magnets attracting metal, attractive appearances and charisma always draw clients in**.

6. Structure.

Many sales remain unfinished. What does that even mean, you may wonder. Oftentimes, a client comes and finds a product he or she likes. However, the client does not purchase the product. It is, therefore, crucial you sneak in some details regarding the purchase of the product while you are discussing its characteristics. If you sell online, you should have a beautifully crafted website and a list of offers that you can send out to clients. You should always find a way to get your client's contact information and reach out to them if they haven't yet purchased your product. You could always ask them if they need any assistance or if you could offer them another product/service. You could suggest your help upon checkout. **That is how you can covertly motivate clients to make more purchases**. Once your clients have paid, you can contact them to discuss delivery details and perhaps some other offers. You should also contact your clients after they've received their purchases, just so you can ask for feedback and show them you care.

The more you facilitate the clients' purchases, the more your clients will buy. The checkout process should be easy, as this will

increase your revenues.

I once consulted for a lady who wanted to sell coaching services. I asked her about payment methods. "How will your clients pay?" I provoked her, knowing this was something she had not thought about. She didn't even have a registered company! This isn't unique to her. Like her, many merchants fail to diversify their payment options, which limits their earnings. A fast and easy checkout page—that offers all sorts of payment options—is the most important thing you should consider when structuring your business.

7. Vigour and Energy.

Sales require a great deal of energy, and salespeople need to be highly energetic. When I feel exhausted after a long webinar, I simply turn off social media and isolate myself. I recharge for a couple of days. I wait. As soon as I feel recharged, I begin working again—even if it is in the middle of the night. I think of new offers, I write emails, and I sell new service bundles. In the mornings, my employees notice all I've done and realise I have found a way to recharge my energy.

Notice when you're most productive. I am most productive at night. I therefore do my best to put my son to sleep, or ask his father to care for him, whilst I work. I often lead live streams on Instagram and write. I am a lot more productive at night. However, there are many people who feel more productive during the day. You should recognize your moments of peak productivity and make sales then.

Also, pay attention to the things that energize you. Igor Nezovibatko as an example. He cannot sell any products seated. He always stands up, even when he is leading a seminar or a meeting online. Bright clothing or perfume may energize you. Perhaps it is coffee and tea that recharge you. Find the things that give you energy. When I need to make an important sale, I prepare by jogging in the park or drinking a ginger smoothie. I also eat, as I cannot work if I am hungry. I only begin once I've done all those things—once I've accumulated the energy a need to make sales. I make sure to always have some high-energy foods around, including nuts, dried fruit, and cheese. Just a couple of bites and I've recharged my energy.

8. Flexibility.

Customer feedback is crucial; so is the monitoring of customer attitudes and behaviour. I always read the comments people write on my posts, just as I stay in touch with my customers through direct messages and emails. I make changes when necessary. Sometimes, people say that the registration deadlines for my courses are too short. In such cases, I extend them. If the times of my webinars are inconvenient for my clients, I make sure to change the time or record them. I always try to be flexible and adapt to my clients' demands, wishes, and needs.

Some people are very rigid: they don't want to make any changes. Their websites might be a decade old; their slogans and colours may be old-fashioned, but these people remain adamant. They do not want to change. "Let's keep things the way they are," such people say, not realizing that outdated website is diminishing the number of sales. **The businesses of rigid people often lose money, all because their owners refuse to adapt to the environment.**

Analyse these eight qualities. Which do you have, and which do you lack? I recommend you discuss this with others; ask them if they think you have any of these eight qualities. You could also ask the people you're talking with about your weaknesses. Ask them if they think you have personal branding. Use their answers to reflect on yourself. Realise what is holding you back. Work on yourself and find a way to develop those qualities you currently lack.

I suggest you read the following books:
• *How to Win Friends and Influence People. How to Stop Worrying and Start Living* by Dale Carnegie
• *Think and Grow Rich* by Napoleon Hill
• *Cold Calling Techniques* by Stephan Schiffman
• *Rich Dad, Poor Dad* by Robert Kiyosaki
• Any of Sergey Rebrick's books

PSYCHOLOGY OF INFLUENCE

"To handle yourself, use your head; to handle others,
use your heart."
Eleanor Roosevelt

People often think that sales are a type of manipulation. Let's discuss this here.

Manipulation involves the use of covert strategies to achieve goals–especially when these goals conflict with the values and morals of the people that are being influenced. Manipulators usually use their influence to lead others to do the things they did not want to do.

TYPES OF MANIPULATION

There are a few types of manipulation:

1. Behavioural Manipulation: we influence others through our behaviour and body language.

2. Verbal Manipulation: we influence others through words.

3. Conscious Manipulation.

4. Unconscious Manipulation.

Oftentimes, mothers consciously manipulate their children with statements like this one: "You will eat this soup, if you love me.; We sometimes manipulate unconsciously—that is, we don't intend to manipulate, but do it, nonetheless. In fact, some people are excellent unconscious manipulators. Others are prone to manipulation. Hence, when we analyse manipulation, the first component we examine should be awareness: I know I am manipulating, or I know I am being manipulated.

WAYS OF MANIPULATION

People manipulate others through one—or more—of these six ways.

1. Through love

Most often, people manipulate through one simple question. "Do you love me?" they ask. Our mothers are the first people who manipulate us that way. "If you love mommy," they say, "you will keep your room clean." There are many variations of this way of manipulation.

"If you love me, you will help me" and "If you love me, you won't act this way" are just two of many.

Women manipulate men this way, too. "You don't love me anymore," we whisper to them.

"That is not true," they respond.

"It is true. You don't love me," we insist.

"What makes you think that?" they ask.

"Well, it is just clear you no longer love me."

"It is clear," "it is evident," and "everybody knows" are among the most used manipulative statements. We turn the love others feel for us against them. We use love as a way to push their buttons, to have others fulfill our desires. The favourite manipulation technique of women is to say: "If you love me, you will give me…" Women often say things like: "If you love me, you will give me flowers every day" and "If you love me, you will pick the phone up immediately."

Manipulation through love works well because it plays on our desire to be loved.

2. Through fear

This method was widely used during the coronavirus pandemic. This type of manipulation works when there is a lack of sufficient information.

3. Through insecurity

This is usually done by narcissistic people. They say things like: "You are lucky you live with me. I have no clue what you would do without me!" Many women accept the affairs of their husbands simply because their husbands have made those women believe they are fat, ugly, stupid, and undeserving. Women feel guilty for their husbands' affairs, too. They think the affairs are their fault, all because their husbands are masterful manipulators who have prayed on their wives' insecurity.

Usually, people with low self-esteem have been manipulated since early childhood.

Bosses also resort to this type of manipulation. "You realise you are not qualified enough, right?" they say to you, not awaiting an answer. "You don't deserve to get a raise—you are simply not competent enough." In these cases, they use the manipulative "You realise" statement before completing it with a twisted, untrue bit of information regarding your qualities or performance. **Learn to recognize the manipulative statements people make.** Manipulative statements stand out. They also attach themselves to your conscience like parasites. They play on your heartstrings. Imagine this: you enter a team meeting, and your boss states, "Everyone is doing well, except for Amanda Jones. Amanda, keep this up if you want to lose your job!" This is a classic example of workplace manipulation.

4. Through guilt

This means of manipulation is used in both personal and professional environments. We often seek a scapegoat. We look for someone we can blame for our problems. "You don't give me attention," we scream at our partners. "You don't give me enough sex" we continue. We also say phrases like: "When I die, you will no longer be able to call me. You will regret it then." Children guilt-trip their parents, too. "I will get sick if you don't buy me this dress. You are a horrible mother. Natalia's mother buys her everything!" People also frequently blame their partners for their own failures.

If you feel a sense of guilt, you are 100% percent being manipulated by someone else.

5. Through pride

If someone says "Only you can do this! I couldn't have done this without you!" your personal manipulation alarm must go off. Our bosses make us feel valuable, just so they can overwhelm us with more work: "You realise we count on you, right? We all depend on you. You are so important to our team. No one else could do what you're doing. You should work on Saturday, too, as there is an important project you must finish. No one else can do it."

You may have plans for Saturday, but your pride overpowers them. You now want to work. "They cannot do it without me," you say to yourself, "I am irreplaceable!" You find ways to justify your behaviour, even when you know you are being manipulated. The situation repeats itself and, as soon as you try to deny it, your boss asks you "You don't want to let us fail, do you?" Now, you're riding a Ferris wheel, rotating around and around two feelings: pride and guilt.

I resort to this type of manipulation in my marriage. It always works on my husband! "How did you do this?" I ask him. "You are amazing! I would be lost without you." That motivates him to do whatever he did again and again. I remember this one time when he bought me a pair of earrings. I thanked him. I also praised him a lot. Now, he is always buying me jewellery. Praise is a tool that wealthy women use; criticism is a tool of the poor. 90% of men can be easily manipulated. "You are my hero" does it quite well. Like my husband, children can be manipulated easily; there isn't a big difference between a grown man and a two-year-old toddler. They both eat up praise like candy. Women are more easily manipulated through a sense of guilt; they can be guilt-tripped quickly and effectively.

6. Through pity

Women are more prone to be manipulated this way. Men often say to them, "My ex-wife was a bitch. She wouldn't let me go out! She never cooked, either—and when she did, she wanted me to help her." Women eat these stories up. They pat their men on the head, whispering statements of care and pity: "Darling, I will never be this way. You can do whatever you want!" Every single time I hear a client of mine utter the words "He had a rough time," I know she is being manipulated through pity. That is why I often pose a question most women cannot answer: "What is this man offering you?"

If your boss complains about barely making the ends meet, about struggling to pay salaries, that boss is manipulating you. You empathize with your boss' situation and no longer ask for a raise. Manipulation is common in the corporate world.

Men also give in to this type of manipulation, especially if they have strong women by their sides. Such men often stumble across a weak, struggling single mother from a smaller town. This woman becomes their mistress, and the men pay all her bills. She is greedy too, taking their money without a hint of remorse. I had this one client, a female, who had been seduced by her husband's mistress; she pitied her enough to buy her a home!

Consider your weak spots. What types of manipulation are you most likely to give into?

Just know that you are being manipulated if you feel any of these emotions: pity; fear of losing your job; fear of losing your relationship; fear of losing money; guilt; love that you need to prove; pride; assurance in your irreplaceability. If you ever feel any one of these, an alarm should go off in your head. You are being manipulated, trust me.

TOOLS FOR MANIPULATION

1. Emotional Display: Sentences like "I am so disappointed. I never expected this from you!" followed by emotional outbursts and crying are a common tool for manipulation. They evoke guilt in the person who is being manipulated. However, emotional display can also be used to foster positive feelings. "I am so happy! I am so thankful. I love you. I love you. I love you!" Such statements are no less manipulative than the ones above. They just pray on people's joy—rather than their sense of guilt—and motivate them to give again and again. **Overt, excessive expressions of emotions** are often manipulative; pay attention to overly expressive mannerisms, loud statements, yelling, and shouting.

2. Incomprehensible Words: Manipulators often use incomprehensible words—or speak too fast—to confuse and manipulate others. Lawyers, for example, use terminology that no ordinary human knows to put others at a disadvantage. Those to whom they are speaking are often left perplexed and afraid to ask, as asking would reveal their incompetency. They are now far more likely to purchase any products.

Recently, my mother bought a cosmetic device for about one thousand dollars. She took out a loan to buy it—all because she felt ashamed saying "no" to the saleswoman. The saleswoman was a beautiful lady, too, well-dressed and seductive. Her appearance played a role in her success. She spoke to my mother with terminology, intimidating her into buying something she neither needed nor could afford. The contract my mother signed was quite horrible: she couldn't find a way out. Instances like this one are quite common, and smart, yet elderly, women are the targets of many manipulators. Sellers manipulate them into feeling small, weak, and insignificant. They push their buttons until these women cave into their demands.

We can be easily manipulated through confusion, shame, belittlement, and guilt. We can also be manipulated through language—when others use words, phrases, and idioms we do not understand.

3. Verbal Repetition: Take, for instance, the statement "You are fit for nothing!" If someone repeats this to you many times, you will eventually come to consider it as a truth. You will internalise it. "I am fit for nothing," you will begin to tell yourself. Beware: this is hypnosis.

> **Let's repeat something crucial: we are manipulated every single time when someone urges us into doing something we do not want to do.**

4. A Sense of Urgency: "You can only purchase this today! This is a limited time offer! If you buy this today, you will receive an additional discount." Statements like this one foster a sense of urgency; in this way, they influence people to make unnecessary purchases. "Don't postpone this purchase," slogans like these ones say, "You only live once! Live your life to the fullest!" These statements are highly-manipulative, and even I find myself manipulated by them.

5. Shredding the Truth: Some manipulators shred the truth into many bits and pieces, and only present those facts that fit their narrative. People wouldn't give in to this type of manipulation if they knew the truth in its entirety.

I worked for a company that told us we had to work on the weekends, just so we could lead seminars at the best hotels in the area. I didn't want to work over the weekend; plus, I wasn't getting paid for the extra work they required me to do. Still, I agreed to work, all because my boss told me I was new to the team and had to prove myself. I was being manipulated through fear. When we got to the resort where we would lead our seminars, it turned out we would need to spend most of our days outside. We would lead team-building exercises in the snow. One of my bosses had me "keep" some ropes "safe," alone, in the middle of the forest, in winter! I obviously objected: "I do not want to be left alone in the forest in the cold!"

"You are new to the team," my boss said. "You must get used to the world. You realise we count on you, right?"

I don't give in to manipulation easily. That is why I resorted to anti-manipulation.

"I will definitely not stay in the woods alone."

"What do you mean? Are you objecting to the task you've been assigned?"

"If I get sick, will you cure me? Will you pay £2,000 – £3,000 for my hospital expenses? In my work contract, it says I am expected to work 9 to 5, five days a week, at an office—not in the middle of the forest, on a Sunday, during the cold winter! How are you, as my manager, protecting my safety?"

My boss quickly realised I could ask for a sizable compensation, especially if something bad happened. She let me continue with my day and sent someone else to "guard" the ropes.

People with low self-esteem are more susceptible to manipulation. They do not have faith in themselves. Such people would never assume they can rebel against the influence of others.

6. Stereotypes: Manipulators use universal truths. "Honey," a man may address his wife, "all successful men cheat! Even Bill Clinton did!" In literature and rhetorical studies, such statements are known as existential fallacies. They allow manipulators to connect their own behaviour to facts and examples that aren't nearly as common as these manipulators portray them to be.

During the pandemic, many companies reduced employee salaries and cut employee benefits packages to the bare minimums. This seems logical, you may think; they weren't making as many profits. Despite common beliefs, the revenues and profits of many companies remained unaffected. Such companies cut their biggest expense—employee salaries—despite the fact they weren't making any less profit.

In cases like this one, you could turn to anti-manipulation. Your boss could say, "Do you know how high unemployment is right now? Do you know that more than five million people got fired in the United States?" By speaking of the wider world—rather than the country you are in—, your boss has now found a way to apply (wrongful) stereotypes to your personal situation.

VISUAL MANIPULATION

Visual manipulation isn't any less influential than verbal and behavioural manipulation. A person who is dressed well—in a well-tailored suit or an expensive dress—will be far better received than a person who does not look their best. This is holds true in any environment, especially the corporate one. The IT sector seems to be the only exception to this rule; IT specialists treasure jeans and T-Shirts.

The point is—we often watch movies to see the effect a beautiful woman can have on people. Sex appeal draws people in, leading them to fulfill a woman's desires immediately.

An elegant appearance will always strengthen your influence. It will also hint at your socioeconomic status. Clothes with defined shoulders—including blazers with shoulder pads—will always inspire respect in others. That is why the uniforms of soldiers have well-tailored shoulders. Jewellery and expensive watches also promote respect towards the person who wears them. It is curious how the same information will be received differently based on the person who delivers it. If that information is delivered by a well-dressed, attractive person, others will internalise it; if it is delivered by a bad-looking individual, people will not take it seriously.

Expensive, simple, monochromatic outfits carry more influence than colourful tacky sportswear.

ANTI-MANIPULATION

"Leadership is not about titles, positions, or flowcharts.

It is about one life influencing another."
John C. Maxwell,
American author

Once we have learned to spot manipulation, we should figure out how to protect ourselves from manipulative statements and behaviour.

Let me give you an example. Imagine your boss says: "You are our best employee! That is why we want you to work in the noisiest, most problematic place—no one else could manage there!"

How will you react?

1. Heed your feelings. Are you happy others appreciate you? Are you afraid of losing your job? Do you feel unworthy?

2. Pause. Don't react to manipulation immediately. Say: "I have to think about this." Personally, I always take a day to think, regardless of the appeal of the deal or suggestion. I usually take the person's suggestion—or invitation—and respond with "Let me consider it." I always pause. That pause is the time I need to make a decision, to see whether agreeing to the other person's suggestion would be "a win" from me or not.

Don't rush into making decisions. All decisions—even the most obvious ones—take time.

This is also true when it comes to your personal life. When my husband proposed, I took a day to think. We were in the Maldives, celebrating my birthday, and when he fell to his knee, I simply said: "Give me time to think."

3. Ask yourself the following: "What do I need this for?" Consider your willingness to work on weekends. Question if this is the right time to get married. Decide if this is the right time to buy a new car.

4. Realise your true desires. "Yes, I can work on Saturday; but I will only do so if they give me an extra day off and compensate me accordingly."

Manipulators view you like a tool they can use to achieve their goals. Anti-manipulation can help you position yourself like an equal, a worthy opponent, who would never allow themselves to be manipulated.

"If you want us to establish a partnership – yes, this would be possible."

A company contacted me once, asking me to promote their platform. I, of course, immediately googled that company and opened their website. I couldn't figure out what that company offered clients! I felt like a fool. I responded to their email, communicating my inability to figure out what the company's products were. "I understand you wish to reach my audience," I noted, "I, after all, have about 140,000 followers on Instagram and about 500,000 on Facebook. But what are you selling exactly? Why should I promote your products/services? How much will you pay me for those advertisements?" This is how you can disentangle manipulation: you separate what's asked of you in many little pieces and clarify each one of them. **You understand what is asked of you, and what—if anything—you will get in return**. The company representative that had sent me the email kept insisting I advertise the company. "Let's sign an advertising contract," I suggested.

"We can't pay you," he answered.

I then applied some techniques for anti-manipulation. "Let me clarify," I said, "your products cost about £20, and you wish to reach my 500,000+ followers without paying me a single cent? With my help, you could make over £2,000,000 and yet you still refuse to pay my advertising fees?"

Facts—and concrete information—can disentangle manipulation. My calculations were pure facts; this company could make two million by reaching my audience. Once I mentioned this to the company representative, he stopped contacting me. I then learned he had contacted many other influencers with the same demands. Despite his failure to offer financial compensation, many of those influencers advertised his products for free.

Manipulators perceive people as tools they can use to reach their goals. As soon as you manage to assert your position as an equal, manipulators will no longer have the same power and influence over you. **That is when you can make partnerships and strive to achieve shared goals.** If the other side has true, honest intentions, you could quickly move to negotiations and reach a mutually beneficial agreement. Still, most manipulators avoid such partnerships. Like parasites, they take without giving while the people they use—the parasite hosts—worry about asking for compensation.

We can only determine what situations, deals, and partnerships benefit us once we have clarified our own goals and desires.

5. Prepare an answer with which you can anti-manipulate according to your goals. Say, for instance, "Thank you for placing your trust in me. Just like you, I know I can manage working on Saturdays! However, I can only do that if you compensate me accordingly and offer me an additional day off during the week."

If a friend of yours is trying to manipulate you, you should immediately demand something in return. **Clarify your conditions and demand compensation.** It is crucial you don't start manipulating your friend; view them as an equal and find a way to make both sides win. Ideally, the agreement you reach should be a win-win. Manipulation, unlike partnerships, only benefits one side. One person wins and the other loses. Furthermore, if you frequently allow yourself to become subjected to manipulation, you will take the role of a victim, developing emotions like shame, anger, dissatisfaction, etc. Relationships that are founded upon manipulation are doomed to fail.

I had a client who worked six months for free. When I asked why she did it, she simply said: "They promise they will pay me." Her bosses manipulated her without a hint of shame. "You are out best employee," they praised her, "we are so grateful to have you in difficult times like these." At the same time, the company was purchasing new cars and equipment; it clearly had zero financial difficulties. My client left, of course. But, prior to our session, she couldn't understand that she was being manipulated—even though this wasn't the first time she had been subjected to manipulation.

The most frequent statements that manipulators say are the following: "Look at how unemployment has skyrocketed. Don't look for other jobs. Stay here, with us;" "Your salary may be low but at least you have a salary. As smart as you are, you must know many people don't even receive a salary;" "We gave you so much! We showed you the tricks of the trade, and you want to leave us for some other company?"

You are being manipulated when you don't receive what you

deserve. In such cases, you, like a tool, are being used to facilitate someone else's goals.

6. Maintain your inner peace while talking. Specify your desires. Be precise in your speech. If you are communicating with a manipulator, they will give up on manipulating once they realise you know what you want. If the person you're conversing with wants to form a partnership, they will readily discuss your wishes in accordance with their own. You will form a mutually beneficial agreement.

Manipulation, especially systemic manipulation, leaves you feeling used. It angers you, and resentment brews deep within your heart. Sooner or later, all manipulative relationships come to an end. I, therefore, do not recommend you use manipulation in the long-term—it may work but it will be harmful to both you and those you've chosen to manipulate.

To avoid manipulation, you should set clear boundaries. Someone feels insulted by you? That is not your problem. You are only responsible for your own feelings. What others do with the things you give them is their choice.

It is easy to guilt-trip people who suffer from psychological complexes, and such complexes stem from mothers. When someone is blaming you, you should use facts to deconstruct their statements. Agree with them: "Yes, that is possible. It happens. I don't deny its feasibility." **You should never argue or try to prove your point—this is one of the most important techniques for anti-manipulation.**

A list of questions we should bear in mind when manipulated:

- **Why are you telling me this?**
- **What do you want from me?**
- **What will I get out of this?**

These questions allow you to display your feelings. They also enable you to assert your position as an equal, as a potential partner rather than a tool for manipulation.

My mother often complains about my father. Every time she does this, I ask: "Mom, why are you sharing this with me? Do you want me to hate my father? Do you want me to attack him? Do you want me to hate men? Do you want me to stay man-less and single my entire life?"

When someone is bothering me, I usually say: "Forgive me for interrupting you. Do you really think I find this information interesting? What do I need this information for?"

When someone is trying to blame me, I respond with: "How am I at fault for your failure to do this? What exactly do you want from me? Why should I get involved with this?"

MANIPULATIVE SENTENCES

- This is the first time I've ever met someone like you. You are incredible!
- Should I help you?
- Don't listen to them! You are doing great.
- Everything is so good when I am around you. With you, I can

finally be myself.

- Everything will be as you wish it to be!
- I understand you so well!
- You are the smartest, prettiest, most ………..
- Stay and you won't regret it.
- I only love you.
- We were made for each other.
- You mean the world to me!
- I will prove my love for you.
- I cannot go on without you.
- I am so attached to you.
- How will I live without you?
- You should know—I am only happy around you.
- You are the only person who gets me.
- You are the only person who can help me.
- I will always be with you.
- I won't let anyone else have you.
- You don't love me!
- What will you do without me?
- If you love me, you will………..
- Why are you behaving this way? What have I done to you?
- Do you remember how we used to……
- I've sacrificed so much for you!
- You cannot live without me.
- I cannot go on without you. I will die.
- Let's remain friends.
- You are responsible for me.

In partnerships, people openly lay their cards on the table. They honestly reveal their intentions and desires—something that isn't so common in personal relationships. Having communicated that, people then decide if the partnership would be right for them.

Expensive presents are yet another type of manipulation.

Once you sense you are being manipulated, I suggest you demand partnerships.

You should know that manipulation is merely a temporary approach. It will not work in the long term. You should always offer something true–something valuable–to your colleagues and partners, especially if you are preparing to enter long-term partnerships with them. You should find a way to make both sides happy. Win-win situations are always desired. If you manipulate others to gain something that is significant for you, you should also offer something that the other side will find valuable. This is the only way to make your professional–or personal–relationship work.

You can **cure the sense of guilt** by consistently reflecting on your own standards. You should find a way to decide what being a good employee, employer, sister, brother, husband, wife, mother, father, daughter, or son means to you. You should set clear boundaries. When you know what your boundaries are, when you have successfully communicated those boundaries with your partners, you will be more likely to enter a manipulation-free relationship.

I recommend you watch the movie **"The Secret Life of Walter Mitty."** It exemplifies how motivation works. Notice the motivation techniques that the movie presents and analyse them.

Your primary task is to learn to recognize manipulation. If you feel guilty, afraid, unworthy, you might be manipulated. If you feel irreplaceable, unstoppable, significant, you might also be manipulated. Stop. Analyse the situation. Ask questions and determine what is going on. Seek your own success without harming others or becoming a victim of someone else.

CHAPTER FOUR
STARTING A BUSINESS

HOW TO DESIGN A PERSONAL BRAND

I am an excellent example of someone who has managed to establish a personal brand. You can't mistake me for anyone else. **We can confidently say we have created a personal brand when others begin talking about us, mimicking us, copying us, even parodying us.**

Our personal brand is what helps people distinguish us; it is also the words—nouns, adjectives—that people describe us with. Your personal brand is what sets you apart! Design a purposeful personal brand, as it is essential for your success.

EXERCISE
PERSONAL BRAND: A TEST

There are a couple stages that go into designing your personal brand. The first one is deciding **what you would like to be associated with.**

Write down your own opinion; note your strengths and weaknesses.

STRENGTHS	**WEAKNESSES**

Contact at least five people who know you well. Ask them to name your strengths and weaknesses. Notice **what qualities are repeated** in the answers of those people. Those are your true strengths and weaknesses. If you are brave, you could post this as a question on Facebook, allowing a wider group of people to contemplate virtues and shortcomings. You could, for instance, say the following: "My dearest friends, I need your help. Please describe my strengths and weaknesses. Note at least three qualities for each category. I thank you all in advance!" You will be surprised, trust me. You will be perplexed at people's tendency to see you in a similar way. We sometimes do not realise our own qualities, or the qualities of those around us, but we all have opinions about each other. **These opinions, namely the way others think about you, is the influence you exert on people.** You should know what sort of influence you have on others. Once you are done collecting your friends' opinions, you can gain a decent understanding of what your influence is like. Determine if you like it or not. Choose if you would like to use it to design your personal brand.

Choose between three and five qualities that you would like

others to find in you. Consider the following adjectives: strong, reliable, dependable, smart, intelligent, intellectual, witty, funny, happy, joyful, pleasant, caring, friendly, professional, etc. Write down the adjectives that appeal to you.

YOUR INFLUENCE

1.____
2.____
3.____
4.____
5.____

Take, for example, Oprah Winfrey. Let's analyse what she communicated through her personal brand. Following her interview with Meghan and Harry, Oprah became the channel through which the scandal that was brewing within the Royal Family floated to the surface. She behaved like a true professional during the interview. It was no surprise Meghan and Harry chose her as their interviewer. Just a single interview with her, a single episode on her show, ensured the royal couple would reach the millions of people they wanted to reach. Oprah's fame, success, professionalism, as well as her air of authority, are all aspects of her personal brand. She is often seen in monochromatic outfits, which aid her neutrality and assert her role as an interviewer. Her hair is neat and well-styled, which speaks of her dedication to detail.

Now, if we were to consider Britney Spears instead, we could note that she is sexy, sweet, soft, unserious, and disorganised. She lacks the authority that Oprah has, just as her career isn't nearly as stable as Oprah's. Britney also has tattoos, dresses casually, and wears extravagant jewellery. This further distinguishes her personal brand from Oprah's.

We know neither of these two celebrities. However, we still have opinions about them. **These opinions are of their personal brand.**

Once you have examined your appearance and the influence you exert on others, you can begin to think about your personal brand's role in sales. Is your personal brand diminishing the total number of sales you are making? **If yes, you must change it.**

I, for example, tinkered with my personal brand quite a bit, and frequently altered my appearance. I first wanted to enhance my femininity, which led me to wear lots of skirts and dresses. I emphasised my sexuality, and most of my clients at that time were women who wanted to do the same. I currently wear jeans, T-Shirts, flat shoes—clothing that is androgynous in style. As a result, I now have a lot more male clients than ever before. This is a fully conscious appearance—a physical persona even—that I created and implemented in the beginning of 2021. I simply decided I wanted to change my personal brand. However, changing my style wasn't the only change I made. I also re-designed my logo. My old logo used to be red, as if to symbolise femininity, and it portrayed a woman holding a heart. My new logo, in contrast, is brown; it's androgynous in nature—neither male, nor female. Just like my logo, I no longer display outward femininity. Through the colour of the Earth Mother, I now radiate stability and security; I am different than I used to be. My androgynous appearance parallels my androgenous courses, which are no longer strictly limited to either gender. This has allowed me to attract a new type of clients—men. I have also managed to maintain my initial clients, women, through keeping some courses focused on feminine success and hiring Nina, who has now replaced me as the sexual, seductive lady of our academy.

Read books that can teach you more about the process of establishing a personal brand.

APPEARANCE ALTERATIONS

Open your wardrobe or, if very lucky, enter your closet. Look around. Which colours—and colour palettes—are most dominant? How do you combine them? What shoes do you wear? Do you wear jewellery? What perfume(s) do you use? What do you eat? What type of restaurants do you go to? The answers to these questions determine your lifestyle, and your lifestyle is a direct reflection of your personal brand. What do you communicate through your personal brand? Can it help you sell? Who is your target consumer? Pin your target group and perform market segmentation. How old are you ideal customers? What is their gender? Is your product expensive? Does your appearance reflect your product?

If you are a feminine businesswoman, let me tell you this: you will not sell to men. I used to wear pink dresses and the only people who purchased my products were women. I began selling to men as soon as I started wearing blazers, jeans, and shirts. I remember consulting with a personal stylist back then, and, asking her if I should start wearing more androgynous clothing. "Absolutely yes," she confirmed. She insisted I wore blazers. I still wear dresses, of course, but I wear them when I lead seminars with women, when I want to accentuate my own feminine energy.

If you sell excursions and exotic vacations, dress in vibrant colours; however, do not forget to look clean and polished.

If you sell jewellery, make sure to wear some jewellery yourself.

Wear simple yet expensive clothing.

If you are a masseuse, clothe yourself in medical attire. Wear clean, loose, light clothes from natural fabrics.

If you offer financial products and services, dress elegantly. Wear pencil skirts or suits, put on a blazer, iron your shirt. White shirts are as business-y as it gets; they inspire trust among your clients. Don't overdo it with lots of jewellery; an expensive watch will suffice.

If your business has to do with therapy, consultations, or medical examinations, your office plays a crucial role as well. "Measured" luxury is always preferred. You can achieve this by purchasing a white couch and always keeping the space pristine.

It was no accident that my company and I began working with stylists and designers. Recognizing this as a significant component of success, we began leading courses on style and allowing our clients to learn about physical appearance, fashion, and design.

DEVELOPING YOUR IMAGE

As you craft your new image, think about social media photo sessions. Your social media presence should parallel your product. If you sell bedding sets, you should establish the presence of the mother. Present yourself as a doting housewife. Take pictures in robes and pyjamas. Radiate joy, cosiness, and care. If you sell cosmetics, make sure to take pictures next to different shampoos, conditioners, and other beauty products. Film beauty tutorials. If you sell food, post pictures you took in the kitchen. Publish meal recipes and tutorials.

You should first consider what sort of clients you want; you can begin crafting your personal image afterwards. You don't have to purchase expensive clothes and jewellery; you could borrow them from a friend or rent them online.

Your website should also be structured in accordance with your personal brand and public image.

A well-crafted personal brand is a manifestation of self-love.

We can rely on research and other people's experiences when crafting our own personal brand. We could, for instance, observe our competitors or the leading figures in the spheres we are about to enter. **This is something I always do before selling a new product. I diligently research all competitors and leaders—in all languages I speak.** I check their websites 50-60 times. I follow their profiles in Instagram and Facebook. I strive to find the similarities among those people, to see what posts perform best, to notice which approaches are well received and which are not. Analyse your competition and adopt their positive qualities. Learn from their successes and failures.

I am assigning you the following:

HOMEWORK
MONITOR THE COMPETITION

Find at least six websites that belong to your competitors. Research the differences between them and your own website. How are your approaches different? What can you learn from them? Use Instagram to see how they interact with their audience.

Note down what you could add to your personal brand to improve it:

I recently researched one of my competitors—a Russian lady who had just changed her Instagram and added an option for client feedback. I, of course, added that option to my own Instagram as soon as I saw it was possible to do so. I also noticed she had posted some photos from her kitchen, and I immediately did so myself. I had to diversify my social media presence to attract a broader audience.

HOW TO DESIGN A SALES STRATEGY

"People won't always remember the product, service or deal you offered them. But they will always remember how you made them feel."

Keith Rosen,
author

GIVE SOMETHING FOR FREE

If you want to make more sales, you can start by offering your clients something for free. In this way, you can awaken their interest in your products and services. That's also how you can improve general attitudes towards your business and inspire trust. One thing you should realise is that **when given something for free, clients often feel**

obliged to give back, to purchase one of your products or services. If you sell beauty products or cleaning products, then make sure to give free samples. If you offer therapy sessions or consultations, give your audience the opportunity to book a personal five-minute session with you and ask some quick questions. Organize online games with rewards, giveaways, and adopt the buy-two-get-one-fee principle. Also, offer discounts. **Every single time to do any of those actions, repeat two or three words that you would like people to associate you with;** these words will help guide you and your business forward. I, for instance, repeated the word "marathon" so many times that it is now a part of my personal brand.

When you offer something for free, do not expect an immediate increase in sales.

I always ask my clients where they heard about me. I will give you a single example: there was this woman who had purchased an expensive bundle of courses that I offered. When I asked how she had learned about my services, she told me she had attended one of my free seminars a few years ago. She had followed me on social media after that seminar and kept track of my online presence. That woman needed two whole years to make that purchase!

OFFER SOMETHING CHEAP

You should offer relatively cheaper—or inexpensive—products. **The purpose of this is to lead your clients to buy your cheaper good or service before moving onto more pricey purchases.**

If you sell cars, this could be a test drive or an additional service. I, for example, hesitated to purchase a car because I did not have the time to change its plate. The seller offered to do it for me, and I immediately bought the car. Something small—a seemingly insignificant act—can sway the decisions and behaviour of your customers. As soon as that seller offered to solve my problem, I paid for my new car. Notice how you can help your customers. If they have troubles paying upon checkout, allow them a few different payment methods. **Give more and you will receive more.** I stay in touch with my clients' problems and strive to solve them. I lead free seminars, just as I lead inexpensive seminars. I sell products for £8-£15, helping people who cannot afford my expensive products solve a problem or two. **Free and cheap products help lead your clients to your main, more expensive products.**

OFFER SOMETHING EXPENSIVE — a VIP PRODUCT, PERHAPS!

I have the following strategy: I lead free live streams, I offer cheap seminars for £15-£25, I lead more expensive seminars for £60-£500. I also offer personal VIP consultations and services, as well as retreats to exotic destinations.

Do your products/services build onto each other? If not, find a way to present them in order, gradually becoming more effective and more expensive. The first product you offer can be, for example, a free workout or a free entry to the swimming pool. The second could be a paid workout. The third could be a weekly or monthly club membership. The list goes on. There are so many things you can do. You should simply realise that successful businesses always offer something for free, all to allow more people to learn about their products and services.

I recently learned about a fascinating service: there are companies that allow clients to find meals online, ship them the products for those meals, and send them cooking recipes. I use this service and, every time I cook, I manage to make a nice meal for minutes! The first four ingredient boxes were free, and they hooked me (and my family) on this service. We are now regular customers. I get fresh pasta and shrimp delivered to my door, and all I need to do is to boil the spaghetti and fry the shrimp a bit. I then add the sauce that is included in my order. That's all. I make homecooked meals every night without having to spend too much time on cooking.

A lady I know used to sell bedding sets. Every week, she invited her clients to tea, and, in the meantime, ended up selling them different products. She is a great saleswoman.

When you give your clients something for free, you should not expect an immediate reaction. Clients need somewhere between one month and two years to mature into buying your products or services.

AD HOARDING IS A THING

Presents are a small part of a long-term strategy. As I already mentioned, I always ask my clients how they learned about me. Many of them share they either joined a free webinar that I led or attended one of my free seminars. They usually follow me for months or even years before making their first purchase. Few of the people who attend my free in-person seminars expect to pay for them. Many of those people, however, purchase tickets for future events.

Don't feel discouraged when you give your clients something for free. It's normal not to get an immediate reaction. Have patience and keep offering your audience free things. Those gifts are the seeds you need to sow for long-term success.

Anthony Robbins conducted a fascinating experiment. A decade ago, clients needed to hear about a product two to three times before buying it. Today, a client needs to hear about a product 24 times to purchase a product. A person may hear about a given product on Facebook, then see a poster or a billboard. The product must stay in the client's mind—there need to be at least 24 impressions with that product—for a client to purchase it. **Today, we need to put in a whole lot more effort to be noticed.** Don't expect that advertising your business in a single newspaper or website would help you increase sales. **Over the course of at least a year, you need to hoard as many advertisements as possible**, in as many outlets as possible. Also, don't rely solely on direct advertisements. Be of use to your future clients, teach them how to use your products, offer them interesting information, and show them how much they need those products.

When handling your social media presence, make sure to remember the 5 to 1 rule. That is, for every five fun, motivational, or useful posts, there should be one post that advertises your products. **You can freely reveal some of your skills or let your audience in onto the tricks of your trade.** If people learn useful information from you, they will happily become your clients. **Consider what valuable things you could give your audience.**

Make sure to show yourself on your social media accounts. You are selling your own product. Make sure your post captions can be read and understood easily. Play with aesthetics and craft visually appealing social media profiles. Lead live streams, as this can help popularize your social media page. Use your social media account to interact with celebrities and comment on their posts. Always provide your audience with a link to take them to your website and show them how to make a purchase.

Post regularly. You should post something every day. You can, for instance, choose to salute your followers with "good morning" or "good evening" posts, training them to expect and await your online engagement. You could also offer useful and fascinating information, including advice, articles, and tests that are related with your products or services. Use a lively, well-maintained social media presence to keep your audience engaged. Your social media accounts are your virtual window shop, the way you attract clients. Analyse successful websites and social media pages and follow in their footsteps. **Make sure to smile in your profile picture.** Clearly describe your products and services. Suggest potential uses for your products. If you sell scarves, for instance, post fashion tutorials and styling tips. Show the different uses of those scarves and use your posts to prove their multifunctionality.

Interact with your audience through comments. Caption your video posts. Make sure to add your email and phone number in your biography, as your clients should have a direct way to reach you. Two-sided communication matters. Always have a direct link to your website. Put up some of your offers on your social media accounts. Make sure your posts are written in the language that you sell in and that they carry a clear message.

18-year-old girls attend my seminars, sharing they have followed me for years, waiting to come of age, attend my courses, and purchase some of my other products. I've been sowing the seeds for events like these—for their purchases—for years, and they've only come to fruition recently.

SEEK PROFESSIONALS

I will use myself as an example yet again: I am not great with fashion. Therefore, I hire specialists who can help me choose and purchase the right clothing. I tell those stylists what I would like to achieve with my appearance and, instead of wandering around stores for days, I purchase the clothes they recommend me. This saves me time and effort. Similarly, when I need to get my makeup done, I hire a professional makeup artist. I trust that he or she will do my makeup better than I ever would. When I need to catch my audience's attention, I hire a copywriter. I know I cannot do everything on my own. You should realise that, too, and strive to hire the best professionals in various fields.

STRIVE TO ATTRACT CLIENTS

You can organize games, lotteries, and giveaways online. You can also advertise your products through social media. Interact with other celebrities and invite them to lead live streams with you. **You will begin to expand your audience as soon as you post fascinating content and keep your followers engaged.** That is also how you can popularize your brand. You may be surprised at how many celebrities and public figures wouldn't mind being interviewed by you. They need the publicity, too! Collaborating with celebrities can facilitate your success, as people will begin to associate you with the rich and

famous; they will trust you to help them grow.
PLAY UP YOUR BRAND'S DIFFERENCES

People are used to me wearing bright red lipstick, having long hair, and being dressed in something scarlet. **As long as they are used continually**, your colours, jewellery, manners, gestures, accent, tonality, and overall presence become your trademark. Even your inability to pronounce a certain sound can be a positive quality if you own up to it. Don't stress over your imperfections; rather, turn them into a mark of character, a trait that allows you to be recognised.

Your personal brand does not require perfection.

I follow an American woman who recently underwent surgery. She had a mastectomy, I think. They removed both her breasts. Anxious, she began showing her breasts on social media, raising awareness about the psychological state of breast cancer survivors. A new psychological service dedicated to helping breast cancer survivors was established because of her! That is how this lady turned something sad and tragic into her personal brand.

As dramatic as this example may be, it illustrates how—as long as you are healthy—you should not be so self-conscious and anxious. Don't fret over your imperfections. Appreciate everything that you have. Everything about you is wonderful. You are wonderful. Accentuate your peculiarities. If you like big, heavy jewellery, then wear it! If you do not like jewellery at all, then don't wear any! This is your story—shape it as you wish! **Don't force yourself to do something inauthentic; stay true to your identity and do what feels natural.**

Come up with a slogan that reflects your values and portrays how you would like to be viewed.

HOMEWORK

WHAT WORKS FOR YOU

Within the next 24 hours, you should analyse your strengths and reflects on what works for you, what propels you forward. Examining both your character and your persona is a necessary step in figuring out which qualities serve you and which do not. Eliminating the traits that no longer serve you is an expression of self-love. If you are a woman, you must have an immaculate manicure and pedicure; if you are a man, your shoes must be polished. Your perfume shouldn't be too intense, as this may push people away. You should be punctual, as this is an important part of your personal brand that people notice. I treasure my time and, if someone is running late, I do not wait for more than fifteen minutes. If that same person is late again, I quit working with them.

Your appearance should be like that of your clients. If you sell boutique clothing, your appearance should be avant-garde and elegant. If you sell medicine, you need to appear clean, strict, and organised—to inspire trust. You should aim to present yourself the way your clients would, as any distance between you two could diminish sales. You cannot be a tattoo artist dressed in a suit; people will feel you do not reflect their free-spirited nature. **You can sell more if you personify the role model of your clients. Use your appearance to appeal to your clientele. Equate yourself to them and accentuate your commonalities. Don't neglect the importance of your appearance.**

When you have a clear personal brand, offer tons of payment options, and have optimised the functionality of your website, you can start thinking of **increasing the prices of your products and services.** You should already have a range of products—from free, through cheap, to expensive—, just as you should have found a way to improve your appearance and use it as a reflection of your products. You should have straightened out the little details before increasing prices. Both my assistant and photographer, for example, keep pushing me to pay more attention to detail, requiring me to match random objects in my pictures with my clothing. They recently had me make sure that my picnic blanket's colour matched the colour of my sweater! Attention to detail matters. As annoying and vain as things like these can be, they do impact the outcome, especially when you are rebranding or establishing an entirely new personal brand. In these cases, every detail should communicate your broader goal and mimic your business philosophy. I have learned that even the type of picture I post—that is, a selfie I've taken or a picture from a professional photo shoot—can reflect a mood and drastically affect the reception of my posts. The latter option, of course, appears more serious and therefore collects a lot more likes and comments on social media.

You will attract those clients who see themselves in you. "We are one and the same," they will think, imagining you have more similarities than you actually do. Every time you post a picture of having eggs for breakfast, people who eat eggs for breakfast will see themselves in you. We're alike, they will think. Similarly, every time you post yourself drinking a latte, people who love coffee will recognise themselves in your habits. Little details accumulate over time, and you gain increasing influence over your followers. Before you know it, you gain the power to post a picture of a car and influence your followers into wanting the exact same car. Your audience sees your post about a family walk in the park and thinks, "we can do this, too." **The more relatable you are, the more your followers like you.** We, people, love success, which is why every retailer attempts to

present their product associated with success. If you sell jewellery, present that jewellery as something that rich people like to wear. If you sell scarves, then have beautiful women take pictures with those scarves; this will improve the public's perception of your brand. If you manage to have celebrities on your social media accounts, especially if you are doing something with your products, this will automatically make your products more valuable and expensive.

I once purchased a pricey purse in Paris. Soon after, its handle tore apart. Even though the purse was designed and crafted by a famous designer, I knew I could find products of better quality in local boutiques around my city. They would be much cheaper, too. I, however, spent all that money, not for the bag or the materials it was made of; I spent it for the brand of the bag's designer. **I technically paid for the logo on my purse and the prestige that came with it.**

EMBRACE DISCOUNTS AS A BUSINESS STRATEGY

We all love discounts. However, we can only afford to make discounts when the discounted price still allows us to profit from selling the product. When choosing the prices of new products, I always consider potential sales, thus setting a price that is can be discounted later without impairing my ability to make a profit. Make your prices just a little higher than necessary; this will allow you to freely discount them later on.

I often speak with people who have clothing stores. They say that if they make discounts, they will end up losing money. Small business owners in the fashion industry have to compete with large fast-fashion brands like Zara and Mango, whose efficiency, quality, and prices they could barely beat. I find that large brands like these sell their clothing on prices that can barely cover expenses; they make a profit by selling a large quantity of products. Therefore, if you have your own boutique, you must have products that contrast with those of Zara and Mango. Use your personal brand to add value. Make sure to overprice items a bit—just so you can then offer your clients "special" discounts.

Let's imagine you bake pastries. Your pastries may be delicious; however, in your city, there are at least 20-30 other bakeries that make similar pastries. There is a lot of competition. In such cases, you should add something small—a free drink, a peculiar taste, a paper wish—to your products to add more value. This will distinguish your pastries from the pastries of rival bakeries. You could further distinguish yourself from the competition by adding a delivery option or opening your bakery before everyone else. I, for instance, like to purchase fresh orange juice from a store that opens at 6 a.m. I don't think there is any other store that is open at this time! **However, the opening hours of this shop are not the only reason I go there. The customer service is amazing!** The cashier there is careful and kind—a wonderful older lady who attracts customers with her warmth. Every single time I go to this shop, there is a long line of people that winds outside its door. Seek extra services that you can offer to attract clients; recognize the value of excellent customer service.

Planned and intentional discounts always work best. Strategies like "buy two, get one for free" or "bring a friend, receive a present" are proven to be effective. That is, **the best discount strategies require customers to do something—purchase a product or bring a friend—before being rewarded.** I find that limited-time discounts are effective as well. Happy Days or Happy Hours always attract clients. Whatever discount strategy you choose to employ, make sure you discount your prices or offer a free product to attract more clients. In fact, loyalty cards are a proven tool to do so. They motivate consumers to keep returning to a single store—or a chain of stores—so they can gain points and win rewards later. Adopt that strategy. Give out loyalty cards only after your customers have registered on your website. Once you get their emails, you could send them a newsletter or advertisements about your product. This will motivate them to purchase more of your products and services. **Discounts speak of your personal attitude towards customers.** Customers love gifts and price reductions, and you must develop and carry out frequent discounts. Still, do not overdo it! If you get your clients too used to getting everything for a lower price, they may never want to purchase anything at your "actual" prices again.

HOW TO CONCEIVE OF A BUSINESS PLAN?

A BUSINESS PLAN FOR YOUR BANK OR INVESTOR

If you want to take out a loan, you should describe your business, note the necessary investment sum, and calculate possible revenues. I suggest you contact different banks, as some would be more likely to loan you capital than others.

If you do not want to work with a bank, you could look for an Angel Investor to back you up financially. There are so many people who have money they want to invest. Find one and offer them a percent of your business—that is, partial ownership—or a fraction of your profits. You should make sure to craft a business forecast, showing your Angel Investor when he or she could get their initial investment back—plus profit, of course.

Always account for 30% of unforeseen expenses. When I first established my business, I had no idea there were so many expenses that went into running a company. I struggled with money, and I quickly learned there were a lot if "holes" in my personal business plan.

AN INTERNAL BUSINESS PLAN FOR YOUR PARTNERS

This type of business plan requires you to note your **goals**. What types of clients would you like to attract? What products would you want to develop? How much do you need to make in revenues? Consider all aspects of running a business, including advertising, sponsors, and sales. Discuss those aspects with your team and conceive of a business plan that outlines your responsibilities for the next year. Make sure to discuss your current weaknesses. What do you lack? What more do you need to do to succeed? You might have to hire more employees or find new partners. You may have to improve your website or your customer service.

YOUR PERSONAL BUSINESS PLAN

What are your goals and responsibilities as a business owner? What steps should you take to carry them out?

When first starting a business, you should register your firm, hire an accountant, inform yourself about national business policies, and figure out how much capital you need to develop your company.

You cannot rely on a single business plan. All three business plans are crucial for success; however, in case you do not need funding from banks or investors, you can forgo the first type of business plan.

TOOLS FOR THE FORMATION OF A BUSINESS PLAN

SWOT analysis is a great tool that can help you formulate a business plan. It includes four points:

1. My Strengths.

Analyse what sets you apart from the competition. What advantages do you have? Aside from the three descriptions that you already used to portray your products, you should also mention some personal qualities: I paint well; I am a talented lawyer; I have many friends; I have a lot of free time; I am great at marketing, etc. Your abilities include hiring employees fast, expanding your brand, and asserting your personal brand can also be considered as strengths. Note at least ten of them.

____

____

____

____

2. My Weaknesses.

Consider your weaknesses. A lack of insurance, inadequate language proficiency, and insufficient capital are just three examples of many weaknesses. Slow process of manufacturing, delivery delays, and unqualified personnel are three more. Write down at least ten weaknesses that you (and your business) have:

____

____

____

____

3. Possibilities.

What possibilities does your business pose? What is the maximum number of sales you could make per month? What's your highest possible profit? Where do the limits lie? Perhaps, the town you are in does not have a certain service/product and you could develop it. Maybe you could popularize it around the entire nation. Determine your possibility for success. Decide how much room for growth you have. Figure out how you can attract new clients and offer new products. Notice ten opportunities for growth and describe them:

____

____

____

4. Risks.

If your products have short shelf lives, there is a good chance you will have to throw many of them away. Other risks include the following:

delivery delays; certification requirements; international shipments; financial crises and diminished purchasing power of clients, etc. Mention at least ten risks below.

Let me use an optics store as an example.

• Strengths: it does not require a large store space; I can sell my products for a lot more than I buy them; I will get my investment back within three months.

• Weaknesses: there is a lot of competition and I have to keep my prices low—just so I can compete.

• Opportunities: I will make more revenues if my optics store is located near a hospital or on a busy street. I could also apply for financial support under a European program.

• Risks: A new lockdown would decrease sales and delay shipments of products.

Once you have clarified this, you can think about bringing your strengths to the fore. Find a way to overcome your weaknesses, optimize your opportunities, and minimize the risks.

If you do not have enough startup capital, you could apply to different European subsidy programs or contact investment funds. If you make your products by hand, you can automate some parts of the creation processes. If you have lots of competition, you can strive to do your job even better—to improve and distinguish yourself from your competitors.

I have strong competition in the Anglo-Saxon countries. Unfortunately, my English is not perfect. To compensate for this, I put subtitles on my videos, add background music, and strive to make my lectures as colorful, beautiful, and as easily perceivable as possible. To maintain a high product standard, I've also purchased good cameras and professional lighting equipment.

Establish a good control system—have cameras in the office, monitor bank transactions, and carefully account each financial transaction. Envisage fines for violating company rules; this will help you establish good employee discipline. Extend your delivery period to account for the potential risk of delayed deliveries.

Your task is to eliminate your weaknesses. Seek those weaknesses constantly, as improvement is a never-ending process. **In business, every detail matters.** If your website is slow, this speaks of a weakness in your business model; improve your website or incur the losses. Lead monthly meetings; get together with your employees and reflect on your business' downsides. Put yourself in your client's shoes. Optimize the payment system.

We once announced a marathon, which awakened a lot of interest on Facebook. However, few people signed up for it. In an attempt to find the problem, I opened our website as a mystery shopper. I had to fill out a long questionnaire. I did it. Then, I had to fill out a second questionnaire, and then a third! Annoyed, I called my employees. "Get rid of those questionnaires," I said. "I want customers to have direct access to the payment system. Only have them fill out their name and surname! Let them pay easily." We made 300 sales on that day—a stark contrast to the 30 sales we had made since the announcement of the online marathon. Our sales increased tenfold only because we simplified the payment system. Over the years, I, as the business owner, have learned to keep track of every detail within my business, constantly checking up on employees and asking: "How could we simplify this?" Lockdown was a bit of a crisis for my company; we went from leading seminars for 200 people to leading seminars for 3-4 thousand people. Our server crashed, but we managed to react quickly.

If you've never had a business before, start small and course-correct as you go.

HOW TO WRITE A BUSINESS PLAN?

1. Goal: What business am I starting? Where am I starting this business?

"I am opening up a new beauty salon in Sussex;" "I am establishing a Pet Boarding Service in London. It will be in Gatwick;" "I am starting an online cosmetics store."

2. Mission: What problems can my product solve?

3. Advantages

4. Target Group

5. Startup Capital

You should calculate the capital you need to start a business. Take into consideration the following expanses: machinery, tools, rent, salaries. Plan three months in advance. Your expenses are fixed and variable. Rent is a fixed expense; you have to pay the same sum every month, regardless of profit. Other examples of such expenses are the salaries and maintenance costs. It is harder to plan for the second type of expenses—variable expenses. The following are all examples of variable expenses: advertising, gifts for clients, Christmas decorations, teambuilding, and events. 30% of your starting capital should be designated for unforeseen expenses, such as machinery malfunctions, market changes, and so on. If you plan to spend £6,000 on fixed expenses, £1,000 on variable expenses, then you must also plan to set aside £3,000 for unforeseen expenses.

6. Planned Income

Here, you calculate the number of clients (and sales) you need to make a profit. If you, for instance, bake cakes, you will have to spend on food ingredients, electricity, machinery, salaries, employee benefits packages, accounting and legal services, advertising. and website maintenance. Let's say you spend £10,000 on expenses every month. Each cake you bake is £100. You can bake about 5 cakes per day, thus making £500 every day. If you sell 5 cakes every day for 20 days, you will make £10,000 per month. You will break even, sure, but this will not be enough to make you a profit. You should make and sell 10 cakes per day to make a profit. In this case, how many clients would you need to have each month?

A significant downside to my business is that I lead live events with small groups of people, meaning I hardly ever make any profits from in-person seminars. In-person seminars are not only unprofitable for me; they also restrict client participation to clients who live or can travel to the city where I am leading my seminar. Online seminars, on the other hand, have allowed people from all corners of the globe to attend. In this way, I have been able to attract bigger groups of clients and make a profit. Because of their ability to solve both my and my clients' problem, online seminars improved my business drastically. Clients are no longer limited by their physical location, and I can make more money. It is a win-win! Remember: there is a solution to every problem.

7. Potential Risks

Analyse potential risks and record your analysis in your business plan.

8. A Time Frame for Profit: how much time will it take you to make a profit?

Here is a **sample business plan for an HR agency**, a company that selects and hires personnel.

1. Goal

We plan to open an HR agency in a town whose population is about one million people.

2. Mission

We intend to facilitate the hiring and employment process, helping companies find qualified employees.

3. Advantages

Most companies seek the services of HR agencies. Therefore, it would be easy to find clients in our city. Furthermore, establishing an HR agency would not require us to rent office space or invest much as startup capital. Initially, all that is needed is a phone, a computer, and stable internet connection.

4. Target Group

Small and medium-sized businesses that can afford to hire a company to optimize the hiring process.

5. Startup Capital

There are a few key expenses that go into establishing an HR agency. First, even if I work from home, I will have to pay rent. In addition, I need a computer, a phone, a Zoom subscription, and even an assistant. I also need to plan for unforeseen expenses. That is, for the first ten months, I intend to set aside £30,000 for expenses.

6. Planned Income

I expect my monthly income to be around £3,000. I expect my investment to pay off within ten months.

7. Potential Risks

Until I manage to establish my brand, I will have to compete with other HR agencies. It is possible not to make sales (that is, successfully be paid for my services) as soon as registering my company.

8. A Time Frame for Profit

Here is a business plan for a pet boarding service.

1. Goal

I intend to open a Pet Boarding Service with space for 45 pets. My service will allow booking via WhatsApp. I will locate my service in a house outside the city. The first floor will only host dogs; the second floor will host other animals; and the garden will be used for dog walks.

2. Mission

I wish to help people find temporary care for their pets. After all, many people do not have anyone to take care of their pets as they travel or do business abroad, and that poses a problem to them. My Pet Boarding Service will solve that problem.

3. Advantages

I will send the pet owners pictures and videos of their pets every day. In addition, I will clean the pets' ears, eyes, and teeth for free. I will also walk the dogs for free.

4. Target Group

Pet owners who need someone to care for their pets.

5. Startup Capital

I need to register my company and gain a license to take care of animals. I need to promote my business, and I could use Instagram to do so.

I need monetary capital to rent the house—the building in which I will locate my service. I also need money to pay employee salaries and ensure benefits packages. Finally, I need money to furnish the building and purchase whatever I need for animal care.

When I first started my businesses, I had a business plan much like this one. I then opened my phone and looked over my contact list. Many of my friends—ones whose details I had recorded in my contacts—helped me develop my business; however, **I was openly seeking their assistance.** With my friends' assistance, I managed to establish my business almost for free. Seek help, ask for it, offer something in return. Do not allow challenges to hold you back! Money and opportunities come as soon as you have a clear idea of what you plan to achieve.

HOW TO CREATE MARKETING MATERIALS

HOW TO DEVISE A NAME AND A LOGO
FOR YOUR BUSINESS

You should first come up with an idea—a general conceptualization of what your business is about and what you want it to be associated with. The name of your business and your logo should reflect your style and people should be able to remember the name and logo easily. Hire a graphic designer to help you come up with a logo. I, for example, worked with four different design companies until I finally found one that worked as well as I wanted! The last design company performed a psychological analysis on me, figuring out my goals and values and learning more about the nature of my work and my clients. I answered 45 questions! The company then went on to ask a hundred people what they thought of me. They picked a couple of words that people most used to describe me. One of these words was "Russian." They therefore suggested I have something Russian about my logo. Two other words were "luxury" and "money." Though there were some other nouns and adjectives that we considered, the graphic designers encoded these three words into my new logo. I loved it as soon as I saw it!

You could contact copywriters to help you come up with a company name. They, after all, are professionals at doing this. Don't try to do everything on your own. You are not omnipotent. For my American website, for example, I hired copywriters. As it turned out, they write a whole lot better about me than I can write about myself. Their product descriptions are so good that I want to purchase my own products! My copywriters, however, watched many of my seminars and are well-aware of my products. Though their services aren't cheap at all, they are worth the money; they helped me gain four times more followers than I was able to get on my own. For a year, my followers grew from 5,000 to 20,000, and that was just on Facebook.

PRODUCT BUNDLES

I suggest you create a couple product bundles. The first should be foundational. The second, which is usually most frequently sold, should include some extras—such as insurance, bonus time for customer service, etc. The third should be for VIP clients and, as such, should offer VIP customer service. Having different product bundles will allow you to cover the different needs of a large group of clients.

VIDEO ADVERTISING

If you wish to advertise your business through video, do not forget we have the so-called **"slide thinking."** That is, we click on a link and, unless the website we are redirected to catches our attention within he first few seconds, we do not read anymore. The same holds true for video advertisements. Like article titles and website designs, **they must be captivating; they should captivate our interest within the first five seconds, and they should not be longer than thirty seconds.** Your business logo should be noticeable at the start of the video. Your video should also have a distinctive theme song. Finally, your video should clearly communicate your business values and objectives. If, for example, you want to portray your cleaning service as immaculate, attentive to detail, and well organised, you should dress the people from your advertisement in pristine cleaning uniforms. Uniforms are a great way to display employee unity and present your business as high-level. All my assistants wear similar dresses at my seminars; this is how everyone else knows they are members of my team. My son wears his uniform to kindergarten. Like him, many private-school students also wear uniforms—a rule which contributes to a sense of order, unity, and discipline.

Every business should have a digital business card—a video. This video should be **either 30 or 60 seconds long. The former format should clearly display your product.** Short clips stimulate sales, primarily because **the modern consumer is a visual consumer.** The modern consumer does not listen carefully—and probably has their sound off—which is why you should include subtitles.

If you want to advertise your cleaning service, you could rely on the principle of contrasting between "before" and "after." You will first depict **pain**—that is, discomfort caused by dirt and chaos—and then **beauty**—the order that reigns in a clean, beautiful household. Make sure the actors in your advertisement smile—**smiles sell.** Include an offer, a discount code even, at the end of your promotional video.

Make this video as good as possible; you're spending money on it anyway.

One of the biggest advertising mistakes you may make is to spend a lot of money on distributing your advertisements and not enough money on crafting them. Invest in the creation of catchy ads.

People enjoy watching videos that help them in one way or another. People want to relate to whatever those videos portray. They also want to benefit themselves. When it comes to video advertisements, you should stay away from videos that are as long as (or longer than) a minute. That's a little too long, and not many would dedicate a minute to your advertisements. It is best to have video ads that are about twenty to thirty seconds. Still, video advertisements are a cornerstone of marketing. They not only familiarize your audience with your products but, in doing so, they elevate your brand and business. It is especially exciting when your video goes viral and many people re-share it on social media!

A video I filmed in Greece went viral. We were on Mykonos, and I was advertising Nammos—an expensive and modern beach, where renting a single sunbed for the day is about £250. Weirdly enough, right next to Nammos, there is a free beach. The two beaches are the same; they are located in the same area, near the same sea, on the same sand. The video I filmed on Nammos was watched over two million times and shared over 130,000 times. All I did in the video, was to walk around the beach and speak about values. I do not know why this video went viral; its success puzzles me to this day. I just know that I somehow managed to grab people's attention. You, too, should provoke people. Motivate them to seek additional information and get to know you. Sure, you may have to resort to scandal to do so, but it is for the good of your business. Do something brave; give people something to discuss. **Brace for negative comments. Learn to take criticism and cope with situations of conflict.**

When the coronavirus pandemic first started, I published a controversial article. People who have sex, I argued, do not get sick. This is partially true; regular sexual intercourse does boost the immune system. However, sex is far from a guarantee that you will not catch COVID. This article had the effects I planned it would. It was translated into fourteen languages! People were even altering the things I had said to make the article even more... scandalous. Yes, I knew that sex did not protect people from contracting the coronavirus; that much was obvious. Still, arguing so allowed me to cause a little controversy that then marketed my business. "Who is this woman?" people wondered. They looked me up, followed me on Instagram, and read my books. This article was no less than a way to hook clients through scandal: scandal, after all, is often closely related with fame and success. "There is no such thing as bad publicity," I tell myself. It is crucial to be recognised by people. If people recognize you, if they know of you, they will also want your product. Develop your personal brand.

To sum things up: focus on short videos. There are many companies whose only means of marketing is short videos. Investing in good, catchy advertisements will pay off.

DESIGNING MARKETING MATERIALS

You should also craft visually-appealing marketing materials. It is best that you hire a web designer to make them for you. Your web designer should also create your logo, just so your advertising materials and your logo follow the same style.

Your logo matters. If you change, you could change your logo as well. You should have an entire logo "line." That is, you should have logos, cover pages, and profile pictures for your social media accounts, website, and email. You should also use your logo everywhere. Popularize it and have people associate it with you.

THE CLIENT'S PAIN AS A SOURCE OF INTEREST

Figure out the sore spots of your customers. Learn if your customers experience any sort of "pain." Then, offer a product that can diminish—or outright eliminate—that pain. Make sure you begin all your advertisements by illustrating that "pain." This will captivate the interest of your audience.

If you offer cleaning services, begin your advertisement videos with the following questions: "Is you home uninviting? Is your home unclean? Do you often wonder how to deal with the stains on the carpet and the couch? Do you struggle to dust all surfaces?" Similarly, if you sell cosmetics to help with acne, start your ads with a direct expression of the client's pain: "Do you struggle with acne? Are you ashamed to go out? Is sunlight your worst enemy?" If you have a pet boarding service, begin your ads with the following: "Do you avoid travelling? Do you avoid it because no one can care for your beloved dog while you are away?" If you sell art, you can begin your ads with the following: "It has been proven that people who notice and appreciate art become smarter! Painting, after all, fosters more neural connections in their brains, leading people to have more confidence, abundance, and opportunities!"

There is this wonderful book by Aldous Huxley, *Brave New World*. A dystopian novel, Huxley's book explored many themes, among which the role of beauty and art. Though a minor part of the novel, Huxley's depiction of art proves that those who grow up surrounded by beauty develop into more authentic individuals. It is no wonder the Communists used art as propaganda. The elite values art. Aristocrats are often art connoisseurs, collecting works of art from all over the globe. Realise that not having any paintings in your home may be a sign of poor imagination; the lack of art around us depletes our psyches. So many qualities can be developed through art.

If you are a personal stylist, you can emphasize the pain people feel after purchasing tons of clothes but never knowing what to wear. Show them they can save time and effort by hiring you. You, after all, will teach them how to choose their outfits, how to match *this* with *that*.

I call this process *putting myself in the client's shoes*. Every single time I create a new program, I try to imagine I were a client of mine. I consider my audience—women without relationships; women with problematic relationships; insecure women; abused women—and imagine I were like them. I stroll around town, pretending to be one of them. I think: "What is my problem?" Many answers float to my mind. "I can't find a partner—no one notices me. And, worse, the men I like couldn't be less interested in me." I record my notes into a tiny notebook.

When crafting my marathon for money, for example, I considered the problems of people with financial difficulties; they can barely pay their loan instalments, always worry about losing their jobs, and are usually doomed to do jobs they dislike. Recognizing this to be the case, I present my marathon for money in the following way: "Do you always stress about paying the bills? Is making your loan instalment the most stressful time of the month? Do you struggle to fall asleep— just because your worries keep you up at night?" People with financial difficulties can relate to all these problems; therefore, when they hear me mention them, they exclaim: "Yes! That's true! This is exactly how I feel!"

We are bound to seek solutions, looking for the person who can help us solve all our problems. Years ago, I purchased a painting for £250. Mind you, I had no money back then. How did they sell this painting to me, you may wonder. Well, they told me it was a "live" painting. The painter explained this herself, convincing me her painting allowed powerful energy to pour into the space where the painting was hung. Yes, I spent my last savings on this painting. However, the work of art decorates my bedroom wall to this day, making me smile every time I see it.

You could also add **facts, data, and comparisons to your advertisements.** You could, for instance, begin by displaying something ugly—allow your audience to find themselves in that ugliness. Then, portray something beautiful, letting your clients know your product will make everything better. The second picture, the beautiful one, stands for the solution you offer your customers.

Your advertisements should illustrate a clear pattern: an initial problem followed by a solution. Your product should be the solution.

Your advertisements may directly present the issue, too. When my team and I worked on the teaser for my book 33 Days to the Dream, we hired a professional ballerina. We had her make mistakes. In the video, she danced ungracefully, making one mistake after the other. Meanwhile, in the background, I spoke about the problems women experience in their relationships. At the end of that video, I went on to suggest a solution—a proven means for change. Once I mentioned this, the ballerina became more graceful and, arabesque after arabesque, captivating the audiences. Like them, she had managed to solve her problem. The ballerina's presence appealed to the audience's unconscious minds, showing them my product would solve their problems.

The third part of your advertisement should lead your audience to **identify themselves with the successful solution of the problem.** Your clients must imagine themselves as the victorious heroes—the individuals that managed to triumph over adversity. Your clients should believe your products will allow them to achieve their dreams and enjoy life.

If you offer online tutoring for students, find a way to stress the time any parent would need to spend on driving their kid to any in-person course. Show your audience the benefit of online learning. Offer them a free tutoring session, just so you **can allow your clients to try out your new products before purchasing them.**

Now, let's do an

EXERCISE
PUT YOURSELF IN YOUR CLIENT'S SHOES

Put on a pair of slippers. Turn on some relaxing music. Take a seat and make yourself comfortable. Calm your breathing and close your eyes.

Imagine you are the ideal client—the client your business is looking for. What's your gender? How old are you? Where do you live? What do you do? What is your lifestyle? Do you lack anything? What do you lack—so much that it causes you pain?

Relax your belly. Breathe.

What do you lack? What do you have that you find is insufficient? What scares you?

Enter the fears of your clients. What worries you? What limits you?

What do you dream of? What could solve your problems? What could astonish you? What can satisfy your needs? What could make you happy—truly happy?

Answer these questions. Say "Yes!" to the answers that float to your mind. Accept them. What should your product be like? What characteristics can make it the product of your clients' dreams? What characteristics make it valuable? What do your clients find valuable? Is it time, convenience, or price? Does your product have any particular qualities that make it stand out, that make it appeal to you? What appeals to you?

Open your eyes, as softly and calmly as you can. Return to yourself.

You can do this practice a couple of times. Keep doing it until you know you have understood your clients. You could even put on the clothes you imagine your clients would wear, taking yourself a step closer to your ideal customers. You could even do this practice at their workplaces. You can only understand your clients if you put yourself in their shoes, if you go through what they go through, if you recognize their needs and desires.

I suggest you return to this practice every so often. This will allow you to learn more about your clients, to figure out some details about their lives, to get to know them very well.

When you portray their pain, your clients feel that you understand them—you know about their problems. To do so, however, you must have experienced that pain yourself. Therefore, if you want to open a pet boarding service, get a pet. If you offer babysitting services, spend time (or even live) with a friend who has a child.

The true nature of your clients remains invisible until you learn where your clients' pain lies. Learn about it and use it to connect with your audience.

I have done this successfully. I have familiarised myself with my clients' pain, experienced it even, and crafted that many seminars to combat it. I know how I felt when I did not have a man by my side. I know how I felt when I was poor. I know how I felt when I could not get pregnant. I know how I felt when I first started my business. When I turn to my clients, I do not speak untruths that sell; I say my truth, communicating the experiences I went through over the years.

Here's the pattern: **Pain—Product—Solution.**

You should remember that the price is never the issue. If people complain about your prices, you've probably failed to convince them of your products' use. Show people they need your products. In case they keep complaining, it is possible your packaging isn't attractive enough or that your customer service isn't as good as it should be. It is also possible that your store is not inviting enough or that your product is not all that different from the product of your competitors. Your pricing—especially when it is higher than your competitors' pricing—should be earned and justified.

POSITIONING A BUSINESS WITHIN THE ONLINE ENVIRONMENT

Advertising on Facebook isn't expensive; offer your audience interesting, useful, and fun information. Stay active on social media and keep the interest of your followers!

Having an idea is never enough; you should develop and implement that idea! We are in the age of Aquarius; **online trade is the future.** Consider how you can position your business within the online environment. Nowadays, successful businesses are those where the business owners take risks, offer their services online, and make contact with customers online.

Remain psychologically stable and confident!

We experience the vicissitudes of life. Sometimes, we find ourselves at the bottom; all we can do then is stay calm and wait. This is the time when we should be collecting resources, making acquaintances, drawing up offer bundles and contracts. Then, as soon as you feel that you've recharged your energy, you should begin taking action. Seek clients and offer them your products.

There will always be people who dislike what you do and how you do it. Some will find your products too expensive; others will think your products are stupid. The masses will always find flaws in you. Ignore them. Delete their comments; don't allow them to disgrace you online. In psychology, this is illustrated by a frame of thought known as Broken Windows Theory. If a shop window is destroyed, and no one fixes it within a month, all shop windows in proximity will be broken. The same holds true for benches in the park. Vandals may break one of them but, unless it gets fixed promptly, all other benches will be destroyed. Negative comments online are no less than the first broken mirror, the first destroyed bench. They are infectious, leading your audiences to believe that if someone else does it, they can do it too. As soon as someone comments on your posts with a nasty remark, you should find that person's social media account and block it. Don't try to argue with such people; don't make excuses; don't waste your time and energy. Block them immediately and move on. **Regardless of the product you are offering, 30% to 40% of your customers will be dissatisfied.** Brace for client dissatisfaction. I often try to offer such clients something else, something that can appease them. However, this is not always possible. The more people complain about a certain product of yours, the more likely it is that product needs improvement. Communicating with clients—and receiving customer feedback—is also essential, as we should always strive to satisfy and delight clients!

All successful businesses have managed to **gain the trust of their customers.** To do so, you should **clearly communicate the terms and conditions** of your business on your website. Explain what you sell, explain payment methods, and clarify the product return process. Allow your customers to familiarize themselves with these aspects of your business before making a payment. The general conditions of your website should be proofread by a lawyer.

I strongly recommend you collect the emails of your customers. You can do this in different ways, the most common of which is offering something for free—in return to the client's email, of course. Clients should give you their email address in order to get their free product. You can also offer clients a discount if they sign up for your newsletter! If you still do not have a website, make sure to clearly communicate your terms and conditions on your Facebook page. In this case, **focus your efforts on creating a website;** your website may be simple, built with a template, but you must have one.

Think about joining a business club. Obtaining membership in some business clubs will give you access to industrialists and people with many resources. Membership will allow you to seek new partnerships, broadening your network and developing your business. If you sell nutritional products, find a way to position your business where health freaks would go! Gyms, recreational centres, and spas are just a few such spots. Lead seminars there! Give a percent of your profits to the gym owners, motivating them to sell and promote your products. You could also decide on a set monetary sum they will receive for each product they sell. The product or the place that sells that product doesn't matter; the principle is always the same.

Catching the interest of mass media—and being portrayed by popular media outlets—isn't as expensive as you may think. You should simply find the most appropriate online environment—social media or online groups—and establish a presence there. Post, comment, and interact with others; this is how you can build a reputation online and get established media channels to notice you.

You can partner with businesses that have the same target group as you but offer significantly different products. I, for example, have partnered up with astrologers; people who are interested in psychology are also often interested in astrology. I also offer partnerships to human design specialists, yoga centres, and psychological support groups, as all of these partners can help me situate myself on the Bulgarian, American, and Russian markets. I also lead live streams, offering gifts and discounts to popularize my business. However, I know I could not do it all on my own; I have therefore assembled a team of professionals. If you create your products yourself, you will probably not have the time to sell them yourself. Hire someone to sell instead of you. Also, whenever you sense a problem arising, tell yourself: **"I do not have a problem to solve. I have a task to accomplish!" Establishing a business is a long process. Don't expect it to become an empire in a day!**

I have been actively trying to enter the Russian market. To do so, I have created a Russian social media account where I post pictures, add stories, and try to gain more followers. Even though my Instagram account has not brought me any clients yet, I refuse to give up. I know it is a steppingstone to success, and I have allowed myself a year to gain followers and succeed. I, therefore, continue to use my Instagram account as my digital business card; meanwhile, I attract customers' recommendations by word-of-mouth. I have also partnered with an affiliate marketing program that allows others to advertise my products and earn money for each sale they make. I do what I have to do until my Instagram gains enough followers and proves itself as the primary marketing method for my products. Every day, I stay active, posting photos and information that can captivate the interest of my audience and entice them into buying my products.

The first step you need to take is to register a firm. You cannot do business without a registered company. You should pay your taxes; they are something you cannot avoid.

Now, let's summarise all of this:

1. Register a firm.

2. Clearly communicate the terms and conditions.

3. Craft a Data Processing Agreement (GDPR) compliance agreement.

4. Hire an accountant who can take care of all financial processes.

5. Register a domain and create a website.

6. Establish a social media presence. Market your products through your social media accounts.

7. Purchase a professional program through which you can send out emails.

8. Make sure you have an official company phone number.

9. Create a managerial email address and allow people to contact you.

10. Resort to advertisement-formation patterns (pain—product—solution).

11. Have three different product/service bundles: cheap, normally priced, and expensive.

12. Publish information targeted to your ideal client. Tell them why

they should purchase your product. Share your story, show how you came up with your business idea, and portray the challenges you had to face. Emphasize how you managed to combat these challenges (hint: your product helped you overcome them).

13. Show your satisfied customers. Publish pictures of them and use their positive feedback as the caption to your post.

14. You can find customers on Instagram. Do so by writing comments that stand out. The more interesting your comments are, the more attention (and likes) they will gather. Over time, your comments will begin showing up right beneath the posts you commented on, leading people to notice you and follow your social media page.

15. Publish your product bundles online. Post them on your social media accounts. Set a clear price.

16. Don't respond to negative comments. Delete them straight away. If you cannot delete the comment, simply write, "Thank you for your feedback." Don't argue. If someone is criticizing your prices, just note that you get what you pay for. Your clients, after all, get products of high quality. Agree with their concerns and say, "Yes, I know my products are pricey. However, they have so many benefits: .... (note all their advantages). Regardless of the function of your product, make sure to present it by illustrating three benefits and emphasizing how it solves a given problem.

17. Seek consumer feedback. Ask your clients what they prefer, which products they like best, and why that is the case. Send out surveys—especially before announcing a new product! This will help you figure out what products will be received best. Don't fear your clients and remain receptive. Value communication. Use social media to do research! Conduct surveys! Develop your social media profiles and show bits of yourself; present yourself as a relatable, helpful person who can solve your audience's problems.

18. Find a way to sell offline. Emphasize the benefits of your

products—benefits distinguish your products from the products of your competitors.

19. Present your products—and product bundles—in a visually-appealing manner.

I stand behind all these recommendations. Follow my advice and you will succeed. Stay brave and persistent. Face the challenges head on and fight. Keep pushing forward. Sooner or later, the seeds you sowed will come to fruition. **Understand your customers, and you will successfully find a way to reach them.**

Multi-level marketing (MLM) businesses have some specificities you need to know. It is best to sell to the acquaintances of your acquaintances and conduct sales in person. Allow your customers to test out the products. Offer your customers useful information. Organize interesting, emotionally charged events, where you can invite speakers; in this way, you can attract people who trust you and would willingly work with you. You could also lead successful events online, especially on Zoom. Still, even then, the **participants should have been invited by someone who recommended you and your services.** The most effective events have between five and six participants, as you can give each one of them individual attention. Establishing this type of business through Facebook would be challenging; however, it is not impossible. It is **full of potential**, which is why I entered it myself, selling Kangen water.

HOW TO ASSEMBLE YOUR DREAM TEAM?

"Give your employees a mission that matches their ambitions. When you challenge people, they surprise you."

Richard Branson,
British business magnate

Many business owners try to do everything on their own—at first, at least. Let me tell you this—you won't get very far if you are trying to make it all on your own. I, therefore, ask you to note the different types of people you will need. You may dream of having someone to take care of sales and adverting; you may wish to hire someone who knows how to grow your social media accounts; you may also want to hire an accountant, a lawyer, an assistant… if you do not know what positions you should hire for, then do some research. Look up companies in your field and see what people work there and what professional positions they occupy.

All businesses need a manager. When starting a business, you will serve as that manager; as your business develops, however, you could hire someone else to perform that role. All businesses also need a salesperson, a lawyer, and an accountant.

8 TALENTS LAY THE FOUNDATION OF SUCCESSFUL BUSINESSES

I will introduce you to Richard Branson's theory of "Wealth Dynamics." This theory presents eight talents that are crucial for the success of any business.

1. Artist (such as Richard Branson): this is the person who invents the product. Artists make something out of nothing.

2. Star (such as Oprah Winfrey): this is the person who presents and describes a product to grasp the audience's attention. This person plays an instrumental role in sparking the audience's interest in each product or service. Everyone wants what the star has.

3. Dealmaker: this person takes the Star's efforts to the finishing line; that is, once the Star has captivated audiences, the Dealmaker offers those audiences actual deals, drafts contracts, makes sales, and accepts payments.

4. Accountant: this person is concerned with the legality of deals and contracts. The accountant also prevents financial pitfalls, takes care of taxes, ensures the business is making profits, and analyses the financial state of the company.

5. Supporter: this person supports the entire business, resolves conflicts between employees (conflict, after all, begins to brew as soon as you hire more than three employees). This person organizes frequent meetings, monitors interpersonal relationships, and helps meet the employees' needs. The Supporter is often in charge of hiring.

6. Business Developer: this person creates and improves the company website, improves the business' social media presence, develops advertising materials and strategies, and facilitates checkout payment methods. Basically, the Business Developer oversees all aspects of the business that have to do with technology. If your business has factories, this person should be competent and have specific qualifications regarding tools, machinery, and manufacturing technologies.

7. Marketer: this person handles advertising outlets and sales. The Marketer seeks partners and plans events. Though previously neglected, this role is cornerstone of business development.

8. Business Growth Manager: this person analyses business development and crafts strategic plans for future growth. The Business Growth Manager pinpoints possible markets into which the business can expand. The Business Growth Manager also communicates the company's goals, objectives, and potential opportunities. New companies do not need this type of person; this person is needed in companies that have already expanded enough to have the opportunity and capital to enter new markets. Until recently, I never needed a Business Growth Manager; I hired one twelve years after starting my business.

The ideal team has members playing all each one of these roles. I first learned about this theory five years ago and found it somewhat unrealistic and impossible. Many new businesses do not have the funds to hire specialists; they can, however, strive to one day establish the dream team. You can only hire more people—expand your business—when you are making enough profits. Invest those profits into developing your business. Personally, I do so by hiring new team members. At first, my business had me, the star, and one other person who played the role of the supporter. I paid her a minimal salary plus a percentage of our sales. I did not have the money to hire more people. I then hired a student who was good at digital marketing; her salary was also quite small, and she was glad to make a percentage of our sales, too. Many of my employees start out this way: their salaries are small, and, over time, they earn a given percentage of our sales. I also promote my employees quite frequently. That motivates them to work hard. Today, my main employees receive concrete salaries and generous employee benefits packages. Meanwhile, some of my partners don't receive salaries but rather a fraction of my business' earnings.

WORK MOTIVATION & HIRING THE RIGHT EMPLOYEES

Some people are not motivated by money. I, therefore, advise you to overcome the fear of "I do not have enough resources." **Few, salespeople included, are motivated by money.** Employees have both extrinsic and intrinsic motivations to work. We will now discuss the motivations for work which Vladimir Gerchikov, the Russian film director, outlined.

1. Patriotic:

This type of person likes your company. All my employees were initially my clients: they liked and purchased my products before working with me. Seek out loyal followers who have the skills and abilities to occupy the position you are offering. Personally, I only hire people who adore my company's products. Most of my employees value being a part of this company. In this case, personal interactions with the business owner, feedback, and praise are crucial.

2. Managerial

These people like to have authority and a sense of freedom. They like being a boss—of themselves and other people. They like to manage others, lead meetings, and make decisions. Personally, I give this type of person as much freedom as possible; I only manage them through results. That is, if I find that something is not okay, I let them know. I then leave them to do their thing and observe them from a distance. They, after all, recognize their duties and responsibilities. I do not give these free-spirited and innovative people set working hours. I only assign deadlines. They choose when to do their work; I do not concern myself with their working habits. Those people's independence, among other qualities, shapes them into successful managers.

3. Professional

There are some employees who value professional development above all else; these employees want to grow in your company. They, therefore, appreciate learning opportunities like seminars and qualification opportunities. These people are motivated by your guidance, feedback, and support.

However, being professionally motivated is not very common. I sent three of my employees to a fascinating professional course, allowing them to obtain a VIP certification. Only one of them appreciated the opportunity. The other two complained about dedicating their free time to additional courses; weirdly enough, these two were a lot younger and less experienced than the first woman. We parted ways shortly thereafter. My company values professional motivation.

4. Monetary

Some people are materialistically motivated. Money matters. Such people are ready to take on tasks and do jobs that they do not like—as long as those jobs pay well, of course. This type of person likes to receive a set salary, a percentage of the profits, and perhaps even an annual bonus. If offered a higher salary, this type of people can be easily persuaded to switch jobs and change companies; they do not feel a sense of duty or loyalty to their superiors or colleagues. These people are like cats, working for themselves, perceiving everyone else as competition.

5. Lumpen

These people work because they need the money. They dislike their jobs and dream of vacations and avoiding work. These people are lazy, constantly spewing excuses and staying as uninvolved as possible. They pick the easiest tasks and never work more than necessary. They only do what is expected of them. They neither seek to grow, nor feel connected to their companies.

What is good about this type of person is that he or she does the jobs no motivated person would ever do. The entire world noticed what happened in Britain after many employees with lumpen motivation left work. Now, Britain is experiencing a shortage of waiters, cleaners, and drivers as a result. This type of person is also essential.

What is motivating you to work? What types of people do you have as part of your team? What types of people do you wish to have on your team?

SET CLEAR GOALS

"Every success story is a tale of constant adaptation, revision, and change."
Richard Branson

When first establishing your business, make sure you do not leave your employees any opportunities to steal. **Do not tempt people**. Stay away from cash and ensure all payments are done online. Keep track of profits and expenses. You will be the one at fault if your employees ever decide to take something that does not belong to them. You should control your assets, especially if you and your employees are separated by international borders.

When you are deciding on salaries, you should do more than promise your employees a fraction of the profits. **You should set clear targets:** there is a minimal number of sales we should make every month. I always set clear goals and craft a plan. **Communicate your expectations with job candidates during interviews.** Let them know what you expect them to do, how much they should make in revenues, and what percentage of the profits they can take home. The clearer you communicate your expectations, the better your staff will perform. **You can craft contracts, include your expectations, and sign them to optimize efficiency.** That is how you can avoid subsequent demands for salary increases. **If you do not know how your business will do in the short-term, offer your employees a set salary. Do not discuss percentages of profits as a potential source of income for those employees.** This will show people they have a guaranteed income for the first couple of months and assure them of the possibility of growth in the long-term.

HOW TO TRAIN EMPLOYEES

The adaptation period tends to last between three and five months. A manager should be making sales within the first five months of employment; if not, this is a clear indication of potential problems. Personally, I don't expect my employees to be making many sales within the first five months.

Expect people in top positions to wish to leave during the first

month of their employment. I suggest you speak with them, as calmly as you can, and ask them to stay for three months. You can plan another meeting once those three months are over; that's when you will discuss how they feel in the workplace. Everyone needs time to adapt. Adaptation takes about three months. I give myself three months every time I start a new project; **I don't expect to make many—if any—sales** in those first three months. I do, however, expect to have expenses. In business, you always have expenses, even when you are not making any profits. I also have projects that are full of potential; yet, I refuse to develop them until I've set aside enough money to fund them for first three to six months without making any profits.

Support people during their periods of adaptation. Work closely with them, just so you can "show them the ropes" and allow them to "feel" the essence of their new job. Few people can stay afloat when thrown in at the deep end. Take your new employees under your wing, keep them close to you, allow them to follow you and attend meetings for you. Do this for the first three months of their employment. Take your new employees to lunch—and dinner— and even bring them with you on a short vacation. Discuss work. Familiarize your employees with your clients and allow them to get used to you. Let new employees hear more of your story, absorb your style of speaking, and mimic your mannerisms. That's how you can engrave your manners, or your "handwriting," so to speak. That is how you transform a part of yourself into new employees, preparing them to serve as extensions and representations of you. Allow your new employees to accompany you at first. Then, ask them to contribute to conversations. Finally, leave them alone, allowing them to finish deals as you go on with your other duties. Your new employees should sense your style of work, internalise it, and apply it daily. Having them read your mind will never work; employees need to be trained. **If you**

do not train your employees well, they will do their work, but the work they do—or the manner in which they do it—may not be what you need. To establish a company that reflects you, you need to hire people who are more or less similar to you. This is a long, often tedious process. Observe the strengths and weaknesses of your new employees. Once you've trained your new hires, go on to challenge them accordingly.

> **If you invest your time and energy into training and mentoring a new employee, that employee becomes a key member of your team. Over time, that employee begins to train and mentor other people, leading to the so-called Matryoshka effect.**

To have a dream team, however, **you should only hire people you find pleasant.** Hire those who make you feel comfortable. If someone is unpleasant and causes you discomfort, you will not want to spend much time with them. You will not take them to dinner, just as you will not bring them on a vacation. At the end of the day, you can learn a lot more about people when you take them outside the workplace and have them relax in an informal setting. That's how you build trust, too. Therefore, hire people you like and then dedicate yourself to training them. Once you've trained them for about three months, you allow those people an additional three-month period to work and improve; expect true results **six months after you have hired a new employee.** Also, remember you can never hire mediocre people and expect them to become brilliant. **Hire talented, creative, hardworking individuals who can manage stress and work well in teams.**

Some people are talented at conceptualizing ideas which they can then pass onto the others for further development. If you are one of them, you should hire employees who can grasp your idea and develop it. <u>You stand at the root of that idea, allowing someone else to branch out and ensure the prosperity of new projects. Meanwhile, you conjure up more ideas, more projects. I am very good at creating and beginning new projects; then, once I've started them, I like to pass them on to my team.</u>

Note down the qualities your employees should have. Describe the responsibilities of <u>each employee.</u>
  Qualities:

Responsibilities:

The most important qualities, in my opinion, are the following: honesty, responsibility, initiative, and resistance to stress.

Your employees should reflect you. They should depict who you are in different aspects of life. **The employees are just like their boss.** It is crucial that you hire your own team; this will allow you to hire people who are like you, who vibrate on the same frequency as you. I recommend you do not try to save on salaries. **If someone does not**

want a salary, brace for peculiar behaviour, lies, and theft. There are cases when people, the wives of successful men especially, aren't too concerned with money; even then, however, those people are not very dedicated to work. Well-educated, qualified, adequate, and attractive people usually want to receive a good salary, as it allows them to maintain their living standard and grow as individuals. Invest in your team and reap good results.

HOW TO SEEK EMPLOYEES

Where can you seek employees? I usually find my own employees by asking friends for referrals. I also publish job postings on Facebook and other social media platforms. In this way, I find dozens of qualified people, who want to work and learn. I sometimes even email my clients about certain vacancies that my company is looking to fill! You can find employees anywhere. Smart people are everywhere, too. When hiring, you should simply make sure your employees-to-be love their jobs and do them with pleasure and professionalism.

Start telling everyone about the employee you are looking to hire. Describe his or her qualities, skills, talents. **That dream employee will show up as soon as you have a clear idea of who you wish them to be.**

I know you may dream of the moment when you will have so much money you can hire as many employees as you want! Well, that will never happen. **Hiring someone new always puts additional pressure on the business owner.** Business owners worry about budgets and often decrease their personal income to pay the new employee's salary. This, in itself, is an act of growth. You know your company will not move forward unless you hire that person. Therefore, you hire the person, taking a risk and investing in his or her salary. Still, over time, you receive an investment return, bringing you more profits than ever before.

Be brave and delegate tasks! Hiring the right people will make you more money than you ever imagined.

If any aspect of your business is not performing as well as you had hoped, this is a sign that you lack the necessary experts. Hire them.

I realise it is quite scary to hire people and become responsible for paying their salaries. I used to think for months before hiring someone. I am now preparing to hire a PR agency in England; I think I've almost convinced myself. **Even today, more than a decade after starting my business, I still feel worried when hiring personnel. However, I hire those people despite my worries, knowing this will help me expand my business.**

Seek the successful. Attract them by offering higher salaries and better employee benefits packages. People like working in companies that offer them better opportunities, respect their efforts, and value their contribution; it isn't all about money. I am great at headhunting. I find beautiful pictures online, contact the photographers, and ask them to meet me for coffee. I see a well-maintained Facebook page and I contact the people who run it. I notice people's work and professional development and I hire the best and the brightest. Do the same.

HOW TO ORGANISE THE WORKING PROCESS

At first, you can hire people on fixed-term contracts. If your employees get paid time spent working, have them register as freelancers and require them to issue you invoices. That is how you can diminish spending on salaries and employee benefit packages. You should clearly understand the motivations of your employees; some find freedom more important than money.

Remain flexible and consider the values of your employees. If you push your employees a little too hard, or disrespect their values, you may lose some of your highly qualified hires.

Lockdown changed our habits and transformed our understandings of how work should be conducted. Before the pandemic began, I used to require all my employees to work from our office. Now, 90% of my employees live in different cities, and most of our collaborative work is done online. I always take their physical location into consideration; some of my employees, after all, are in different time zones and on different continents. Prior to the pandemic, I used to think people could not work well from home. I was wrong. One my friends, the multimillionaire I often talk about, helped me realise my mistake. We were in Bali, having lunch near the beach. "Natalia," he said, "don't you think having an office is an unnecessary expense?"

"How could I work without an office?" I asked.

"It is very easy! My wife and I have a successful online business and work from home. We make sales from our living room! We can live wherever we want."

That was a conversation we led in February of 2020. A month later, the United Kingdom—and the entire world—went into lockdown, pushing us to change our strategy. Still, even before lockdown began, my friend had managed to show me the advantages of allowing employees to work from home. This story once again illustrates why you should communicate with successful individuals!

My friend's advice calmed me down, too. Because not having an office space worked for his business, I assumed the lack of an office would also work for me. My friend helped me figure out a major **drawback to my established business model:** I was spending too much money on rent and utilities, both of which were unnecessary expenses. I felt relieved when we shifted to working from home; and I wasn't the only one! My employees also preferred to work from home—as they do until this day. Not requiring my employees to work from our official office also allowed me to expand my team; I could now hire professionals from all over the country—and the world— without asking them to move. **Flexibility leads to money.** The more emphatic you are, the more you set your expectations in stone, the more limitations you will experience. Limitations prevent you from making money; they also lead to unnecessary expenses and loss. Therefore, I advise you to listen to employee and customer feedback; you may need to change a thing or two!

Save as much as you can during in initial phases of your business lifecycle! Many spend on clothes, restaurants, and redundant luxuries. Don't make that mistake! Invest the profit back into the business; do not spend it on yourself. I bought my first nice car ten years after starting a business and began flying business class on the twelfth anniversary of my business. Set yourself a clear salary and only spend the money from this salary; your business needs perpetual investment of past profits to grow; buy more equipment, hire an employee, and set aside enough money to pay that employee's salary. Know you will spend three months training that employee, then waiting for another three months for them to actually begin making sales. Your investment will return in six months—at minimum. As soon as it does, save the new profits you make and invest them back into your business. That's how you propel your business forward. **Business development is a slow process.**

You can only begin taking in profits in the fifth year after establishing your business. Even then, you should remain careful; investing always comes first.

Some people tell me I can afford a higher standard of living. They are right—in a way. I could afford to purchase more expensive clothing, live in a better area, and drive an even more expensive car. However, I prefer to reinvest money into my business, knowing I'm sowing the seeds of success. I also realise I need to pour money into my business; I am, after all, attempting to enter both the American and the Russian markets. I know where I am going, I know what my business objectives are, and I know how I wish my business to be in ten years.

At the end of the day, everything about business is risky. Business is built upon risks! Some of your employees will do better than others; some will learn more quickly and deliver better results. Others will struggle. You should remain aware of the motivations of your employees; figure out if they are materialistically or intrinsically driven. They may be directed by a desire for self-actualization! Figure out what strengthens the motivation of your employees. My female employees, for instance, appreciate my praise and support. I have some employees who value boundaries and privacy; I try not to contact them outside of working hours. These people often refuse salary raises and promotions, as they have other responsibilities— family included. There are other types of employees. There is, of course, the freedom-appreciating type; these people usually work part-time or as freelancers. We decide on their duties and tasks before every major project. I observe them closely, trying to figure them out as individuals. I even ask them about their goals and aspirations during job interviews. I suggest they explain what the ideal job would be for them. Sometimes, these people share they would only like to work for five hours per day; however, as many of them get far more work done in five hours than others would in eight, I agree to that. It's a win-win! As an employer, you should remain flexible, **figuring out what works for both you and your clients.** Remember—you are the foundation upon which the business is built, you are the person everyone else will mimic. Your employees, as we already mentioned, are like matryoshka dolls. They are little "you's." If they happen to displease you, remember it was you who hired and trained them! Implement the following principles:

1. Be honest with your employees!

2. Give your employees concrete job descriptions.

Use job descriptions to guide your employees. Realise that a clear job description can specify the goals, duties, and responsibilities of every employee. Clearly state how many hours your employees are expected to work, how much they will be paid, and what employee benefits they will receive. Make sure to specify their future working conditions.

3. Organize informal activities!

Teambuilding, informal company dinners, and thematic events all help bring your team together. Personally, I also offer annual bonuses and **gifts**—chosen in accordance with the tastes and needs of my employees. **Establish personal relationships with your employees**

but do not befriend them. Your team shouldn't be aware of your personal problems with men, family, and money. For them, knowing this would be unnecessary. Your team should be focused on completing tasks, making sales, and solving company problems—not on your personal issues. Find a way to motivate your employees through nonmaterialistic means. Do something with them in your free time. Plan something fun—at least once per month. You could even bring your employees breakfast, have meals with them, lead more informal conversations. Doing this is crucial. Many people work for those exact moments, especially if they have a patriotic motivation.

Good interpersonal relationships among employees are also crucial for the success of your company. **Consider which people work well together, and which do not.** Don't force people to work with colleagues they do not like. If conflict brews in your company, approach it carefully, analyse it, and find a way to eliminate it.

4. Offer your employees clear information about potential opportunities.

Offer your employees a clear idea of how much they can grow in your company. Tell them about potential opportunities, mention what they can learn, and show them they can simultaneously work for you and for someone else. Many of my employees do projects for me and for others at the same time. I encourage them to have a side hustle, as this is an additional source of income.

5. Conduct meetings.

Conduct meetings and encourage your employees to share ideas for business development. Consider every suggestion carefully. Ask everyone to share their opinions—even the cleaner! A single word can give birth to a powerful idea.

6. Train your team to function independently.

You need to train your employees to get tasks done without your direct guidance. You can foster business development by passing more responsibilities to your subordinates. Do the negotiations yourself, and then allow your employees to seal new deals.

7. Analyse the weak sports of your business.

Reflect on your business and strive to improve its drawbacks. Come up with products that could bring good results. **Usually, 20% of your products bring in 80% of your revenues.** Keep track of your "premium" products and find a way to sell more of them. For example, two restaurant owners recently told me they made most from selling coffee and water! Conceive of ideas, steal ideas, and hire people who would contribute to your business. Multiply your best-selling products—sell in ever-increasing quantities. Make sure to maintain three product categories: cheap, normally priced, and expensive.

Seek new ideas. Analyse the competition. Figure out what your competitors do and realise what makes them successful. Bosses that are egocentric, unwilling to listen, and conservative don't lead successful businesses. Recognize your employees may know something you don't and allow them to speak up. **Embrace feedback. Everyone has something worth sharing!** It is a huge problem if you are the only "brain" on the team. Seek synergy. Ask your employees: "What do you think? Could we do this in another way? What are our competitors doing?" If you have successfully hired smart, creative, and ambitious people, your team will be full of ideas. Give your employees the opportunity to express opinions. As their boss, strive to remain receptive.

8. Organise meetings with colleagues

I love organising meetings. Every now and then, my employees and I meet to discuss our work and brainstorm. These meetings help us motivate each other. Though there are not many people who have adopted this attitude, I am certain of the positive benefits of collegiality.

CLEARLY COMMUNICATE
YOUR COMPANY'S VALUES

"A business is simply an idea to make other people's lives better."
Richard Branson

If you want loyal and honest clients, you need to clearly communicate your company's values. If you display and adhere to those values, so will your clients. If you love your products, clients, and company, your employees will love them too, becoming more interested in their work and following in your footsteps.

Clients hold authority over everyone within a company, including the business owner.

I, for example, often communicate with my clients. They text me and send me emails, and I respond to them, knowing that "the customer is always right." When a crisis happens, I react immediately, even if doing so means working at midnight. I take charge of the situation, do what is necessary, and solve the problem by morning. My employees observe my behavior and shape their own accordingly. **Always give**

your clients a little more than they expect. This is an important rule we all must follow.

You should respect your employees if you want them to respect your customers.

You, above all, should adhere to your company principles. Do not insult your employees and do not raise your voice. Treat your employees like separate individuals. Value their individuality. If someone has made a mistake, ask them how they would react if they were you. That person will then decide on their own punishment and compensate for their mistake. When your employees do not perform their duties as expected, **you can resort to questions.** "How are you doing now?" is a question you can ask to check on their progress. This question often leads your employees to offer you a solution such as, "I will work for two additional hours today to get this done." Demonstrate respect, love, and understanding; you, after all, are team players working to achieve the same goals. Use questions to encourage your subordinates to put themselves in your or your clients' shoes: "How would you feel if you receive similar customer service elsewhere?" I always try to make work pleasant for my employees, just as I attempt to satisfy my customers.

The love and care you give your team often translate into the love and care your team offers your clients.

If your team is rude, you should question your own behavior. How do you treat your employees? You and your employees are a system of two parts that constantly interact and influence each other. Make sure that influence is positive, as it will be reflected on your clients.

Here are some key company values that you may wish to adopt: security, honesty, responsibility, goodness, love for your clients, attention to detail, high quality, etc.

HOW TO ORGANISE PROCESSES

"What do you need to start a business? Three simple things: Know your product better than anyone. Know your customer, and have a burning desire to succeed."
Dave Thomas,
founder and chief executive officer of Wendy's

PHASES OF BUSINESS DEVELOPMENT

Every company passes through four phases of business development.

1. Chaotic Phase

Between the first and third year of establishment, your company is like a baby. Everyone is doing everything, getting involved with all tasks. At this phase of development, there aren't clear job positions or rules. You can be the boss, the manager, and the cleaner all at the same time. This is absolutely normal. At this phase, you also work between 10 and 15 hours per day; your brain is busy with tasks, and you do not have the time for anything other than your company. You give your business your all. Your business is exactly like a child, consuming all your time and requiring constant care in its infancy.

2. Bureaucratic Phase

Between the third and seventh year of establishment, your business is quite like a child at the same age. At this phase, you need to start planning and organising processes. You set clear job descriptions, assigning specific roles and duties to your employees. You also develop clear company rules and policies, and company values, and decide on a distinctive attitude towards your clients. All company employees have specific roles and goals. Your business develops a certain dose of stability and security, allowing you to loosen the reins and relax a bit. You begin delegating roles, and hiring people to perform lower-level company duties.

3. Team Phase

Within the seventh and the fifteenth year of establishment, your company is like a teenager. Your team works well, and your employees are more independent than they used to be. Everyone knows his or her own responsibilities. You have hired a specialist to carry out important roles within your business. You delegate tasks. Your company is like a well-functioning machine that yields results. At this phase, your company is flourishing, and you are making more money. Your company has a stable flow of profits. You are reaping what you sowed. As the business founder, you can slow down a bit, hiring a manager to lead the team while you oversee the business in its entirety.

4. Decline Phase

Your company splits into multiple sub-companies, each of which is busy with its own distinctive project. Each of these sub-companies goes through the four phases of business development. The dissemination of these sub-companies also leads to the creation of new businesses. Richard Branson, for instance, started out as a business owner of recording studios; he then went on to open gyms, transportation companies, and internet companies. At this phase of business development, new models of business management take over the old. You, as the business owner, can also use one company's profits to invest into the establishment of new companies.

HOW TO CRAFT A JOB DESCRIPTION

As I already mentioned, a clear, well-written job description stands at the root of a truthful and honest relationship between you and your employees. The job description is handed to the employee in written form and signed by both parties. It should include the following information:

1. Job title
2. Job duties and responsibilities
3. Working hours
4. Additional opportunities for growth
5. Direct supervisors and superiors

You do not have to be everyone's boss. It is so much easier if you hire a manager who can keep track of the team. In this case, you only have to communicate with the manager to figure out more about your team's morale. You should establish a well-functioning hierarchy at the workplace.

6. Preferred qualifications and experience

I strongly recommend Svetlana Ivanova's book Motivation for 100%.

HOW TO CONDUCT INTERVIEWS

Here are a few questions you may ask:

1. What type of work do you enjoy doing?

We are best at the work we love doing. This is an unspoken law. I do not make people do things they hate.

2. Were you ever satisfied working on any of these positions, at any of these companies?

3. Why?

4. Do you struggle to work well with a certain type of person?

5. What would make you resign?

6. What type of work do you dislike doing?

7. What do you expect from your new working environment?

8. What matters most to you?

9. If you were choosing between two job offers, what would impact your decision?

10. How do you improve your professional qualifications?

11. Who are the experts within your field of expertise?

12. What are your professional goals?

13. How and where do you plan to fulfil those goals?

14. What proportion of your working hours do you dedicate to communication and planning?

15. If you could change this proportion, what tasks would you remove from your official job duties?

One of my friends once shared a funny remark she had found online: "If you do not have money for therapy," she said, "attend a job interview. There, you can also talk about yourself, share, cry even."

To summarize, let's discuss the employment process. Once you have crafted your business plan, figured your company values, and come up with distinct job position, you can begin seeking employees. Employees usually "appear" when you have a clear idea of what and who you need. You should give those new hires clear job description, clarifying their duties, responsibilities, and opportunities at the beginning of their employment. You should train your employees. If you have managed to find and train the right people, your business will be propelled forward with their assistance. These people can, for instance, develop old ideas or polish new projects, helping you carry out projects that have been in the making for a little too long.

Even if you do not have to hire an employee right now, you can still write a job posting and publish it online. State the desired employee's characteristics and allow your audience to understand what you are looking for. Begin conducting interviews. This, according to quantum psychology, means you are ready to take the next step. **Allow yourself to meet with job candidates.** You could even find people who wouldn't mind getting minimum wage or a set percentage of revenues. The possibilities are endless, but they will not reveal themselves to you unless you start. **You cannot develop a business if you work alone.** Even if you dedicate your entire life to your business, you will remain limited, resting—or hustling—at the same level. Be brave. Experiment! **Allow yourself to try!** Nobody will criticise you for your efforts; plus, the job applicants you interview couldn't possibly be harmed by a single job interview! If anything, it is additional practice for them! Job interviews may actually motivate candidates, urging them in the right direction. **Confidently assume the role of an employer.** Notice yourself as an employer. I am certain this will bring some of your long-hidden talents to the surface, bringing you resources and the opportunity to grow. Take the first step. Success will follow!

You must be all in to succeed. "I want to do business!" you must convince yourself. **Burn your bridges. Don't allow yourself to head back to where you started. Fight at all costs.** Make it work. Saying things like "I will try it for a day or two" will not lead you to success. As I already clarified, businesses become successful only after the fifth year. You will have to fight tooth and nail to keep your business running in its first year. You may not break even; you may be losing money! You will worry about budgets and finances every month, not knowing if you cover your expenses or not. Every month!

People who lead businesses they are not passionate about are doomed to fail. You must have faith in your product to establish a successful business. You must know your product will help humanity.

If you trust that your product will help people, people will also become convinced in your product's usefulness. Your enthusiasm should be contagious. Infect people with enthusiasm and love for your product. Failing to do so will result in a failing business.

The first rule in business is: "Kill all doubts."

If you do something, give it your all. If you doubt or worry about your product, people will sense your hesitations and internalise them. You cannot allow yourself even the slightest hint of uncertainty. You should readily sacrifice for your business, working day and night, persevering in the face of adversity.

My first year as a business owner was challenging. There were times when I could not put food on the table! I sometimes cried to my friends about it, whining about my hunger. "Come over," they said. They often took me into their homes and fed me. This happened for months on end. I spent the little money I made on the rent for my office space and on the salary of my only employee. Understanding my situation, many of my friends helped however they could, supporting me, calming me, feeding me food, and showing their pride in my idea.

I didn't have spending money and my friends lent me their clothes, giving me beautiful dresses I then wore to my seminars. They also did my hair and make up for free. **Back then, I often asked my friends for help.** Still, I had faith in my idea, and they could sense it. As a result, they had faith in me. Now, I sometimes wonder how I gathered the courage to do it; I can't really come up with an answer other than, "I was young and stupid." I had no other choice, either. I was living in a country whose language I could not speak—not well, anyways. I did not have a job. All I could do was pour in my efforts into something I found significant. I kept trying until I succeeded.

I moved to the United Kingdom, and it isn't all that different here. Doing business is hard—regardless of your geographic location. I learn every day—I do not have a choice, after all, and staying the same would lead to failure. I need to gain the trust of my audience—and entice new followers—which takes years. Still, I believe in my idea and take calculated risks.

One of my clients once shared she receives a good salary but wants to start a business. "Why would you want that?" I asked.

"I want to be free," she replied.

"You're joking, aren't you?" I uttered in surprise.

"No."

"Business is slavery. You don't sleep, eat, or spend on luxuries. You invest everything into the business—for the first five years, at least. You don't achieve success easily. You pay for it in blood and sweat. But, if you love your work, your inner flame—the passion—keeps you going, and you don't notice the difficulties. You do business because you can't live without it."

As I live in England, I often hear people say things like this. Sometimes, I think to myself: "Oh lord! How can people live without my seminars?" I also notice the positive changes I make in their lives; many of my clients give me feedback, noting how much I have helped them over time.

Doing business isn't easy. It requires passion, persistence, perseverance, dedication, and faith in your business idea. You will succeed as long as you have those qualities. Yes, I am free now. I now have financial abundance; I can afford nice vacations and other luxuries. **Still, this is only possible because I enslaved myself to my pursuit, allowing it to subject me to hardship and difficulty. I persevered.** You should, too. You will do this for the sake of your future. If you receive a salary, you are a slave, too, but you will never get the chance to become a master unless you take a risk. Choose happiness. Choose long-term satisfaction and do what you love.

For homework, I ask that you conduct a couple of interviews. Doing so will be very useful for you, as it will allow you to see yourself as an employer. This will also allow you to better understand your former employers.

THE NATURE OF SALES

"Nobody likes to be sold to but everybody likes to buy."
Earl Taylor,
Trainer in Leadership and Sales

CONNECTING WITH CUSTOMERS

You should always be happy, friendly, and welcoming; remember you love yourself, just as you love each of your customers. First impressions matter most!

Nowadays, **most companies connect with customers online.** Customers open your company's Facebook page or scroll through your Instagram profile; they read about you and pay attention to your posts and picture. Contacting customers doesn't require your direct involvement anymore; with social media, you can connect with people through past and present posts. You must already know the influence you exert on to others; asking your friends to describe you should have helped with that! **Abstain from posting serious, edifying pictures! You should always smile on photos!** When I was learning how to sell, I had a photoshoot, where the photographer instructed me to make different facial expressions. Let me describe them to you:

Face Photos:

1. Surprise: your mouth should be open in "O" shape; your eyes should be wide open. This facial expression sells best! Use it when you make sales. Use this facial expression to communicate your own surprise at the gigantic sale you've organised for your website! You may think posing like this is ridiculous; do it despite your skepticism and notice your sales increasing.

2. Admiration: Your mouth should be slightly open. Your eyes must look up at the camera.

3. Emphasis: your face should mimic the face you make when saying "hmmm." Have a little cunning smile playing on your lips! Your hand should be folded, and your index finger should be pointing upwards. The message is clear: "Did you see this? Pay attention. This is for you!"

Full-Body Photos:

1. Your arms and gaze point in the same direction. The graphic designer then edits the picture and lays out information next to your body. Your body shifts the viewer's focus towards the caption.

2. Same position but turned to the other side.

3. Your hands are in the same position but your face gazes at the viewer. Your facial expression speaks of surprise.

4. You bend forward. Your hands point at the camera.

5. You are bent forward and extend your hands, pretending to hold an imaginary product. Your graphic designer will place a product or a message in the empty space between your hands.

6. One of your hands is on your back and the other holds an imaginary object.

7. The same position but the other way around.

You must have these pictures. You need them to sell. Find the online profiles of Marie Forleo and other successful entrepreneurs. Notice they all have those pictures on their social media feed. For my first photo shoot, I hired a professional who taught me how to pose; I paid this person well, of course.

When you have in-person meetings, they usually begin with a handshake! That is the first contact you make with the client. Make sure your palms are dry. Don't be sluggish. A strong handshake speaks of confidence. Make eye contact as you shake the client's hand. Hold a soft gaze and smile. Your blazer should be unbuttoned. Don't wear polo shirts. Clothes that are very "closed up" give the impression that you are hiding something. Your perfume shouldn't be too intense. It's best if people recognize your specific smell and associate you with it. I have a friend who has not changed her perfume for years; when meeting her for dinner, I usually "smell" her before I see her. Select an introductory sentence and start all your social media lives and videos with it: "My dearest friends" or "my lovely ladies" would both work. The options are endless; choose one and make it your trademark.

Start and end the conversation with a compliment!

If you are speaking in front of a large group, find a way to compliment your entire audience: "You are all so smart! You understand my lectures very well! You respond well, too. I am so happy I can communicate with you!" If you attend a business meeting at an office, you can say: "I found a parking spot quite easily! The location of your office is awesome." You could also note: "The receptionist was so kind!" or "Your office smells so good!" You could also compliment the company whose office you are in: "I am so happy to finally meet you; you are the best of the best!" In my case, **these phrases come straight from my heart.** I truly love my clients and I love finding their good qualities. I thank you, my dearest readers, for spending so much time with me! My clients are the best. My clients are the smartest! I love you all!

Record the compliments you give most frequently:

It is crucial to connect the compliment to your client's personality. If he is trying out a suit, saying "It's perfect" will not be enough." It would be far better to say: "This blazer—especially the shoulder pads—emphasise your strength!" I often hear comments that are just wrong. "This is a beautiful dress" is one of them. This is a compliment to the person who designed the dress not the woman who is wearing it. It would be far better if we said something like "This beautiful dress emphasizes your femininity!" or "This dress shows your youth and vibrant energy!" These comments will flatter the woman a whole lot more.

Still, make sure that your compliment **is not too personal**. This will incite the opposite effect. The compliment should focus on a trait that the person has; the compliment should exaggerate that trait to flatter the person. It is best if you address the person by their name while giving them a compliment: "Peter, this suit looks absolutely fantastic on you!"

Many of my seminar participants are surprised by my ability to remember names. This is a special talent of mine. However, I also have a little secret: when I meet someone, I **immediately repeat their name**: "Peter, is it so nice to finally meet you!" Then, I try to **say the person's name again**: "Peter, where did you park your car? Was it hard to find a parking spot?" Repeating a person's name three-to-four times helped me memorize their name. "Oh, Peter, you are a master of finding parking spots! I always struggle to do that." **I make sure to repeat the person's name a few more times**. Doing this is so important.

What should we do in case **we forget our client's name?** There is an elegant way to ask about it: "What would you like me to call you?" I use this question quite often, especially when communicating with foreigners who have specific names.

It is best to compliment women's appearance. "You are such a sunshine! You brightened up our office today! We love it when you come." **It is best to compliment men on their skills, knowledge, or status:** "You are so organised. Your employees are trained very well!" **Give people compliments; give compliments everywhere you go.** I walk into a store to buy myself orange juice. I say, "Your store is so cosy. I love it here!" That is how I train myself to make contact with people by **offering them a compliment.** Do this everywhere: at the restaurant, at the gym, at work… this is a principle of behaviour. I remember this one time when the doorman did not let me in into the building. I just looked at him and said: "Nothing escapes a doorman like you! The building must be so secure! You are just wonderful. How do you manage to do your job so well?"

"Well, I have been doing it for twenty years!" he replied.

"Twenty years? You are such a stable man!"

Flattered, he straightened up. "What do you need? Let me help!"

That is how I entered an embassy recently—even though I hadn't booked an appointment/ Compliments facilitate communication. Use them everywhere you go.

Your compliment should not have a double meaning. Make your compliments as concrete as possible. Make sure they are connected to the person you are trying to compliment. If someone got their driving license a month ago and you say, "You are such an experienced driver!" your compliment would appear fake. It will provoke a negative reaction. **You should exaggerate just a bit—don't overdo**

it. Don't tell a voluptuous woman she is skinny. **Your compliment should not be banal.** If you call a beautiful woman "beautiful," then you will not be saying anything she does not already know. You'd be far more successful to point out she has beautiful fingers—very classy and aristocratic. Your compliment should be short and specific; long monologues are tedious.

Your smile is a must-have! You will hardly ever manage to sell without a smile on your face and a compliment leaving your lips.

GAINING THE CLIENT'S TRUST

Once we have established contact with the client, we should shift our focus to gaining the client's trust. To do so quickly, we can use the **Principle of the Three "Yeses."** You ask questions whose answer you know will be a "yes!" Then, you ask a fourth question that has decisive power.

"You are Peter, right?" you ask.
"Yes," the client answers.
"We have a meeting scheduled for today, don't we?" you continue.
"Yes, we do."
"Is this where you would like to sit?"
"Yes."
"Would you like to sign the contract?"
The fourth answer comes in automatically. "Yes," the client responds.

The three "yeses" that his client said out loud successfully fostered a sense of trust in the unconscious mind.

There are other methods I use to build trust. At the beginning of seminars, I often ask: "Is there anyone here who has never attended one of my seminars before?"

People raise their hands. There are always those who've never been to one of my events before.

"Is there anyone who has attended my seminars before?"

Many raise their hands. Satisfied, I say, "Let's applaud our new participants!"

Everyone applauds. **This is how I get everyone to participate, to do something that I have tasked them with.**

Sometimes, I organise chairs into long rows. Then, in the middle of my seminar, I say: "Let's make a circle!" People immediately begin moving their chairs and interact in the process.

**We can gain the trust of our customers by giving them a clear task.
Once clients do what we tell them to, once they follow our rules,
they establish a sense of trust towards us.
This is an unconscious process.**

"You can sit here," you say, waiving your hand towards an empty seat. This is one simple way to provoke your client to do something. Offering your clients coffee and water is yet another way to promote trust. Offering them special, luxurious tea is even more effective. It is best if you have an attractive young assistant who brings your customers tea in a beautiful cup!

If you communicate online, start with: "How are you today? What's the weather like?"

Comparing yourself to your clients, emphasizing your commonalities, is also effective. Saying "Oh, yes, me too" can do wonders! You could also say things like: "You are wearing red today? This is my favourite colour!" and "Like you, I also travel a lot!" Find similarities and verbalise them. Equate your experiences to the experiences of your customers. Show them you are alike! Name at least three similarities, as this will allow your clients to appear closer to you, developing trust and feeling understood. Clients are a lot more likely to purchase your products if they can relate to you.

The effective salesperson quickly figures out the values of their clients and orients the product presentation accordingly.

It is important that we understand the values of our clients immediately after making contact. Imagine a well-dressed woman in her mid-forties is your client. She shows up at your store wearing a beautiful black shirt; her hair is tied into a neat low bun. She clearly values cleanliness, comfort, and freedom. The dark colour of her clothing speaks of her desire to remain practical. She wears tiny studs, proving she doesn't like to have everyone's attention on herself. She is smiling; her lips are painted red and full. They've clearly been "done" by a professional; this symbolises her sexuality—her femininity. Now, how could we sell her our product? We need to find a way to show her that our product will emphasize her sexuality. If I were to sell to her, I would possibly say something like: "Maria, you look very sexy! You could take amazing pictures with this phone! Not taking a photo of your lips would be a crime! Your children will proudly show these pictures to others. Your husband will be happy every single time you send him one of those photos. This phone's camera really does wonders. It is not only practical and easy to use, but it will serve you to take photos for years! Plus, this phone model is so elegant; it is perfect for a classy woman like you!"

As I speak, I will pay attention to her reactions. I will notice what flatters her most. In this case, what flatters her most is the compliment I gave her regarding her lips! If I try to sell her a cell phone with a long presentation, Maria will probably fall asleep! Bored to death, she will say: "I have a phone. I don't need a new one!" Figuring out your client's values is such a significant component of the selling process.

If your client is a woman dressed in sportwear, you can approach her very differently from the way you'd approach the woman we just discussed. This woman is wearing a pair of leggings and a sweater; she values comfort. She is probably free-spirited and honest! She might love nature, physical activity, long walks, and all things that are simple and honest. To her, I would say the following: "This phone has a very special program that records the steps you make each day. This isn't all it does either! This program also tracks how fast you run and how many calories you burn! It also comes with a ginormous music library, just so you can play different tunes while jogging and hiking. The phone is also fall-proof! It will survive every drop! It is also waterproof; you can take pictures under a waterfall or on the beach! The battery lasts very long—about twenty hours. The batter will never let you down, especially if you happen to be mountaineering and in need of navigation. Oh, I almost forgot! The phone's camera is so good! It takes excellent landscape pictures!"

This woman would not be amused if I told her that young, rich women love this phone model. However, she will be glad to hear my kid dropped the phone into the pool, and the phone "survived."

I present the exact same product differently; I alter my

presentation to appeal to the client and reflect the client's values.

I remember buying a car. My ex-husband and I walked into the car dealership; I was dressed up to the nines, wearing high heels and a dress. My husband, on the other hand, wore sports shoes and a pair of jeans.

The car dealer turned to me. "I have a car—all beautiful women want to drive it."

Then, he addressed my husband and said, "This is a very practical car. It also doesn't consume too much fuel! It's also quite easy to park—it has parktronic. Even your wife will manage to park it!"

The car dealer wasn't finished with his presentation yet. "It was featured in *Vogue*," he noted, looking straight at me. "A famous actress drove it! We can personalise the car—just for you. You can choose the car's interior!"

The car dealer then turned to my husband again. "The car has an airbag. It's very safe."

That car salesperson was a master at figuring out our values. He figured it all out just by looking at us! We ended up purchasing a car that was a lot more expensive than we had planned. We paid for extras, too. This salesperson's ability to understand our values convinced us to buy a brand new car—even thought we had planned to get one second hand—and spend so much money! A true master, he earned our trust! Unfortunately for us, the car was horrible; I barely managed to sell it later.

Carefully analyse your clients and figure out what programs they would appreciate.

Big groups are different. If they come to one of your seminars, or if they purchase one of your products, this is usually a sign that their values resonate with yours.

Analyse your values and understand why your clients chose you! You could also try to understand what attracted your clients to you. Notice how your customers dress and see what makes them react.

My clients, for example, are mostly women. Like them, I attend many seminars. I remember participating in a seminar where the host was a weird woman. A follower of Osho, she looked like hippy dressed in a long loose dress. Everyone in the seminar group looked exactly like her. I stuck out like a sore thumb. People looked at me weirdly, openly judging me for my shorts and skin-tight top. Even though I knew why I chose to attend the seminar, I still asked myself, "Natalia, what are you doing here?" I wanted to try something new. The problem was—I could not fit in. Both my appearance and my values were vastly different from those of most seminar participants. All of them were single, childless; nothing tied them down. At the end of the seminar, they told me how they were soul brothers and sisters who have sex with each other. I ran out as soon as I heard this.

There was this other seminar that I attended. Its host looked like a butterfly; she wore pink dresses and chirped when she spoke. All her students looked like her. Dressed in bright, colourful dresses, they chirped along, echoing her words and actions.

When clients come to you, they usually resonate with you. Their values align with yours. Therefore, **the clearer you articulate your values, the more aligned your customer base will become.**

Now, let's clarify our values. What matters to you? Is there anything you could not live without? Beauty, liberty, comfort, luxury, ease, goodness, punctuality, clarity, honesty, and so on. What are your values?

Write them down:

1.

2.

3.

4.

5.

I value beauty. I therefore lead all my seminars in elite, beautiful hotels. I dislike ugly spaces. I love luxury and I insist on offering my clients courses in clean, comfortable, and luxurious spaces. I lead seminars about money and success, as both are important for me. People whose values are largely different from mine lead different seminars and focus on different topics. Their products are vastly different from my own.

DISCOVERING THE CLIENT'S NEEDS

You can discover the client's needs by asking questions. Customers tend to have one of three types of need:

1. Customers are experiencing a certain problem but either refuse to notice it or purposefully ignore it.

I was in Greece and needed a haircut. I booked an appointment with a luxurious beauty salon, just so I could get my hair cut and dyed. The beauty salon was huge; it had more than twenty hairdressers! As I walked in, the owner noticed me. "I will do her hairstyle!" he decided.

One of his assistants dyed my hair and then sent me over to the owner. "What's your name?" asked the beauty salon owner.

"Natalia," I responded.

"Natalia, do you recognize you have a problem?" he continued.

"Uhm, no," I muttered, "what sort of problem?"

"Your hair is dry and thinning. You also have split ends!"

"Well, it's the summer!" I knew I had a problem but refused to recognise it.

"No, Natalia, this is not right. I have a solution for you. Here, we offer professional hair treatments that will infuse your hair with vitamins and moisture! You will no longer have split ends!"

The beauty salon owner began to present his product. Interestingly, the entire presentation rotated around my problem—my problematic hair. Once he was done, I told him I would think about it. I did not know such hair treatments existed!

I returned home, googled the treatments he was offering, and convinced myself to try out the Keratin treatment he suggested. That man helped me realise I had a problem! Unfortunately, lockdown happened shortly after. I am now looking to do those treatments in London!

Of course, this is not the only time someone has made me aware of a problem I failed to recognise. My employees often inform me of problems on our website and then suggest ways to eliminate those problems.

Let's imagine that you are a personal stylist. You could, for instance, say: "Natalia, you have such a beautiful body! I would suggest you three different outfits! If you like them, I would be delighted to work with you." As a stylist, you will show me clothing that I do not own; this is what will get me hooked to your services.

If you sell scarves, you can look at my most recent photo and say, "Darling, I saw you wearing this exquisite dress. And, you know what? I have the perfect accessory for it! Here is this scarf. It will bring your entire outfit together! Gaze at it and imagine how it would look on you!" Send me a picture of that scarf. I am certain that if you were to send out one hundred messages like this, you would sell at least twenty scarves.

2. Customers recognise they have a problem but do not know how to tackle it.
We often procrastinate for appointments such as going to the dentist. Recognising this tendency, our dentists tell us things like: "Come back in 3 months."

Let me give you one more example! Think about a store that sells suits. A man walks in; he has skinny legs and a big tummy. He knows nothing will look good on him. You know that, too, which is why you suggest he gets his new suit tailored! You could even ask the tailor to come to the store to get his measurements. That's how you offer this person a solution and seal the deal.

3. Customers acknowledge the problem and strive to solve it.

These are the so-called "warm" clients. They know what they want. They walk into your store, saying: "I need a scarf for this dress!" They come into your travel agency with a clear demand: "I want to go to the Maldives!" All you need to do in this case is to ensure the client is convinced and seal the deal.

I suggest you consider how to expand the first and second type of clients. Scroll through social media, look over your friends' social media accounts, and figure out **what and whose problem you could solve.** Note: "I see you have not travelled in a while. Well, luckily for you, I offer amazing trips to Cuba. So many of my friends and acquaintances went to Cuba and came back delighted! It was such an enriching experience for them. I am sure you would enjoy it, too. Do you want me to send you an offer—just so you could see what the trips are like?"

We can imprint needs into our clients! We can convince them they need something.

My team and I recently organised a "Business Academy." One of the participants lived in England. She contacted me. "Natalia," she said, "I have a travel agency. Would you like to book a trip?" Mind you, we were in the middle of a pandemic!

Noticing my hesitation, she continued: "well, as soon as the pandemic is over, everybody will want to travel! It's best to book now. Otherwise, we may run out of hotel spaces and tickets! You really want to travel, don't you? Let me show you what we offer."

Bit by bit, she figured out what my problem was: I love to travel, and I was longing for a vacation!

It is crucial to remain active and persistent! This woman was not annoying or insolent; on the contrary, she was sweet and tactful, knowing exactly how to approach the situation and convince me to travel. **The key to selling successfully is offering your clients enough products and then letting them choose for themselves.**

Another woman recently shared she struggled to lose weight.

"You know," I began, "detox and Kangen Water are my go-to's when losing weight."

"How is this possible? What is this water?"

"I can connect you with a friend of mine; she sells Kangen Water machines. What sort of water do you drink?"

The "real" conversation began as soon as I learned her problem: she drank water from plastic bottles, and we both knew that wasn't the best for her health! Around the end of our conversation, she noted: "Oh! How could I have lived without this water?" She happily purchased a Kangen Water machine soon after.

How can we figure out the needs of our customers when selling online?

We could discount the products that sell the least. We could also analyse why some products are often returned. We should also read comments and consider customer feedback. We can send out surveys.

There are four types of questions:

1. Situational:

Figure out what is going on. Ask: "What are you looking for? Do you have any problems? Do you need anything? Is there something you lack? What would you like to happen now?

2. Problematic:

Use this type of questions to unlock the needs of your clients. Bring those needs to the surface and make your clients realise them.

Imagine you are selling scarves! A client shows up. You say, "What types of scarves do you usually wear?"

"I don't really wear scarves all that much. I have very few scarves."

"Oh!" you exclaim. "You are missing out on an invaluable accessory! Scarves solve so many problems! They warm you up and make your outfits... so much more complete! Also, having different scarves eliminates the need to always purchase new clothing! Scarves can drastically change your outfit—always for the better, of course! You don't need more clothes; you just need more scarves. In this way, you will also have more space in your wardrobe. You won't have to throw old clothes out to fit the new ones in!"

This example clearly exemplifies how a salesperson can amplify the problem.

3. Deductive:

Show your client what will happen if he/she does not tackle their problem. Say, "If you continue using your old phone, you will not be able to update your software. Android won't maintain the old software either. Your phone will work worse and worse, and you will not be able to take pictures or even call you loved ones!"

4. Guiding:

These questions show your clients what would happen if they purchased your product. "If you buy this new cell phone model, you will get access to all new updates and have a wonderful camera! Your phone will function meticulously—for more than three years."

You could also ask such questions online. Do it through posts and stories.

Here is a cool example about the practices of a call centre:

"What phone model do you use? How many calls do you take per day?" (*situational question*)

"Are your clients ever unable to reach you? (*you allude to the problem*)

"Yes, I have that problem," responds the client.

"On average, how much money does a missed phone call cost you?" (*what will happen if the problem remains unsolved*)

"A lot."

"If you could decrease the number of missed calls, would you do it?"

"Yes, of course. I would like my clients to reach me easily."

"I could offer your this service bundle. It will solve all your problems…" (*what could your client do to solve the problem*)

Maria Solodar, who leads the best sales courses in Russia, always offers something for free on her website. She has free books, webinars, and talks. Also, as soon as a client subscribes to her website, they receive a voice message: "Hi! How are you?" Maria says. "I am Maria. I couldn't be happier that you are now my client! I congratulate you on your choice! Why don't you download one of my free books or webinars? I am waiting to see you at our next seminar! See you soon!"

Maria's voice is pleasant. Her message is friendly and impresses all new subscribers.

It is best when the business owner manages to reach the client! "Thank you for joining our community," the business owner may say. "It is my personal mission to teach others! I am so delighted to help you too! I can't wait to learn from you! Natalia."

You use questions to show your clients why they need to purchase your product. You present all your product's benefits.

Don't worry about asking too many questions. **It is best to ask between five and eight questions.** This will help you figure out why your client is seeking your products and services.

Here are some other questions you could ask:
• **What are you hoping to get out of this product?** (*if you are selling a scarf, note what matters: beauty, utility, warmth, material, etc.*) If you have regular clients, you should figure out who looks for discounts and who purchases things for their entire family. If your client buys in bulk, give them a special offer! Realise which clients like to purchase the newest and trendiest items! Figure out which clients buy the most practical products! Offer them exactly what they need.

**Clients are happy when they receive exactly what they need.
They are satisfied when they receive what they expect and
feel your concern.**

If you sell scarves, you could also crate product bundles. I would, for instance, create a mother-daughter product bundle, offering my loyal customers promotional product bundles. Write to them and inform them of your new offers.

If you sell trips, figure out what your client is looking for. Do they want a cheap, mediocre, or luxurious vacation? Do they want to go skiing or do they want to go scuba diving? Offer them some terms and see how they react. Notice the exact desires of your clients. Understand what your client values and desires. Ask clarifying questions:

- **Am I right to think that** ……………………… (*mention your client's requirements*). What would be best for you?

    o Then, go on to clarify! Say: "**Have you used similar products before?** Was there anything you disliked? What did you like best?"

    o "Well, their customer service was horrible! They never picked up my calls! But they did have good offers!" the client says.

    o "We offer non-stop customer service. We always respond to your calls and messages! Both our products and services are of high quality."

Realise that clients who whine and complain a lot usually do so to catch you attention. Specify what your client wants.

If you offer psychological counselling, you can craft programs with concrete topics: "Are you sick of working all the time and not being paid for it?" You could also have topics like "Are you afraid someone will steal your husband?" and "What if you just don't like yourself?" **When naming people's problems as questions, you show you understand your customers and know how to combat their issues.**

If you offer educational or babysitting services, your main customer base would be parents, especially mothers. Your business message and social media pages should appeal to those mothers. Your appearance should be reminiscent of theirs; this will invoke their trust. Post pictures and, in their captions, give parenting advice. Show your qualified employees. With parents' permission, show your experts working with children; make sure not to show those children's faces.

Invent different activities on social media. Post controversial pictures, organize giveaways, and motivate people to give positive feedback regarding your work. Dare them to "See this video!" and "Share some personal experience!" Motivate them to share your posts: "Repost this!" Also, ask them questions: "What excites you?" and "What would you like to talk about?" are just two of many. **This is how you can hear your clients' needs.** This is how you figure out what products you need to create.

I never invite speakers who do not do free live streams. When negotiating with Lise Bourbeau, she let me know she did not lead free live streams. That was an important rule of her franchise, as she put it.

"I understand," I said. "Miss Bourbeau, I have been a follower of your work—and a student of yours for many years. You are my guru. I bow before you! However, I also know it would be nearly impossible to 'sell you' in Eastern European countries like Bulgaria if you refuse to lead free live streams or recorded webinars. How is it possible that you do not record your webinars? They are priceless!"

She looked at me and a smile played on her lips. "Natalia," she said, "you are a wonderful businesswoman!"

Getting her to agree to this was a hefty task. We even edited the contract and included free webinars and live streams into it! I am the first (and last) person who has managed to get her to record her seminars and lead live streams! I gathered about 500 people, those who joined online included. Lise was shocked, "My seminar groups in Canada are about 100 people. I've never had such big groups!" Even in St. Petersburg, Lise had only gathered 120 people to attend her seminars. I, however, managed to convince her of live stream's utility, as well as the need to record seminars, and, as a result, her success skyrocketed. I had the same terms when working with Larisa Renar, an author.

If you franchise, you will possibly encounter limits to the total number of sales—and profit—you may make. This may therefore not be the best business model. Reconsider your contract or seek another company to work with. Always offer free content on your social media pages! **Positive customer feedback is essential.** There is a solution to every problem. Remain flexible; I, for instance, am always changing things around. I was planning a seminar in China. Apparently, it's forbidden to talk about sex there! I say, "We will not speak about sex. We will discuss bananas!"

You will always find a solution! You should figure out where the money is "hidden."

Let me return to my "scarf" example. Create a survey. Start with a simple question: "Darlings, what sort of scarves would you prefer?"
- Bright scarves
- Pastel scarves
- Colourful scarves
- Large, square-like scarves
- Large, rectangle-like scarves
- Tiny scarves
- Sling scarves
- Children's scarves
- Offer bundle: scarf and face mask.

Unfortunately, I hardly ever see such questions on the webpages of most of my clients. How could you figure out what your client needs if you do not ask first? How could you know what products to create? **I insist you begin asking questions; publish those questions on your social media pages. Send them out as surveys via email. Pose them when meeting clients in person!** Analyse feedback and use it to improve your job. I, as a mother and wife, look for clothing in similar style for myself, my husband, and our son. Think about a line of products that people like me would love to purchase. If you sell scarves, create a family line. Market it with pictures of a happy family whose members are wearing your scarves. Present your product line as a trend. Figure out what would work in the market you are trying to enter. Here in England, for instance, scarves (and umbrellas) are a necessity. People use them every day. Scarves are also essential in countries like Germany and Austria. Find influencers who can help promote your products.

For a client to comment on your photo, he/she needs to invest some resources—time, effort, responsibility. Why should your audience interact with your posts if they won't get anything out of it? Give your audience an incentive. The incentive could be a gift. **People love presents. Use presents to motivate others to comment on your photos.**

PRESENTING A PRODUCT

Once you have figured out what your client needs, you can present a product that satisfies that need!

Personally, I like sharing stories about some clients of mine who have managed to solve a given problem with the help of one of my products. There is this story that I like to use; it is about a client of mine whose mother was on her deathbed and whose husband was an alcoholic. On top of that, she also had two kids that she had to feed and raise. She took my seminar "Geishas" and, soon after, met a man online. An English aristocrat, he had her move to his property in England, where she lives to this day. This man loved and cared for my client until his death; he also left her a huge inheritance, ensuing stability for her and her children. I know many women have similar problems; therefore, when they hear this story, they become interested in my product. They hope it would transform their life. When presenting a product, I **often refer to success stories.**

The best presentation would include you showing how your product changed someone's life for the better.

However, you could also present your products through a skillful **description**.

Here are a few common mistakes that people make when presenting a new product:

1. Too much talking.

2. Lack of awareness regarding the clients' needs.

3. Arguing with clients during the presentation.

4. Unpreparedness.

5. Putting too much emphasis on product qualities that are insignificant to the client.

At the end of your presentation, your client should say one and only thing: "I want this!"

SMOOTHING OUT THE DIFFERENCES

"In sales there are usually four or five "nos" before you get a "yes."
Jack Canfield,

Objections are a sign of interest. The lack of objections is far worse; there is nothing worse for your business than the client leaving without saying a word. If this happens, you should do everything you can to figure out what is stopping your customer from making a purchase. "Is there a problem?" you may ask. Your client might have missed a significant point in your presentation. Your client might have misunderstood something. Many of my clients, for example, say that my seminars aren't conducted at a convenient time. I immediately explain that I always record my seminars, and my clients quickly make a purchase. It is also possible that your clients find your payment methods inconvenient; therefore, you should allow them to pay in a way that is comfortable for them. You should even allow them to pay in a few instalments, especially if you are selling a more expensive product. You could also offer a discount—but only if your client makes another purchase or brings a friend to your seminars. We've already discussed the need for flexibility.

"I don't have money" is not a true objection. If a client wants your product, they will always find the money to purchase it. They will take out a loan, sell something, and even change jobs to get a higher salary—just to afford your product. Convince your customers that your product can change their lives, increase their vibration, and bring in more money.

There are overt and covert objections. A lady I know, for instance, wanted to sign up for my "Academy for Winners." She was experiencing financial difficulties and could not pay the fees. "Would paying in instalments be better for you?" I asked her.

"Well, I have a newborn and may not have the time," she responded.

"I can give you the recordings of our seminars."

"Well, no, that will not work either. I don't like showing myself on camera," she said.

"What are you afraid of?"

"I don't want my ex to see me!"

As she and I continued talking, I figured her objections had nothing to do with money or new newborn child. "Technically speaking," I started, "you don't have to turn your camera on. However, if you make sales with your camera off, you will sell a lot less. That's why our "Academy for Winners" tries to train you to show yourself on camera and solve your problems on your own."

"Okay, then, I will do this my way," she agreed reluctantly and purchased my program.

Money is hardly ever the reason behind your clients' objections. Money is a side factor, a complement to the true cause of your clients' unwillingness to buy.

Here are the most common objections and how you can approach them:

1. "This is too expensive!"

Start by agreeing. "Yes, it is not cheap. But this is a first-class product. You are a person of taste; you can see this product is the best of the best! Sure, it is a little more expensive than some other products, but its quality is unsurpassed. And, at the end of the day, you get what you pay for."

Don't argue; agree with them!

2. "I have to think about it"

This is a covert objection. It speaks of the client's uncertainty. Agree with your client, "I understand you. It's normal to feel that way. Could I just ask you… what worries you exactly? Is it the price? Is it the quality? Could I help you solve the problem?

When working to eliminate your client's concerns, you should always begin by agreeing with them. Statements like "Yes, this is expensive" and "Yes, this is hard" become your best friends. Validate your client's concerns. Then, ask your client a question.

Imagine your customer says, "The delivery fee is quite expensive. It makes the entire purchase more costly."

"Yes, this is true," you respond. "Are you comparing this delivery fee to the delivery fee of another company?"

You learn if your competitors offer a cheaper delivery. As it turns out, their delivery fee is £2 less. That's an insignificant difference. Keep posing questions.

"Are there any other characteristics—other than the delivery fee—that matter to you?" you can ask. "Perhaps you have free time on your hands; if this is the case, you could come to our office and pick up your product form there! I recognize our prices are a bit higher than most, but so is the quality of our products. They are not consumer goods. They are luxury goods. So, as you have chosen to be a luxury client, I presume you only seek the best. I assume your time is a valuable resource, and I can assure you that our delivery service will help you save time."

"Let me think..." says the client.

"What are you worried about?" you continue. "I just want to clarify that this is the last product we have in stock, and someone might buy it soon. You don't have much time to waste. If you really want it, I could book it for you, just so you can decide if you will go through with this purchase or not. Of course, you could also purchase it now and return it tomorrow—in the unlikely event you don't like it!"

Allow your clients to see, touch, and examine your products. Foster a sense of urgency; make your clients think they are running out of time.

3. "Your competition offers the same product for less."

You should know your competitors. Therefore, when someone mentions them, you can say: "Who exactly are you talking about? What is the name of their company?"

That's how you get the client to name the competitor, allowing you to automatically refer to your own knowledge and verbalise the differences between your product and the product of your competitors.

"Yes, I know this company," you reply. "However, their products do not include ……………… (describe everything). If you wish, we can remove these extras from your offer; then, you will notice that our prices are actually lower than theirs."

4. "I don't like it."

"Why do you not like it? What sort of product would you prefer?" Describe your product again; present it well.

5. "I don't have time."

"When would be a good time to talk about this?" you ask.

6. "It is of poor quality."

"What makes you say that?" you can ask. "Why don't we examine our products and find what is best for you?

In this case, if you do not offer the product your client desires, you can recommend someone else—some other company. **Your client will be grateful, and they will come back to you in the future.**

7. "I have everything I need; I do not need this product."

"Oh, I am sure this is the case. Still, would you mind if I still showed you this product? It is so good! It would be a waste not to see it! You don't have to buy it now, of course, but you can at least learn about it—and know where to purchase it in the future."

You must get to the root of your client's worries. Figure out what the client's true objection is. You can do this by asking questions. Remember that objections are a sign of interest; don't let them worry you. You just have to figure out what your client is worried about and assure them that purchasing your product is a smart, rational decision.

I was a member of an online group; its admin used to delete my posts. I began asking people about it. I had to know why she was doing that! People told me the woman who managed the group loved wine. I, of course, bought her an expensive bottle of wine. She never deleted my posts again. You should realise that sometimes the solutions are not directly related to the problem. Still, there is a solution to every problem.

SEALING THE DEAL

Powerful energy is required at this phase of the sales process. It is often the case that a client is preparing to pay—they've taken their credit card out, ready to buy—when that client decides not to go through with a purchase. Customers often choose not to buy something at the checkout line! This is even worse if customers are shopping online, as technical difficulties often make the payment process complex and unpleasant. People fill up their baskets—physical or virtual—but they hardly ever purchase all the things they initially wanted. Customers allow products to sit in their baskets, seldom making an actual purchase. When I figured out that this was happening with my own clients, I hired an employee whose sole task was to phone customers who had not completed their online purchases. When phoned, people shared a plethora of different reasons that prevented them from completing their online orders! Some forgot; others got distracted by their children. Many simply did not know how to use the website well enough to make a payment online. As soon as we managed to kindly urge people to pay and complete their orders, our company's revenues increased by a couple of thousand per month! **Use Google Analytics.** Figure out who visits your website and leaves without making a purchase; phone those people, seal the deal, and thank them. Discount codes or small-sum vouchers always motivate clients to return to your website and make more purchases in the future!

Don't allow your customers to procrastinate on making a purchase; procrastination is often a telltale of uncertainty. If your clients take too long to make a purchase, offer them the opportunity to pay a small proportion of the price in advance. Although clients may have doubts, once they have paid for a certain purchase, they know they can no longer go back. They become happy, waiting for their product to be delivered. At this point, your clients know they've sealed a good deal.

Know that sales are a wonderful thing!

Have beautiful people market your products. Post their pictures on social media. Attractive people always get the audience's attention. You could even entice those beautiful people into marketing your products by offering them a gift—or two! Take good pictures of yourself, too. Make sure to smile. Have a distinct presence, a clear personal message. Post twice a day!

Keep promoting your product! Don't expect clients to come on their own!

Sell to people you do not know. It is far easier to sell to those you do not know. Oftentimes, your closest people prove to be most resistant to your products.

Don't sell to your friends; sell to the friends of your friends. Be brave, promote your products, and keep trying until you find a method that sells. **Polish your products, test them repeatedly, and, once you've perfected them, make them public.** Always look for new opportunities! **Switch up your packaging, organize discounts, and offer product bundles... find a way to surprise your clients.**

If you make sales offline, it is crucial you select an effective payment method, deciding if it is going to be done through cash or card. **Don't stop improving your customer service. Don't procrastinate on doing the things that matter.** Closing the deal is often the hardest part of the sales process. **You put in effort and invested your time— finish what you've started!** Help your clients, make things easy for them, and don't leave them alone until they pay. We all love buying stuff; it gives us immense pleasure. Therefore, offer them your help, ask them if you can facilitate the payment process, figure out what prevents them from finalising the purchase. Clients usually admit they worry about the delivery period or the payment method; offer them at least two options of payment and delivery. Offer your clients the possibility of paying by card and PayPal. There will hardly ever be more than ten changes to your business. **Put yourself in your clients' shoes, figure out where they are coming from, and improve yourself consistently.**

HOW TO REACH CUSTOMERS

DIRECT SALES

1. Phoning customers

Call customers to maintain contact. "Hello! How are you today? How are you liking our product? Could I suggest our newest product? I am sure you'd love it. Do you need anything else? Would you like my assistance? Let me know how I could help. Would you like to make another purchase?"

It is crucial you do this without worrying you will be a bother to people.

2. Inviting clients to something special

People love to have your attention. Pay attention to them, offer them interesting meetings, articles, courses, concerts, etc. Do not forget to mention that these offers are exclusive. They are only valid for your clients and for your own team; they wouldn't possibly find offers as good as yours.

Here is the next

HOMEWORK

SELL ME THIS PEN FOR £20

You have 24 hours to sell a couple £20 pens. I bought one such pen once—the salesman presented it to me as the pen that makes dreams come true! The pen wasn't anything special. I could have probably bought it for a pound at the supermarket. The salesman, however, explained this pen would affect my Feng Shui, that this pen will help me write dreams into existence. Convinced this pen would bring me luck, I bought it.

Come up with a story and use it to sell the £20 pen. Sell at least a few pens. **If you manage to figure out what your client needs, and accordingly change your story to appeal to the client, you could sell the pen for a whole lot more than £20.**

If someone is in a bad mood, then sell them a pen that writes joes and improves one's mood. If someone has been cheated on, sell their partner a pen of monogamy; if the adulterer writes with this pen, he/she will never cheat again! If you manage to sell a pen for £20, you can manage to sell anything else. The nature of sales remains the same, regardless of the product you are offering.

Don't forget: people are actually purchasing you–they are buying your ideas and your energy!

Just remember how many times you've bought an unnecessary piece of clothing just because you liked the sales assistant!

Are you keeping track of your thoughts? Did "I cannot do this; it is too hard" show up? Command such thoughts to stop immediately! Say, "I can, and I will. I will sell not just one but twenty pens!"

HOMEWORK
<u>COLLECT FIVE "NOs"</u>

My goal is to teach you to accept denial and objection. Ask people for things to which you know they will object. "Will you marry me?" you may say to an attractive person on the street. "Would you like me to photograph you naked?" you may ask a random person at the supermarket. "Would you like to give me £5,000?" There are a lot of things you could ask for. Demand those things, ask for them despite your fear and discomfort. Take a risk! Risk, as you now know, is a crucial component of business! **Don't let "no" affect you.** You, after all, asked for some unreasonable things and expected to hear "no" as an answer. Adrenaline will help you bear fear, discomfort, and disappointment.

You are capable of this, trust me! If you don't take risks, you don't drink champagne! Accumulating affluence is a risky process that makes you do some crazy things! You do what no one else is willing to do. You don't know what results your efforts will yield; yet you put in the work. That's how you succeed. Prepare yourself for success. Realise that risk and wealth often home hand-in-hand.

HOW TO TUNE IN FOR SUCCESS?

331

"The stars will never align, and the traffic lights of life will never all be green at the same time. The universe doesn't conspire against you, but it doesn't go out of its way to line up the pins either. Conditions are never perfect. 'Someday' is a disease that will take your dreams to the grave with you. Pro and con lists are just as bad. If it's important for you and you want to do it 'eventually,' just do it and correct course along the way."

Tim Ferriss,
American entrepreneur

Now, let's mark your homework. Did you sell a pen for £20? Did you at least try? If no, what was holding you back? Did you have to overcome any obstacles?

I want you to know that I am not judging you. All I am attempting to do is encourage you to examine yourself and your behaviour. You are doing this for yourself, not for me or anyone else. I am not the strict teacher who will give you a bad grade. I just want you to examine your psychological wiring and comprehend your attitudes. This homework clearly presents your strategy for success or failure. Personally, I feel motivated by failure; however, this may not be the case for you.

If you did not even try, this shows you have adopted the strategy of failure. It is preventing you from heading towards success. You postpone things and make excuses. All you had to do was pick up the phone and call the right people! Or, perhaps, you could have used Facebook and sent out a couple of messages. Analyse why you did not even try.

EXERCISE
PEOPLE NEED YOU

Close your eyes. Recall one of your successes. It should be something that you managed to achieve despite difficulties circumstances. What skills did you resort to achieve that success? What qualities did it bring out in you? How did you behave to make it happen? What was your energy like? Memorize those answers. They illustrate the painting of success.

Now, recall one of your failures. You wanted something, but struggled to achieve it. Things weren't working out. You felt fear, worrying your desires would never come true. Record that feeling.

Expand your "success painting." Imagine it getting bigger, first as big as your TV screen, then as big as a screen at the cinema. You are astonished by your own successes. You are happy! You made this happen! "I did it!" you tell yourself, "That's right! I did this on my own! I faced the challenges and succeeded! I fulfilled my dreams. I achieved this on my own. I followed my dreams, took my risks, and invested my own energy!"

Shrink your "failure painting." Imagine it contracting, shrinking into a tiny image. As it shrinks, imagine your "success painting" expanding even more, becoming vibrant and three-dimensional. You render that "success painting" into existence. Observe your body. Notice your happy face, your wide smile, your shining eyes. Feel your victorious stance. Breathe in and breathe out. Affirm yourself of your abilities. Say: "I am a winner! I always succeed! I always find a solution, and I always win! I always succeed!"

333

Your "failure painting" is now small and barely visible. It is black-and-white, too. It lacks colour and livelihood. Your past failures no longer define you. That picture is so frail you can crush it with the clap of your hands. Clap your hands! Imagine the picture turning into sand and falling into the ground! Imagine the breeze sweeping those unwanted grains of sand away from you! Breathe in. Breathe in. Align yourself with the breeze of success. You are a winner. You know everything is working out for you! Your entire life—and everything in that life—is shaped and reflected by your "success painting." It is the most accurate representation of you! You can do it all!

Imagine you are holding a pen you wish to sell. Envision how you take your phone, call someone, and say: "I have something you need. You may not have realised you need it yet, but I know you do. I've been dreaming about it—about you. I am not sure if you believe in miracles, but I am sure we all deserve a miracle to occur in our lives. I have a miraculous pen! As I was holding that pen, your image floated into my mind. I know you must own it. This is a magic pen, trust me. It allows you to connect with your desires and better understand your heart. That pen helps you write what is true for you. It helps you render your wishes on paper before you render them into existence. What is most exciting is that this pen ensures your wishes come true through the most miraculous means possible! I am selling you this pen only because I want to secure a proper energy exchange! Giving you this pen for free would devalue it. It is also crucial you buy it from me. The pen is worth £200 but, for you, I will make a huge discount. You, as my friend, can buy this pen for £20! I really want you to have this pen, and I know you will appreciate it once you have it! My intuition shows me you need to own this pen. I know this it true!"

Allow your conscience to imagine someone you know; this person can be a man or a woman, a colleague, or a friend. Let the image of that person float to your mind. This is a person who needs to connect with themselves, who needs to return to their heart and validate their desires. Sense that person's gratitude. Your product has appeared just at the right time! That person has accepted it gladly. Imagine that person paying for the miraculous pen. Imagine yourself wrapping that pen in colourful packaging. That pen is no less than a gift from your own heart—a gift that can change lives. Visualise how that person tells everyone they know about the miraculous pen you sold them. All their friends want a miraculous pen now! Imagine that this will always be the case. People need you, just as they need your products. Every product you sell—whatever it is—has the power to change lives. People seek to purchase your products. **You are a winner. People need you. Don't worry about sales; strive to respond to people's needs.**

Breathe in. Breathe out. Softly open your eyes. Return to the present. Memorize the sensation; forever engrain the feeling of being a winner into your heart. You are someone who offers others opportunities. Allow this to be true.

Note the name of the person whose image appeared in your mind during this meditation.

If you have tried to sell this pen but have not managed to do so quickly, your failure is merely a reflection of your strategy. You must change your strategy and remain persistent.

Your doubts are your biggest enemy! You must exterminate them. When you **find yourself besieged by doubt, you should find a**

random stone, project all your worries onto it, and throw it as far away as you can! Once you've done that, console yourself with the following words: "I've liberated myself from doubt! Now, I am moving forward."

I shush every worrisome thought that pops into my mind. "Stop!" I scream. I quickly shift my focus to something better—something more optimistic. I often workout to disassociate myself from negative thoughts. I simply shift my frame of mind! Why should I stress over something I cannot change? If there is something I can do, I go and get it done as soon as possible. If there is a problem I must solve, I solve it quickly. But, when there is nothing I can do, I simply stay put, not worrying about things I cannot control.

STRENGTHEN YOUR FAITH AND WILL

Nowadays, getting rich is an act of faith. As long as you have faith, results happen—sooner or later. Years ago, I was invited to Paris. However, as a Russian citizen, I needed a passport to enter France. I responded I could only come if I showed my marriage certificate. Still, because I travelled without my husband, they would not let me get on the plane to Paris! I had not even translated my marriage certificate. Anyway, I demanded to be allowed to board the plane. They called one of the airport managers, who explained that even if I made it to France, I would be denied entry into the country. "They would fine you, too," he noted, "the fines are about €5000!" I did not care; I kept insisting. I spoke with the main airport managers and called people from the French airport. I explained my situation and, as I waited for them to make a decision, I walked around the airport, whispering: "There is a solution for every problem!" I imagined myself on Champs-Elysees, drinking champagne. They finally allowed me to board the flight. Of course, they repeatedly cautioned me that the French custom officers would never let me into the country. The plane took off. Throughout the entire flight, I maintained the vibration. The customs officer barely gave my marriage certificate—written in Cyrillic, which he couldn't possibly read—a second gaze. He let me into the country, and I headed towards Champs-Elysees. I drank some champagne, too!

The Universe is on my side; I am fully convinced this is the case.

**The strong and successful have faith;
they trust that things will work out.**

If you tend to procrastinate, your life will enter a period of stagnation. Opportunities won't come your way, and neither will motivation. Things won't be working out for you. You should therefore plan your days carefully. Choose a couple of tasks and get them done. It is far **better to have one or two things on your to-do-list and get them done than to have ten things and not get anything done.** Postponed errands and tasks you've procrastinated on doing eat up your energy. I cannot procrastinate; I always do everything, here and now. I stick to my schedule and get things done. That is why all my employees are punctual and my company runs smoothly, charged with powerful energy.

Your mind may be inclined to procrastinate. You can, however, train it to become punctual. This is a matter of **will**. Adopt the following attitude: "Once I make a decision, there isn't a challenge or a hurdle than can stop me from going after my goals."

My husband and I honeymooned in Miami. We travelled around,

attended parties, and ate delicious food. Every night, however, I sat down and worked until the early hours of the morning. I had deadlines to meet! My book, 33 Days to the Dream, was nearly finished, but I had to make some final tweaks before submitting it to my publisher. Of course, I finished the book on time. I also presented it on a date we had selected months in advance! **You can develop your will. Strong will is at the foundation of wealth; you need it to make and save money. Your will is also a respectable quality; people need to respect you to purchase your products.**

Consider why you do not keep your promises. Figure out what makes you procrastinate. Note and analyse your excuses; eliminate them. If you have set out to learn a new language, I am certain you can stay awake for an additional hour; find the time, do the exercises, and do not betray yourself.

OPPORTUNITY LURKS AROUND EVERY CORNER

The third condition is opportunity. Opportunities are everywhere! However, if you only focus on problems, you will never notice the opportunity that lurks around the corner.

My husband and I strolled around Tulum, walking near the coast. There were so many restaurants around, and smells flew and mingled in the air. "Why isn't there a souvlaki place here?" my Greek husband wondered. "If there was, there would be a long line of people trying to eat some Greek food!"

My husband was right. A little street food truck would have been a massive hit there, near the beach. As we continued our walk, we noticed at least five other opportunities to do business. Doing so was only possible because of the state of our psyches. You have to tune yourself in to notice opportunity. That is why this book teaches you to "smell" money, to see where it has been hidden. Opportunity lurks around every corner; money is everywhere, waiting to be found.

EXERCISE
UNLOCK THE ENERGY

Imagine an orange. What can you use this orange for? Write down ten ideas.

1.	6.
2.	7.
3.	8.
4.	9.
5.	10.

What vibrations did you sense while thinking about these uses? What helped you come up with ideas?

The orange is neutral, which is why it awakened your creative force. Isn't that true? Unfortunately, this is not the case when it comes to your own product. Your creative energy often flees your body as soon as you begin thinking of your products. To prevent this from happening, you must realise that your product, just like this orange, possesses great potential. Your brain should internalise this truth, unlocking the energy, knowing that "Everything is possible." You should think big, never doubting the possibility for success. Your products can help the entire world—not just your town or country.

**Even when we do not realise it, everything we do impacts humanity.
Our actions–and inactions–influence everyone else.
We are a united whole.**

I posted a picture from Mexico during lockdown. Many people criticised me for it, leading me to delete it from my social media accounts. However, I also stopped for a second, thinking about the picture and my trip. It was thanks to crazy people like me, I realised, that flight attendants kept their jobs in aviation despite the pandemic. Restaurants and hotels also survived because of people as peculiar and travel-addicted as I am. When I shop, I help people that work in the fashion industry; I spend money on their products! The economy will die as soon as people stop spending money. As long as we all spend and earn money, the economy is in circulation, bringing in revenues and profits. This is a crucial exchange of energy.

YOUR RESERVOIRS

Please note the things and activates you avoid or procrastinate on.

These are your reservoirs. You reawaken the energy each time you do any of those activities. This is also how you set your goals in motion.

A friend of mine and I were having dinner, at a restaurant in Thailand. In between bites, she said: "Natalia, you should find someone to cover our bill."

I had already given her all my money; my wallet was empty. I stood up and walked over to the two men that occupied a table nearby. "Hello," I greeted them kindly, "could you help us?"

"Yes," they agreed.

"Could you pay our bill?" I asked.

The men, a French gay couple, were surprised. "What do you mean pay your bill? How could we pay your bill?"

"Oh, it is easy," I noted, "you could do it with cash or card!"

They were shocked, and I could not let that happen. I continued, "I forgot my card." Then, I took out my wallet and opened it, "and I do not have any cash. Please help us."

This experiment was totally worth the discomfort it made me experience. The men paid for our dinner, though unwillingly, and we thanked them. I don't think we harmed them all that much. They could surely afford to spend £65 on dinner to gain the privilege of saying how they had once saved two unfortunate women in Thailand. They were our saviours; they were winners. People feel good when they do something good. They also begin attracting the good into their lives. Urge the people around you to be truly good.

It is crucial you overcome discomfort and the inability to ask for help. Therefore, I am assigning you the following:

HOMEWORK
REQUEST A PRESENT

Go out. Request something for free at a store—or two, or three—and receive a present! Then, thank the sales assistant and move on with your day.

You may often miss on presents (and opportunities) only because you are scared to ask. You think you don't deserve them. You pay money for things others receive for free. I've seen this happen hundreds of times. To prevent it from happening in your own life, you should do this exercise. Do not forget to then give someone else a present, as this will keep your energetic equilibrium in check. This is the law of giving and receiving. Tell yourself: "I find it so easy to give and receive. I stimulate the flow of energy!" Give others presents; ask for presents—requesting a gift isn't all that difficult. Notice how your psyche reacts when you ask for presents.

Shame squanders opportunity.

Train yourself into believing you only deserve the best. Develop your discipline and strengthen your willpower. Finish what you've started. Stop procrastinating. Keep trying new things—do what you've never done before. Give and receive; do it slowly, calmly, easily. Don't blame yourself. The braver you are, the easier you will find and seize new opportunities.

Everyone can do business. Yes, some succeed more easily than others. However, if you put in the effort to work and learn, you will obtain your dream life.

I will share one of my favourite stories about sales. Two men, good friends, lived in the same town. The first one was a happy, joyful person. The second one was plagued by sadness.

One day, the first man bragged a bit. "I bought an elephant!"

"An elephant?!" the second man exclaimed in bewilderment.

"Yes, you cannot imagine how nice it is to have an elephant! The kids play with him, and they leave me alone! He runs after them and lifts them up with his trunk. Our neighbours ride the elephant from time to time and give us gifts—as a sign of gratitude. My wife and I have more free time now. She is happy we have a big—pun intended—helper at home. Seeing my family happy, I too feel better than before. I am full of ideas. I also got a promotion at work! My life feels like a fairy tale."

Interested, the second man asked, "Would you mind selling me your elephant? My life is miserable, and I have so many struggles. My family isn't doing well. My career is bad, too. Please, please let me buy your elephant."

"What do you mean? My elephant is precious to me!" responded the first man.

"You've already enjoyed your elephant. Sell him to me!"

"He's very expensive," said the first man, pensively.

"It doesn't matter; I want the elephant!"

The two men negotiated for a while. Finally, they sealed the deal. The elephant was sold for a sizable sum. The second men took his new pet—the elephant—and walked home.

A few months later, the two friends met again. The joyful friend was happier than ever before, and the sad friend was sadder.

"How is the elephant?" asked the first.

"Don't even ask me about him," replied the second. "He stunk—and the neighbours kicked us out because of him. We had to move. My wife left me; she did not want to have an elephant in her garden. Scared of the elephant, my kids moved out with her. I am alone, sad, and miserable. I stink like an elephant! I was fired because of that. I am now jobless, childless, and divorced… but I have an elephant."

"Well, man, you will never sell the elephant with an attitude like that!"

Your attitude is just important—regardless of the sale you're trying to make. Ultimately, sales are a frame of mind.

Let me share a short personal anecdote. I dreamed of traveling to Mexico; I also knew most Mexican hotels only hosted and served adults. Despite my husband's concerns, I said: "Don't worry about it! We'll figure it out when we get there!" We caught a flight to Mexico.

We stayed at a good hotel. As soon as we walked over to the beach, however, an employee stopped us. "You can't go to the beach with your son," he said to us.

"Okay," I replied, "would you recommend us another hotel that would be happy to have our family?"

"Yes, there is a nice hotel right next to ours. You can do there."

We changed hotels. Together with our young son, we went to the beach at our new hotel. I wanted to take some photos on the beach. I asked my husband to do it, but he refused. I then asked a waiter and a few passers-by, but none of them managed to take a remotely decent picture of me! I finally spotted a swimsuit vendor that was walking around the lounge chairs. I went over to her, and, in my half-broken English, suggested to give her £10 if she took good photos of me. As soon as she heard this, she left her sacks next to my husband's sunbed and then took me to the most exquisite parts of the beach. I had put a nice dress on, too, and she helped me find the most appropriate way to pose. Her photos were excellent! "Who taught you to photograph others so well?" I asked.

"I studied photography and cinematography in the Netherlands for two years," she answered.

I was shocked. I couldn't believe that a woman who sold swimwear on the beach turned out the be the specialist I needed!

Solutions are everywhere! Train your brain to locate them. Even though I knew bringing my son with us would be challenging, I still got my family on a flight to Mexico. We managed to find a nice hotel! My husband refused to take photos of me. I managed to find a professional photographer! There is a solution for every problem. You will achieve guaranteed success as long as you internalise this frame of mind.

Doubting your product will squander your chance to make sales. Your first motivation should therefore be finding why people simply cannot live without your product—even if that product is a stinky elephant. Like a pen, your product can be simple and commonplace. Still, if you have faith in it, you will always find a way to sell.

The client notices and internalises your hesitations. You cannot be congruent if—deep within—you doubt your product's utility. You can only be congruent if you are certain in the absolute necessity for your product. It is often the case that clients do not really need your products; motivated by you, however, they realise your products can be useful, deciding to purchase them: "This product is exactly what I needed!" they squeak happily. Keep track of the energy you put into sales. Notice what energy helps you sell your own pen/elephant.

If you have set yourself up for failure, your actions will only prove the following: "Well, I knew I wasn't going to make it but, at least, I tried." **Your faith determines the outcome.**

How can you strengthen your faith?

There is this Russian practice which suggests you use **positive affirmations formed as questions:** "Why do I make sales so easily? Why do I make money this quickly? How am I always this lucky?" Such questions activate your unconscious mind, training it that everything is possible.

There is one more way to strengthen your faith; to do it, you should **connect things and concepts that have nothing in common.** Say, for instance, "If I see a bird this morning, my entire day will run smoothly." Of course, you will see a bird today. When forming this type of affirmation, try to select things and ideas that are nearly guaranteed. Tell yourself you will make a lot of money if you see a man dressed in black. Promise yourself you will make a successful business deal if you pass by a blonde woman on the street. Over time, make your affirmations a little more complicated. "I will sign a contract if I meet someone wearing yellow shoes." It isn't all that easy to find someone wearing yellow shoes. Then, when you finally encounter that person, you will trust that signing a contract is the right thing to do.

I once shared this frame of thought with one of my clients, who lives in Norway. She objected to it! "Natalia," she said, "you basically want to say that I will succeed in life as long as I see a blue butterfly?"

"Yes," I responded.

"But there are no blue butterflies in Norway."

"Darling, just visualise the butterfly. It will show up, trust me. What do you want to happen in your life?" I asked.

"I want to get a raise," she answered.

"Okay then, as soon as you see a blue butterfly, your wish will come true—in a way that is most appropriate for you!"

That same evening, my client emailed me a picture of a big food truck. There were tons of little blue butterflies decorating its doors.

"You were right," she wrote, "as long as you focus on your chosen sign, you will encounter it when you least expect to."

Connect with a symbol that can represent a wish or a goal. This is how you can set yourself up to think that success is near—if you see the symbol, you will achieve exactly what you desire. This is how you can send the Universe an order, which it will then deliver to you. **The ease at which you notice and seize opportunity will surprise you; things will begin happening a lot faster than you expected.**

When you feel that you've depleted your energy, do something that makes you happy. Walk to a special place, get a massage, invite a friend to your favourite restaurant, go for a long drive, etc. Do something that can help you recharge! **You are responsible for keeping yourself at a high energy level!** Men, for instance, can increase their vibration by wearing a suit—even at home! This allows them to feel more authoritative and powerful.

HOW TO ONLY TAKE THE BEST

Your self-confidence is decisive for your ability to sell. It will also help you succeed in all other aspects of your life.

Think about what a clear sense of self-confidence could bring into your life. How could having more self-confidence impact your lifestyle? Write it down:

Our society is structured into dominance hierarchies.
Alphas take the best.

Let's start by describing alpha, beta, and gamma people. Konrad Lorenz was awarded the Noble Prize for his illustration of a theory of alpha, beta, and gamma behaviour. Though Lorenz conducted many different experiments, one of the most fascinating ones is the following: he placed food and water in one corner of the room and an electroshock in the other; then, he let rats into the room; the most insolent rats, the alphas, headed straight for the food; the betas reached the food, too, eating a bit; meanwhile, the gammas waited, only getting the remainder of what used to be a rat meal. The second part of Lorenz's experiment was even more interesting: in a smaller room, he placed some food and water in one corner and the electroshock in the other; he only let the alpha rats in; these new conditions show how some of these rats prove to be leaders while others remain followers. What Lorenz's experiment shows is that our entire society is founded upon hierarchies. **There is an alpha, a beta, and a gamma in every group. The environment matters: people—and animals—assume roles based on the environment.** You can be a big fish in a small pond; but, once you move to New York City, many are better than you, leading you to become a small fish in a big pond.

I was in grade three when my school had us do IQ tests. My IQ was average. I was placed in a class with children of mediocre intelligence. My mother, however, is an ambitious woman; she met with the headmaster, yelled a bit, and moved me to the "smart-kid" class. This was an experiment that the Americans were doing at my Russian school. It was my mother—not my IQ score—that placed me within the 30 smartest kids in my class of 150! They were alphas. Our teachers were constantly telling us, "You are smart! You are strong! You are geniuses!" They sent us to competitions and Olympiads. Their attitude towards us was so different from the attitude they had towards the other kids; they told everyone else things like "It is clear you wouldn't be able to achieve much more than this." Had it not been for my mother, I would have been told that, too. Interestingly, when we met for our 20-year reunion, it turned out that my class, the alpha class, had the highest number of successful individuals. I remain grateful to my mother to this day. She put me in the right environment where everyone praised my "greatness," even when I wasn't even that great. **I believe a lot of my success is a direct result of this; when people call you smart and successful, you become smart and successful.**

You should do the same with your inner child. Praise it. **Realise that alphas are allowed everything; they are privileged.** In natural habitats, they are the ones that choose and conquer new territory. They are the ones that allow new members to join their packs and tribes. They choose which males will enter a battle and which females will breed. They only breed the strongest, most beautiful females. After all, one of the main roles of the alphas is the dissemination of their genetic material. Alphas have many female partners. If you wish to be an alpha male, you have to understand continuation of the species is a main role of alpha individuals.

Alpha women are both a blessing and a curse. Alpha females were not created for marriage; they willingly choose to get married—if they ever do. Coco Chanel, Angelina Jolie, and Meghan Markle are classic examples of alpha women. They give their partners a sense of direction, choose the path, and make the decisions.

A leading quality of alpha people is their proclivity to **enter battles** and fight until they achieve their goals. Alphas would rather die than lose. **Also, when conflict occurs, alphas, unlike betas, never back down.** If there is a conflict between two alphas, they know one will be victorious and the other will die. **Alpha leaders know they are allowed everything. They set their own rules, coming to conclusions like, "I can do this, but you cannot."**

Betas are monogamous, dedicated to family. They do what alphas tell them to do. Betas are great at executing commands. They take others into consideration, submit themselves to the strong, and respect authority. Oftentimes, betas are prettier, smarter, better professionals. Betas usually come with ideas that the alphas then adopt and sell as their own.

There are so many examples of short, ugly, and unattractive company owners whose employees are tall, beautiful, strong men. Women, however, choose the former. Years ago, a beta man was flirting with me, trying to tie me down. As soon as we got to the point where he could have finally managed to seduce me, he became hesitant. Beta males aren't decisive enough; they are often insecure despite their intelligence and attractiveness.

Gamma people are those individuals who do not have ambitions and goals; they don't live—they just exist. They understand someone will hire them to do an insignificant job, and they do their work quietly, without expecting too much. They only obtain the most basic necessities.

Data shows that **10% of people are alphas**; 30%-40% are betas, and 50% are gammas.

It's been proven that these qualities are partially hereditary; 50 percent of us is what we inherit from our kin, and 50 percent of us is what we develop. That is, it's **50% nature, and 50% nurture**. You might have been born a beta; with the correct upbringing, however, you can become an alpha. That is exactly what happened with me. You could have been born an alpha but, after years of abuse, degraded into a beta. If you are born a gamma, you may turn into a beta but becoming an alpha would be nearly impossible. Your relationship with your parents, your upbringing, and your familial environment play a key role here. Big, happy families raise alpha children; the opposite happens, too. Sometimes, in their pursuit to prove themselves to the world, the children of dysfunctional families become alphas.

You are an alpha if:

1. You always assume the role of a leader.
2. You fight for your goals.
3. You make decisions.
4. You take risks.
5. You manage people and situations easily.
6. You delegate tasks and responsibilities easily.
7. You impose your point of view.
8. You know what you want.
9. You fight for your dreams even when you face adversity.
10. People respect you; they are a little afraid of you, too.
11. People follow your lead; they admire you.
12. You enter conflicts easily. You prove you are right.
13. You are highly sexual.
14. Your family is important, but it is not your priority. Your mission stands first.

You are a beta if:

1. You are intelligent, have a nice job, but do not seek to become a business owner.

2. You seek peace, stability, and security.

3. You want to have a stable source of income.

4. You find happiness in family, children, and your loved ones. You are monogamous.

5. You're often smarter and more competitive than your superiors.

6. You are not insolent; insolence puts you off.

7. You strive to keep the peace, even if that means taking a step back.

8. You are conflict-avoidant. You don't impose your opinions.

9. You are not very sexual.

You are a gamma if:

1. You don't have goals or aspirations.

2. You are often bored.

3. You dislike your job but do it anyway; you must survive, after all.

4. You aren't sexual.

5. You struggle to find a partner and, when you do, you become obsessive.

6. You fear your partner will leave you.

7. You experience financial difficulties.

8. You don't have valuable qualifications, skills, or knowledge. You are not ambitious.

You can recognize alpha personalities through their clear, charismatic presence. **They captivate your attention; they cannot remain unnoticed.** You feel drawn to them. There is a sense of chemistry between you two. **The alpha's clothes and appearance don't matter; everybody wants the alphas regardless of their physical appearance!** It is so interesting to notice how—as soon as an alpha male enters a room—all women fix up their hair and makeup. They twirl their hair and look up playfully. This happens organically; I do it, too. Married or not, we are never blind to the alpha male. Our instincts are at play here, making us like the alpha man. We know that even when he is not monogamous, his genes will produce the best, strongest children. If you have an alpha male as your partner, realise that limiting his freedom is the surest way to make him leave you. **Alpha males love freedom: they prioritize it, together with their mission, placing it above all else.** If someone dares steal their work, alphas will tear everything down, just so they can reclaim their power and work. **An alpha's spouse will never be a priority; work occupies a sacred space in their hearts.** Your alpha spouse will always be attractive to others, and you do not have the right to be jealous. Alpha women don't cheat; they are too busy. Living with an alpha is challenging; alphas are often egoistical. They are allowed everything—but their beta mates are not. Alphas often seek people who can serve them; they therefore often marry betas. Two alphas cannot coexist.

You can do business with alpha men; however, you should expect them to always be right. They are stronger and better than the alpha females; well, in their own minds, at least. If you are an alpha female who does business with an alpha man, expect him to compete with you, potentially trying to take over your company. **He probably thinks he is allowed to do what you cannot do.** Insolent, he will do everything he wishes. He will never feel as if he is doing something wrong; he's allowed to do everything he pleases! When alpha males begin to degenerate, they usually become bandits. That's the beginning of the fall for them. Even then, they always have admirers and followers. Betas may be far more beautiful than alphas, but their pull is never as strong or compelling.

Now, we will do a little exercise to improve your self-confidence!

EXERCISE
HOW TO SELL YOURSELF

Note down first strengths and weaknesses.

STRENGTHS	*WEAKNESSES*

Let's imagine your PR manager noted your strengths and your biggest critic mentioned your weaknesses. The former needs to market you, bringing out the best in you and showing it to the world. The latter, on the other hand, aims to destroy you, making you feel small and insignificant. **You must strengthen your inner PR executive; that is, you should praise yourself and admire your own skills; this is how you learn to sell yourself!** Silence your inner critic; if you can, eradicate self-criticism. Criticism is a breeding ground for doubt, and doubt leads to failure.

Stand near a chair and imagine yourself sitting there. Softly point towards yourself—the imaginary you that rests on the chair—and say:

"I would like to introduce you to a wonderful man/woman. He/she is successful and talented; everything he/she touches turns to gold! He/she is energetic, vibrant, full of ideas. He/she accepts change and always strives to become better. He/she seizes opportunity. He/she is respected by his friends, partners, and subordinates. He/she is precise in his/her speech, honest, and always on point. He/she is punctual and always sets clear goals…" (speak about the five strengths you mentioned above.)

Notice how comfortable you feel marketing yourself.

Stand up straight with your shoulders back. Place your hands in front of your chest. Point your palms to the sky. Draw your fingers together. Say this out loud: "I am allowed to do everything I want!" Now, expand your fingers, turn your palms towards the floor, and draw a semi-circle to your right. Verbalise this: "You are not allowed to do this!" Repeat this again: "I am allowed to do everything I want. You are not allowed to do this!" Keep repeating this until you sense power bubbling up within your body. You are strong. You can achieve all that you desire!

Now, return to the chair. Stand next to it. Yet again, imagine yourself sitting on that chair. Introduce yourself, describing your character and skills in third person pronoun. "I wish to introduce you ………………………………………… (say your name). He/she is a wonderful men/woman ………………………… His/her strengths are …………………………………………"

Speak confidently. Do it with pleasure.

"He/she is so good at business ………………………………………

Everyone admires him/her for his/her ....
Plus, he/she is ...."

Now, take a seat. Sit on that chair! Breathe. Merge with the formidable presence—the person—you imagined there, aligning yourself with your higher self. Straighten up. Stand up with your shoulders back. "Yes, this is me," say to yourself. "I am great. I am respectable. I am allowed to do everything I want!"

What would you like to do right now? What would you like to allow yourself? Write it down.

I will assign you one more:

EXERCISE

SING ON THE STREET

Go out and stand on a street. Remember: **everything is allowed. Sing! Sing at the top of your lungs!**

This exercise will convince you that you just don't care! In your life, everything is allowed. You want to sing—you sing. This is allowed for you. Singing on the street will stimulate the creation of new neural connections in your brain. **You don't have to put everyone else first anymore! Don't worry about it too much! Don't care about other people's opinions!** You want to sing, and you do it. You are a free individual. No one can tell you if and where to sing. Observe your personal limitations and fears as you sing. Feel yourself growing more confident. You can handle anything that comes you way! **You are not afraid! You get what you want!**

I was 18 when my teachers assigned me this exercise. It was so difficult! I was a shy, beta, even gamma-like individual. My exercise was to meet 25 people and sing on the street. This task changed me forever. I found strength, bravery, and confidence! Yes, I can do it all!

Has this exercise led you to think about something? Has it, perhaps, caused an internal dialogue? What are your thoughts, feelings, and sensations? Are you worried about people judging you? Do you fear they'd find you insane? In the unlikely occasion they do, their opinion won't be your problem! You worry that you don't sing in tune. You may be tone-deaf, too. Well, that's even better! You become more authentic this way! Are you still worried about other people's reactions?

The path of any Alpha individual is the path of the pole. You stand out like a pole, irritating everyone else. People begin to criticise you. "Who do you think you are?" they exclaim. "Have you gone mad? What are you doing?" they ask. In cases like these, there are two courses of action you can take. You can either let people crush you or keep on going, letting them realise you do what you set out to do. Over time, people will cave in. Meanwhile, you continue to assert and communicate your new rules. **If you wish to grow as an alpha individual, you will have to craft new rules.**

Other than singing on the street, I've done my fair share of other shenanigans. I once kneeled on a street, extended my hand, and begged for money. There was this other time when I put on my underwear on top of my regular clothes; I went to work like that, too. At a store, I once asked a random man to clasp my bra's band together. As crazy as these things were, they **gave me a new sense of confidence.** You can obtain that confidence as well—not by reading books about it but by doing things that challenge you. It's much like riding a bike. I can explain how you should ride a bike but, until you hop on and do it yourself, falling a few times here and there, you will not learn. **Your confidence is directly positively correlated to your goals and standards. Your ambitions grow proportionally with your confidence, and so do your standards.**

ASSERT YOURSELF

If you were alpha, what would you require from your boss, your partner, your family? Bear in mind: even alphas do not receive what they are demanding unless they provide clear justifications for their demands. Even alphas must be deserving.

You must know your strengths; this is how you allow your internal PR to keep working, to help you assert yourself in public. I am certain you have enough good qualities to convince you of your awesomeness. You could always develop the qualities you lack. I, for instance, did not feel confident in my housekeeping abilities; during lockdown, however, I improved my cooking skills and gained more confidence. Put your internal PR to work and **advertise yourself whenever possible.** This is a skill you must hone.

Try to describe yourself in a single sentence. Use seven-eight words that communicate the best and most important things about you. Don't be humble. Describe yourself in a way that would impress people that do not know you. Wow them! You could even exaggerate a bit, as, in time, this will be your new reality:

This sentence is your business card and must always remain within reach. You should remember it when you feel anxious and insecure. Call that sentence to you mind and whisper, "Hold on! Do you remember who you are?"

EXERCISE
I CAN, AND I WILL

Now, let's work on the second column—the one that your inner critic crafted for you.

Turn on some pleasant music. Close your eyes.
Breathe in.
Breathe out.

Remember all criticism you received as a young child. Do you still blame yourself? Is there anything you dislike about yourself? If yes, what is that thing? Do you judge yourself?

What does your inner critic look like? Is it a man or a woman? Is that person tall or short? What's that person's body like? Does your inner critic remind you of anyone? How is he/she dressed? What clothing does he/she like to wear? What accessories does he/she wear? Why does your inner critic want to trample you? Does your inner critic deplete your energy? What sort of situations does your inner critic bring to your mind? What are his/her criticisms?

Feel that inner critic living inside you, residing deep within your body. You let that critic in only because you are a loving, caring person. You allowed the inner critic to possess your body only because you loved someone else. You trusted that person. But that person's criticism is not your reality. It is not true.

Breathe in. Breathe out. Slowly open your eyes.

Describe your inner critic. Note down everything that you felt; record every little detail.

Close your eyes again; imagine that everything is possible in your life. You are a confident alpha personality. What your biggest desire? What do you pine after? What matters to you? What do you want to get out of life?

Sense your dream coming true. You have an inner dreamer. Sense that inner dreamer. Locate them. Where are they? Why did your inner dreamer allow your inner critic to exterminate you dreams? Your inner critic limited you with statements like "Have you gone mad? This will never work out. People will not like your idea. They won't purchase your products. You couldn't pull that off!"

Remember how your inner critic walked all over your dreams. Recall how he/she had you walk away from them.

A dream has to be born before it can be fulfilled. Your inner critic must let it live. Once he/she has done that, your inner logician must outline the steps that dream is to follow. Then, your inner observer should observe the environment, figuring out how to adapt your dream to your circumstances and make it feasible.

That's when dreams come true.

Breathe in. Breathe out. Open your eyes.

Find four pieces of paper and, on each of them, write the following: DREAMER, CRITIC, LOGICIAN, OBSERVER.

Order those pieces of paper into a rectangular shape on the floor. Step on top of the piece of paper that says DREAMER. Think about your greatest desire. Describe it, as concretely as possible. Say, for example, "I dream of building a village that is ……………………………"
Dream, describe all our dreams out loud.

How are you feeling? What is your energy like?

Now, step over the piece of paper that has critic written over it. Assume the stance your critic took during your meditation. Act like your inner critic. Is he/she confident? Is he/she aggressive? Is your inner critic trying to insult you? Is your inner critic ignoring you? Is your inner critic dissatisfied? Is he still criticising you? Verbalise his criticism! "What sort of dream is this?" ask out loud. "This will never work out! You couldn't possibly make it happen." Utter the words and sentences you hear from your inner critic! Notice who your inner critic reminds you of! Is it your father? Or is it your mother? Keep repeating their criticism. As soon as you've had enough, clench your fists, raise your hands into the aid, and yell: "I have had enough!"

Feel your power. You can ignore and stop other people's criticisms! Repeat this: "Stop! It's enough! Stop! It's enough! Enough is enough! Get out of my life! I can, and I will! No one can tell me what to do! Enough is enough!"

Straighten up. Stand up straight with your shoulders back. Breathe in. Feel your inner critic disappearing. Open your fists and banish him/her from your life. It's enough! Enough is enough! You don't need that inner critic anymore! Imagine your inner critic shrinking, turning into sand, only to be carried away by the wind. Your inner critic is gone! A new sense of power has taken his/her place! You can achieve anything! You are capable of it all! You can fly! Your hands are your wings—spread them and fly! You're headed towards your dream. You have the strength to make your dreams come true. You have the power to create! You have the power to succeed! You move on, flying upwards, knowing you are capable of everything. "I can do this," you assure yourself. "I am a winner! I am doing well!"

Waive your hands, spread your wings, and fly. Recall all the times you did something that seemed impossible! Say this out loud: "I have already achieved…… (say, for instance, I learned how to drive; I graduated with honours; I speak a foreign language).

Put your palms on top of each other. Place them in front of your third chakra. Feel your inner power. Sense your willpower. You have achieved so much. You are doing so well.

Maintain that power. Don't move your hands. Step on the piece of paper that says LOGICIAN. Consider what you should do to achieve your dreams. Take a seat. Write it all down:

1.

2.

3.

4.

5.

6.

7.

Observe yourself from aside. Describe yourself using third person pronouns. Say, "This is a man/woman who dreams of ……………………….. To do so, he/she will take the following steps ……………………………………………………………….. (read what you wrote above)."

Why do you have to observe yourself from afar? Well, once again, it comes down to the psychological concepts of association and disassociation. It is hard to comprehend what is going on when we are a part of the process—that is, when we are associating. Once we go outside, however, we find it a lot easier to understand the situation. It is therefore easier to speak about other people than it is to speak about ourselves. When we talk about the man/woman who "wishes to ……………," we actually disassociate from ourselves. This lessens our worries. I therefore advise you to disassociate every single time you set out to pursue a dream. Use this exercise; it will help you fulfil your dreams. **Follow this pattern: formulate a dream; destroy your inner critic; consider the steps you need to take; think about**

those steps from the position of an objective observer. Start by disassociating; once you figure out what the steps are, it would be far easier to associate with them. Your plan becomes clearer than ever before.

DO WHAT FRIGHTENS YOU

All problems in life come from the prohibitions others imposed on us. I will share a story that continues to amaze me. It is a warm summer day. The sun is shining, and the weather is as good as it has been in months. A mother walks on the beach with her son. They get to the lounge chairs. Wanting to rest, the mother turns to her son and says: "You can go into the ocean—but only if you don't get your swimsuit wet! Get it wet, and I will beat you."

Her son knows the mother isn't joking; she'll beat him if he gets his swimsuit wet! The boy reaches the ocean; he goes in, too, careful not to wet his swimsuit. The sun is shining, the temperature is getting warmer, and yet he is too afraid to go submerge himself in water. He'd be punished if he did! He stands in the ocean, water reaching up to his knees, watching everyone else swimming happily. Children invite him to play with them, but he refuses, moving further away to avoid being splashed with water. At some point, the mother screams, "We are going home!"

The mother and son leave, returning home unhappy.

Many people are like that little boy, too afraid to get their swimsuit wet. They waste their entire lives standing on the sand, waiting for someone to allow them to dive into the ocean. They think deciding to swim would result in something bad; they could not possibly make such a decision on their own!

Life is risk. Yes, alpha individuals get punished, too; sometimes their projects work out and other times—they do not. Alpha individuals, however, do not worry about getting their swimsuits wet! They dive right in, taking the risk, knowing well it is worth bearing the slaps just so they can spend some time with other children, playing happily in the ocean. These people realise there is no worse slap than the one that insults your cheek when you gaze at yourself in the mirror, old, wrinkled, and unsatisfied. You see the face of someone who never swam in the ocean.

The behavioural models and principles of our parents live within us; they are encoded in our genetic memory. They begin to manifest more clearly as we age. One day, we slow down and say: "This is not who I am! I am acting like my mother/father! I've turned into my mother/father!" People with alpha personalities have the strength to declare: "This is not who I am. This is not my story. Yes, you stayed on the sand, fearing your mother's punishment. I did not. I swam in the ocean. My life is all about trying—going into the ocean, testing the limits, and doing what I know is right. I recognize I might get a slap on the cheek, but even that is not certain. Things may work out just fine!"

I dare you to do the things you fear. Fear is what transforms a beta into an alpha! We worry about finding a better job; in spite of that fear, however, we sign up for courses, attend seminars, and obtain qualifications that will help us improve our competence and find a better position. We communicate our boundaries to our partners— even when we are afraid to do so. We do it, ready to lose everyone else but ourselves. If others do not get it, then this is their problem. The reactions of other people should not concern us; we don't have to try to imagine it in advance and neither should we try to act in a manner that will be appreciated by others. We stay true to ourselves.

Both my mother and my husband fail to understand many of the things I do. My mother once saw the photos I took for Playboy and called. "Natalia," she said, "I saw your Instagram. It is too… open, too honest—if you know what I mean."

"So?" I asked.

"Well, nothing, I just wanted to tell you."

Oftentimes, all you need is a little "so?" that can stop people from arguing with you.

People accept your truth when they sense you are willing to fight or it. You must know you are ready for everything, even those things you will not need to do.

I DESERVE, AND I SHALL RECEIVE

I was recently invited to speak at a seminar. I postponed personal errands, bought my plane ticket, and travelled to another country. However, I was not paid the money I was promised. The more I asked them, the more often the repeated the same sentence: "We are going to send you the money shortly." It was a huge event. I also learned that the event organisers had lied to other people, too. When I got there, I refused to get on the stage.

"But so many people came here for you!" they said.

"I understand. Let me count to five. Unless the money shows up in my bank account right now, I will not go on stage. I refuse to play your deceptive games!" I stated.

I was paid shortly thereafter. I got on stage, delivered my talk, and returned to Greece. I then learned I was literally the only speaker they had paid. **I do not try to take what is not mine; however, I will not give what is mine to anyone else.** I don't tolerate disrespect, especially one towards my work and labour. The event organisers sensed I would not let them use me. **If you are an alpha, you don't even have to get into conflict; when people know you can bite, barking becomes redundant.** They value you as soon as they see you. Alpha leaders speak quietly, frightening everyone who tried to take unfair advantage of the situation.

Consider if you are betraying yourself in one way or another. Had I gone on stage without being paid, I would have betrayed myself and my principles. How could I talk about confidence and self-respect when I disrespected myself enough to do work I wasn't being paid for?

Alphas set clear boundaries. They don't give in to pressure. Think about your life and find the things you dislike. Why do you put up with them? Are you afraid to change them? Start small: sing a song of the street, not caring what people think about you. Whatever it is that they are thinking, it is not your problem. That is their story, not yours. Seek situations where you can communicate your standards and say: "I will not allow this. This is not how you treat me!" Of course, you could tone it down a bit and say: "Yes, this could be possible, but only if ...." **When you stand your ground and confidently declare "This is who I am," people begin listening to you. "Okay," they respond. Things also start to fall into place. Everyone is giving you exactly what you wanted. But this is only possible because**

you know your worth and defend your points. Meanwhile, others sense your confidence and self-belief.

I therefore advise you to enter an alpha state. Destroy your inner critic. You can write down all your weaknesses—as you did above—on a new piece of paper, step on them, and scream: "This is wrong. Get out! You don't deserve a place in my life!" Tear the piece of paper apart and kill self-doubt! Repeat the following: **"I deserve, and I shall receive. I will make my dreams come true. This is my life, and I will do whatever I want. So be it!"**

Observe your posture and your behaviour. You should exude strength. "I am allowed to do this, and you are not! I allow myself to do whatever I please." **The first three defenses of your position are usually the hardest. Once you do this more than three times, you become increasingly better at standing your ground.** You can no longer betray yourself. It is as if a part of you that you kept hidden has now floated to the surface, expanding, coming to dominate your character. You do not betray yourself! **You respond to every injustice immediately! You state your standards, rules, and boundaries. Alphas decide for themselves, here and now. They do not wait for better times to come, just as they do not seek excuses. They stand up straight, dominating the space, letting others know they are capable of everything, flying included.**

Let me tell you a story. There is this wonderful fairy tale that Elfika, a Russian author, wrote. Once upon a time, a family lived: a mother, a father, and their two children. Once she was done with work, the mother returned home every afternoon, busying herself with housework. She always went to bed exhausted. She repeatedly prayed for a change—a positive transformation. She prayed to her angels, asking them for a set of wings. One day, she received her new set of wings! She put them on and flew into the sky. It was so good for her! She enjoyed the ease of flying and the beauty of the world! She appreciated her strength and freedom! A few moments later, she heard her husband call out, "Darling, come back. The dishes are dirty!"

The woman fell right into her dirty kitchen. Her husband was sitting on the table, waiting for her to bring him a beer. The kids were sitting nearby, demanding her attention.

"Darling, I can fly! I have wings now!" she shared.

"What do you mean?" asked the husband. "What wings are you talking about?! Look at the stove and the fridge! It is time for you to cook and clean. I couldn't care less about your wings!"

She then called her boss. "I have wings," she said to him.

"What wings are you talking about?" responded her boss. "Your working hours are from nine to six. It would be better if you worked after six, too. Don't dream too much and earn your salary quietly!"

The woman then called a friend of hers. "Darling, I have wings!"

"Mmmmmm, you found yourself a lover, huh? What's he like? Who is he? Nothing else could make you fly!" said the friend.

She called her mother. "Mom, I have wings!"

"Honey," responded the mother, "I was young and stupid, too. I used to dream of having wings! But those are just dreams. Life is misery and pain. You better get used to it. Your life ends as soon as you give birth to a child."

Sadly, the woman took off her wings. "No one needs my wings," she said to herself as she put her wings into the drawer.

Some time passed and her angels showed up. "Dear," they said, "give us back the wings if you won't wear them! There are so many people who wish to fly! You must decide if you will give us those wings back until tomorrow! You either give us those wings back and continue living as you always have or you put them on and fly!"

The woman spent the entire night thinking. "I will keep them," she decided. She began flying.

At first, her husband ridiculed for it. "What are you doing?" he asked. "What is going on with you? You are attending seminars, taking yoga and Pilates classes, going hiking! Who do you think will clean the stove?"

Instead of arguing with him, she smiled. She remained calm and happy. Some time passed and he said, "Maybe I should go hiking with you! I used to dream of conquering those hills when I was younger!" The two went hiking and reawakened the romance!

The children noticed their parents' happiness and decided to study more. They declared: "We can fly, too!" They began helping their parents, studying more, dreaming big.

The woman's mother called and said: "You made it! You, at least, figured it out. I know I have not lived in vain!"

The woman's boss offered her a promotion; she became the new marketing director! Her boss finally noticed she had talents that he had never seen before! Under her direction, both the marketing department and the company grew successfully. She was even offered the chance to become a partner at the firm!

When another woman heard this story, she left her job; she only made £500 per month anyways. She soon found a new job and began making £1500! She also started working out and developing her skills. When her husband noticed her successes, he, too, changed for the better. He also got a promotion! Their children who never wanted to study before, were now A-students!

The second woman noted: "Her story is now my reality."

Alphas seize the opportunity to fly.

They know they have a right to do so.

No one can take this right away from you. No one can make you forget why you are here.

I therefore assign you this

HOMEWORK
PUT ON YOUR WINGS

This homework is the most important process you will go through! It will begin now. It is your responsibility to keep working on it in the future! Do not forget this.

Take a seat. Make sure you are comfortable.

Breathe in. Breathe out.

Return to your youth. Remember your dreams. What mattered most to you back then? If someone gives you wings, what dream of your will you fulfil? What are the little wonders you can do for yourself every single day? Could you buy yourself a beautiful bouquet? Could you make some coffee and enjoy it in silence? Could you go for a walk, establish new business partnerships, or invest into a new idea? Could your business enter a new market? Think about the dreams your inner critic used to silence.

What did you excel at as a student? What talents do you parents and grandparents have? What have you always wanted to try? Allow yourself to try. It may not turn out to be your thing, but you should at least try doing it. Life is a process. You put on your wings every day, preparing to do something you love.

Write down your dreams below:

I CAN SEE YOU SPREADING YOUR WINGS!
YOU ARE READY TO FLY!

You are ready to transform your life, to undergo the metamorphosis of your life! You are ready to love life!

All my feelings are feelings of love.
All my words are words of love.
All my thoughts are thoughts of love.
All my knowledge is knowledge of love.

May there be love around the world! May there be love inside your home and heart!

I SUPPORT YOU!

Remember: failure does not exist. Failure is only real inside your own mind. Gain experiences throughout your entire life. Keep trying until things work out for you!

When I first started by business, I told my friend—the one who has businesses in eighteen countries—that I was afraid. "What if I fail?" I asked him

"You will try again," he said.

"Is it really that simple?" I wondered.

"Yup!"

Every problem can be solved, just as every challenge can be tackled. Things will fall into place.

I wish you prosperity! Be blessed, wealthy, and happy! Keep on going and grow!

I will be delighted to know this book motivated you to realise your mission, start a business, or find a better job! Don't ever give up on your dreams!

Наталия

ACKNOWLEDGEMENTS

I would like to thank Margarita Lozanova—the patient publisher who is both the editor and the "godmother" of this book. I could not have done this without Margarita's support.

I would like to thank my dearest team, some of whose members have been with me since 2009. Together, we have worked to build an empire. This is a task at which we have succeeded, reaching milestone after milestone as members of my team fell in love, got married, and had children, only to then return to the office, just so we could keep going forward and bring you the products and support you deserve.

I would like to thank Boriana Damianova—the best layout artist. She readily accepted my (changing) ideas and masterfully reworked this book's layout as many times as it was necessary to fit my vision.

I would like to thank all people who had faith in my dreams and supported me on my way to success.

I would like to thank my therapists, teachers, and the people who helped me grow professionally and taught me how to expand my business.

I would like to thank my amazing, smart, and loving client-friends, who accompany me on the path to progress every single day.

I am thankful to my son Philip, who knows how to entertain himself quietly while his mommy is writing books.

I am also grateful to all my friends, who lead by example. They inspire me with their love and support. It is no wonder they are of such high significance in my life!

I would like to thank myself for the love that I feel for people, for the strength and bravery that I allow myself, for the dedication with which I pursue my goals, and, finally, for the discipline and persistence that allow me to fulfil my dreams.

Most importantly, I would like to thank you for completing all the exercises I gave you in this book. Thank you for trusting me to guide you forward. Thank you for finishing what we started.

You could learn more about our products here:

Website: www.kobylkina.com
Facebook: Natalia Kobylkina International
Instagram: nataliakobylkina_

If you have any personal questions or ideas, you can reach
me at natalia@natalia.bg.

If you have any advertising inquiries, you can reach us at
denitsa@natalia.bg.

If you have any questions regarding my courses
and seminars, you can contact
clients@natalia.bg.

Our company phone numbers:
+359 894361191
+359 893220801

Some other books of mine:
33 Days to the Dream
A Woman's Guide to Happiness
The Wise Woman